Patent, Trademark, and
Copyright Searching on the Internet

Patent, Trademark, and Copyright Searching on the Internet

by

CHARLES C. SHARPE

McFarland & Company, Inc., Publishers
Jefferson, North Carolina, and London

Cover image © Index Stock Imagery *and* Jean-Francois Podevin 1999

Library of Congress Cataloguing-in-Publication Data

Sharpe, Charles C., 1935–
    Patent, trademark, and copyright searching on the Internet / by
Charles C. Sharpe.
      p. cm.
    Includes bibliographical references and index.
    ISBN 0-7864-0757-3 (sewn softcover : 50# alkaline paper) ∞
    1. Patent searching—Computer network resources. 2. Trade-
mark searching—Computer network resources. 3. Copyright—
Computer network resources. 4. Internet searching. I. Title.
T210.S53   2000
025.06'608—dc21   99-48014
                                                    CIP

British Library Cataloguing-in-Publication data are available

Manufactured in the United States of America

McFarland & Company, Inc., Publishers
 Box 611, Jefferson, North Carolina 28640
  www.mcfarlandpub.com

Contents

Part IV: Appendixes   127

Preface

In the fall of 1998, the United States Patent and Trademark Office introduced two major innovations in patent and trademark searching on the Internet: (1) a searchable database of the full text and drawings of all patents issued since January 1, 1976, and (2) a searchable database of all federally registered and pending trademarks. The Full-Text Database for patents went online on March 26, 1999.

This book was researched and substantially written in anticipation of these databases' becoming available for online search by the general public. What formerly required costly and time-consuming trips to a Patent and Trademark Depository Library can now be easily accomplished in one's home or office using a PC—if the searcher knows how and where to look. The purpose of this book is to present and explain in detail the procedures, resources, and steps to be used in conducting an online search for patents or trademarks. It is a guide, a handbook of search methods, and includes step-by-step exercises for an online search for either patents or trademarks utilizing a large array of sample Web pages illustrating starting points through end results of a search.

Part III of the book discusses copyright, the third principal area of intellectual property law, and one which often engenders some confusion vis-à-vis trademark. The title of this part is "Searching for Copyright Information on the Internet." At the present time, you cannot conduct an online search for registered copyrights. There is very little likelihood that such a search capability will ever exist because of the nature and complexity of the subject. The emphasis here is on where the reader can find *information* and resources online to assist him or her in preparing and filing a copyright application.

The book was written for the layperson, particularly the amateur inventor and or aspiring entrepreneur, for the attorney or paralegal in the area of intellectual property law, for the librarian, and for those authors or artists uncertain about protecting their works. It is hoped that it will prove to be an invaluable resource to all of these.

There is a brief overview of both patent, trademark, and copyright law. A discussion of these topics is provided as a general introduction to each. This background material takes a "what you will be looking for and what you will be looking at when you find it" approach.

1

Unique to this book are detailed, step-by-step instructions on how to efficiently and effectively search for either a patent or trademark on the Internet—a capability of which relatively few persons are presently aware. It is hoped this book will change that.

Part I

Searching
for Patents
on the Internet

1. Patents

WHAT IS A PATENT?

Exactly what is a "patent"? Before you undertake what can be an expensive and time-consuming task of searching for patents, you should have a basic knowledge of exactly what you are looking for—and what it will look like when you find it. In order to search the Internet efficiently and effectively, you should understand a few key elements of patents, patentability, and patent law.

A patent, also known as "letters patent," is a document that conveys a grant of a property right by the United States Government to an inventor (or to his or her heirs or assignees) of a limited monopoly. In exchange for disclosing the details of your invention in your patent application, you will receive such a monopoly. The language on the cover sheet of the sample patent in Appendix 1 describes this monopoly.

Once a patent issues, no one else may legally make, use, import, sell, or offer for sale anything that has the same or an equivalent structure or function without the inventor's (or patent owner's) permission. This includes any and all products made in the United States, or in any foreign country. The inventor, or his or her assignee is given the right to *exclusive use* of that invention for a limited period of time—the "term" of the patent. The term of a patent will be discussed in chapter 2.

The patent itself is issued by the Commissioner of Patents and Trademarks in the name of the United States of America. It is bound as a booklet (Form PTO-377C) with dimensions of 7¾" × 11¾". On the cover is the embossed, gold seal of the Patent and Trademark Office and a crimson satin ribbon. (See Appendix 1 for a black and white facsimile of the cover sheet.) A color photocopy of the cover and or selected pages may be framed. If the invention from which the patent issued has no commercial value, it can be a most impressive, but very expensive, decoration.

To encourage the creation of inventions that might benefit society, and to protect such inventions from being stolen, our legal system has developed the concept of "intellectual property." In law, this is defined as any product of the human mind—anything that is the tangible or perceptible result of intellectual, creative processes. There are four classes of intellectual property: (1) patent, (2) trademark, (3) copyright, and (4) trade secret. Copyrights are registered with the Library of Congress. They are not searchable on the Internet. Locating

4

copyright information and resources online is the subject of Part II of this book. Patents and trademarks come under the purview of the United States Patent and Trademark Office (USPTO, PTO, the Office). These are now searchable on the Internet, and they are the focus of this book. Trade secrets will be discussed in chapter 11.

After you have come to an understanding of the definition of a patent, the criteria of patentability, and a few basic points of the relevant law, you may find that there is no need for you to proceed further—a search may be unnecessary or unwarranted. You may realize that your invention is patently unpatentable. This is highly unlikely—as you will see. Virtually every inventor who considers obtaining a patent will, out of curiosity or necessity, personally undertake a search, or commission one before filing an application.

WHAT CAN BE PATENTED?

In the words of Thomas Jefferson, the father of the U.S. patent system (and a number of other things), anything "devised by man" is patentable as long as it is useful and novel. Any thing or process created by the human mind that enables humans to do something that was heretofore undoable, or even unknown, if fully disclosed, is patentable. Laws of nature are not patentable; utilization of discovered laws of nature are. Inventions offensive to public morality are not patentable. The definition of "offensive to public morality" seems to be given rather wide latitude by the Patent Office—as a search of certain classes and subclasses will show. There have been any number of patents for devices and apparatus to "enhance," "assist," "exercise," and "improve the performance" of various organs and parts of the human body and or their physiological functions.

As defined in the "Statutory Provision" (which is discussed in more detail in chapter 2) there are five "Statutory Classes" that are the proper subject matter of any and all patents. If, in the virtually impossible event that your invention cannot be assigned to one of these five very broad classes, you are not going to get a patent (perhaps a Nobel Prize). In theory, the five statutory classes should embrace virtually everything that might possibly be conceived, created, or discovered by the human mind, including the methods and processes of conceiving, creating and discovering.

THE FIVE STATUTORY CLASSES

1. Art
Art refers to the manner, the technique of making a thing rather than the thing itself. This includes any new or improved process or method.

2. Machine
This includes any device, implement, instrument, or apparatus.

3. Manufacture
The term manufacture refers to any and all articles or commodities that are produced in any way, by any means. This would include any item manufactured by hand or by machine.

4. Composition of Matter
This encompasses all natural and chemical elements, and any creation, combination, or reformulation of these.

5. New and Useful Improvements on Any of the Above Categories
This has been the most common point at issue in lawsuits for infringement. The definition of "improvement" is usually the question the courts must resolve. An improvement cannot be merely minor changes in the structure or function of a prior invention. If this were allowable, no invention would have worth to its inventor. Simply altering size or appearance, rearranging components, or incorporating alternate parts without changing the constitutional construction or function of an invention would not be considered a new and useful improvement. The improvements must be significant.

THE THREE TYPES OF PATENTS

The five statutory classes of subject matter of patentability are assignable to one of three principal types of patents: (1) Utility, (2) Plant, and (3) Design. A fourth, Trade Secret, is also protected under patent law. Trade secrets, by definition, are not searchable.

Patents are creatures of the legal system. As such, they apply to inventions only, and only if an invention falls within one of these three legally defined types. Anything that cannot be assigned to one of these three categories cannot be patented.

UTILITY PATENT

A Utility patent may be granted for an invention that falls under any of the five statutory classes. This type of patent covers any new and useful method, process, machine, device, manufactured item, or chemical compound. Virtually anything that can be produced can be the subject of a Utility patent. These are granted for any invention that enables a new function. This type of patent protects the form and function of an invention as these are presented in the patent application's "claims." (See Appendix 1 for samples of the wording of claims.) Most inventions fall into the category of Utility patent, and our discussions in this book will assume a Utility patent as the subject.

DESIGN PATENT

A Design patent may be granted for any new, original, or ornamental artistic rendering of the *form* of any manufactured item or article of manufacture. This type of patent protects the appearance, the visible aspects of a product. It addresses *form rather than function.* Any aspects that are inherent in the structure, function, or the operation of an invention would be covered under a Utility patent rather than a Design patent. Infringement of a Design patent could be claimed when the configuration, the form and shape of another product appears to be exactly the same as, or substantially similar to, an already patented design.

PLANT PATENT

Plant patents may be granted to anyone who invents or discovers a new plant variety that can be "asexually" reproduced. Asexually reproduced varieties of plants include those such as grafts and spores. Other new plant forms would be protected under a Utility patent as new compositions of matter. A Plant patent excludes others from asexually reproducing the new plant for commercial use.

A patent of any type applies not just to its subject invention but also any succeeding invention whose form or function might fall within its scope—that is, if any subsequent invention incorporates any of the aspects of creativity of the original—even if subsequent inventions are created independently by another inventor.

ADDITIONAL REQUIREMENTS
FOR THE GRANTING OF A PATENT

To be patented, your invention must not only fall within one of the five statutory classes set forth in the Statutory Provision, it must also fulfill three other requirements. These are: (1) novelty, (2) utility, and (3) nonobvious (the Patent Office's term).

NOVELTY

The invention must be new. It must have at least one element that is *new* in an unqualified, absolute sense. It does not have to be totally new. Any proportion of new-to-old can be acceptable. It can be one or more improvements of an existing product and, as such, could become a profitable invention. As noted previously, any improvement must be significant; it cannot be just some minor adaptation or change. Differences in size, shape, or materials, or substitution or reconfiguration of components, or other obvious modifications are generally not patentable.

Another, and most significant, definition of novelty also requires that your invention has previously been *unknown* to the public. It is *new*. It has never been publicly shown, used, or sold anywhere in the United States or described in any form of printed material anywhere in the world more than one year prior to the date of your patent application. The importance of this for patentability will be discussed in more detail in chapter 2.

UTILITY

Being new or different is not enough. The invention must have some degree of usefulness. It must be useful in some way and in some measure, no matter how great or trivial that use may be. It must have a purpose—any purpose. The invention must have "operativeness." The machine or device must be able to perform its intended function. If it cannot accomplish this, it would not be considered utilitarian and, therefore, nonpatentable. Virtually everything made has some utility—even if only as a form of amusement or "recreation." This requirement is usually not a point of contention.

NONOBVIOUS

Your invention, when compared to all presently or previously known inventions of its kind, must have been nonobvious to any person "skilled in the art" at the time you invented it. This requirement is the one that usually raises the greatest number of questions and problems regarding the patentability of a particular invention. One "skilled in the art" is generally defined as any individual who would normally make and or use the subject matter of the patent, the method, application, or that which is the closest thing to it. "Art," as defined previously, refers to the process of making a thing rather than the thing itself.

Now that you have learned what a patent is, what can be patented, and what is required to obtain one, you may be better prepared to make your decision to begin the application process. An understanding of a few of the basic points of patent law is also in order.

2. Patent Law

THE LAW

In *The Devil's Dictionary*, Ambrose Bierce defined litigation as a "machine which you go into as a pig and come out of as a sausage." For the aspiring inventor with dreams of prosperity, ignorance of the basics of patent law could mean the difference between the knock of opportunity or … knockwurst!

PATENT LAW

Several hundred years ago, before patent systems were created by law, patents were exclusive rights (monopolies) granted by a monarch. A patent may have been granted in recognition of an inventor's accomplishment, or for a "fee" to help replenish the royal coffers.

The United States Constitution gives Congress the authority to enact laws relating to patents. Article I, Section 8, of the Constitution states: "Congress shall have power … To promote the Progress of Science and useful Arts, by securing for limited Times to Authors and Inventors the exclusive Right to their respective Writings and Discoveries." Individual states have no statutory powers in matters directly relating to the issuance or continuance of patents. This is the function of the United States Patent and Trademark Office. State courts do try lawsuits in which issues of patent rights or ownership, or claims of infringement are in dispute.

Over the years, Congress has enacted numerous laws regarding patents. The first was enacted on April 10, 1790. It was signed into law by President George Washington. The body of patent law that is now in effect represents a general codification that was enacted on July 19, 1952, and which took effect January 1, 1953. This codification, known as the Patent Act (the Act), is set forth in Title 35, United States Code (U.S.C.) Sections 1–376.

The law is formaldehyde in print. There really is no need for you to know, let alone attempt to understand, all of the provisions of patent law. However, there is one that you must understand before initiating the patent process, and that is the "Statutory Provision" (the Provision). This specifies the general fields of subject matter that can be patented and the conditions under which a patent may be obtained. These have already been discussed in chapter 1. The language of the Statutory Provision is quoted below.

9

> Any person who has invented or discovered any new and useful art, machine, manufacture, or composition of matter or any new and useful improvement thereof ... not known or used by others in this country before his invention or discovery thereof, and not patented or described in any printed publication in this or any foreign country, before his invention or discovery there, or more than one year prior to his application, and not in public use or sale in this country for more than one year prior to his application, unless the same is proved to have been abandoned may upon payment of the fees required by law, and other due proceeding had, obtain a patent therefor.

In summary, the Provision includes four principal points:

1. The invention must be one of the five classes listed as subject matter;
2. it must meet the requirement of novelty; that is, it must be new;
3. it must be useful; and
4. a patent application must be filed within the period prescribed by law where there has been any public use, sale, or publication of the invention prior to the filing.

These are the essential elements of patent law that each inventor should understand. If you grasp these four points you will be able to situate your invention at the outset of the patent process. Your attorney will carry it through the process. If your invention does not appear to be covered by the language of the Provision (that is highly unlikely) you will have to go back to the drawing board.

TERM OF A PATENT

The term of a patent is determined by its type. Utility and Plant patents are granted for a term that begins on the date of issue (publication) and ends twenty years from the date on which the patent application was filed. Design patents are granted for a term of fourteen years from the date of the grant. The cover sheet of the sample patent in Appendix 1 defines the term of the utility patent shown. It states:

> If this application was filed prior to June 8, 1995, the term of this patent is the longer of seventeen years from the date of grant of this patent or twenty years from the earliest effective U.S. filing date of the application, subject to any statutory extension.

> If this application was filed on or after June 8, 1995, the term of this patent is twenty years from the U.S. filing date, subject to any statutory extension. If the application contains a specific reference to an

earlier filed application or applications under 35 U.S.C. 120, 121 or 365(c), the term of the patent is twenty years from the date on which the earliest application was filed, subject to any statutory extension.

When the term of a patent has expired, anyone is free to make, use, or sell the invention without permission of the patentee—provided that matter covered by other unexpired patents is not used. The terms may not be extended except by special act of Congress.

An inventor cannot renew his or her patent when its term expires. However, a new and useful improvement of something that has already been patented (an active or expired patent) as well as a new use of a preexisting device or product, may be the subject of an application and possibly a new patent.

THE INVENTOR'S PATENT RIGHT

The right conferred by the patent grant is "the right to exclude others from making, using, or offering for sale, or selling the invention throughout the United States or importing the invention into the United States" and its territories for the term of years prescribed by law—subject to the payment of maintenance fees as also provided by law.

The inventor should understand the exact nature of the right conferred. The key is the phrase: "right to exclude." Note, the "right" is negative rather than positive. A patent is best defined by what it is not, rather than what it is. A patent does not grant the inventor the unlimited right to make, use, or sell the invention, but grants only the exclusionary nature of that right—that is, to exclude others from these activities in the absence of authorization from the patentee.

Since the patent does not grant these particular privileges, the patentee's own license to do so is dependent upon the rights of others and whatever laws might be applicable. A patentee, merely because he or she has received a patent for an invention, is not thereby authorized to make, use or sell the invention if doing so would violate any law. A patentee may not engage in such activities regarding his or her own invention if doing so would infringe the prior rights of others as granted to them by a patent that is still in force.

Even though an invention is patentable, it could be seen as an infringement on a previously issued patent. The result could be a lawsuit for damages. The grant of a patent is not a guarantee that it does not infringe some prior art, or that it could not, at some time in the future, be declared invalid in the event of a legal challenge. However, until that challenge arises the patent bestows all the rights and privileges on the inventor as previously described.

HOW A PATENT RIGHT CAN BE LOST

If the invention has been described by anyone (including the inventor) in a printed publication anywhere in the world, or if it has been in public use or on sale in this country or anywhere in the world more than one year before the date on which an application for patent is filed in this country, a valid patent cannot be obtained. The inventor will forfeit any and all rights to a patent on his or her invention. Under patent law, it is immaterial when or where the invention was actually created, or whether the printed publication of, or public use of, the invention was by the inventor himself, or by another person or entity. If it had been known by anyone, anywhere, anytime—it is not new.

FOREIGN PROTECTION

A United States patent protects an invention in this country only. Normally, a license must be obtained from the Commissioner of Patents and Trademarks before an inventor can file for a patent in another country, unless that filing occurs more than six months after the filing in this country. In that case, no license is necessary unless the applicant is informed otherwise by the Patent and Trademark Office.

3. Deciding to Apply for a Patent

SHOULD YOU APPLY FOR A PATENT ON YOUR INVENTION?

In 1899, Charles H. Durell stated unequivocally: "Everything that can be invented has been invented." At the time, Durell was the Director of the U.S. Patent Office. In May of 1849, Abraham Lincoln was granted a patent for "A Device for Buoying Vessels over Shoals." The patent number is 6,469. You will not be able to retrieve it in an online search, but you can order a copy of it from the Patent Office—of which Lincoln once said: "The patent system added the fuel of interest to the fire of genius." Mark Twain was granted three patents. Thomas Edison received 1,093 patents—several posthumously. Edison, in describing his gift for invention and creativity, stated: "Genius is one percent inspiration and ninety-nine percent perspiration." He also affirmed that "anything that won't sell, I don't want to invent."

As we have seen, an invention is defined as any innovative idea; however, a patent cannot be granted for an inventor's idea per se. Notions, conceptions, or inspirations are not patentable—no matter what their merits might be. A copyright might be obtained on the form of expression of these, but not a patent.

An inventor does not necessarily have to comprehend the science that may underlie his or her invention. Some of the greatest inventions have been serendipitous—the celebrated "stroke of genius." The key factors are originality and novelty. Fame and fortune have come to many ingenious tinkerers who toiled in garage and basement workshops instead of university or corporate laboratories.

SOME POINTS TO CONSIDER BEFORE YOU BEGIN THE FORMAL APPLICATION PROCESS

Before you undertake your search for patents, and certainly before you commit to the time-consuming and expensive process of applying for a patent, you should ask yourself a number of questions—and answer each as truthfully and objectively as possible.

- Does your invention meet *all* of the criteria for patentability?
- Do you believe it is likely to be patentable?
- Does your invention solve a problem or answer a need? How?
- Will your invention sell?
- To whom will it sell? Who and where will your market be?
- Can it be manufactured economically?
- Will you make money from it? Will you at least recover your expenses?
- Do you realize that a patent application is not simply filling out a form? A patent application consists of a detailed technical description of an invention, properly rendered drawings (where required), and specifically formatted claims. To appreciate the requirements of the application, review the sample patent shown in Appendix 1.
- Do you understand that you really must have a patent attorney to assist you in filing an application? There are many authors and websites that say otherwise. The Patent Office, however, confirms this need.
- Do you know what an attorney will charge per hour for this service?
- Do you accept the fact that you will be required to do a lot of patent spending before "patent pending"?
- Do you have what will be large sums of money to spend on what could be a futile effort?
- Can you take the risk? Is it worth it? Can you afford to invest in your dream?
- Do you understand what you have to lose?
- Do you have the patience and perseverance it will take to apply for, prosecute, and obtain a patent?
- Are you willing to accept failure at any step in the process?

If you can answer each of these questions with an unqualified "yes," you can start the application process. You can start your patent search without answering any of them.

4. Applying for a Patent

WHO MAY APPLY FOR A PATENT?

The patent law states that only the inventor may apply for a patent. There are certain exceptions. If someone other than the inventor, or his or her authorized agent, would apply any patent that he or she might obtain would be null and void. If the applicant had falsely stated in the application (by an oath or declaration) that he or she is the "true inventor," he or she could be subject to criminal penalties.

If the inventor had died before the application could be filed, it may be initiated by a legal representative, that is, his or her heirs or the administrator or executor of their estate. If the inventor has gone mad in the creative process, an application may be made by a guardian. If an inventor is unwilling to apply for a patent or cannot be located within a reasonable time, a co-inventor or any person having a proprietary interest in the invention may apply on behalf of the inventor who is reluctant, or who has gone missing.

If two or more persons invent jointly, they can apply for a patent as co-inventors. An individual or company that provides only investment capital, no matter the amount, is not considered to be a joint inventor, and cannot be joined as such in the application. The applicant does not have to be an American citizen. Any foreign national may apply for and obtain a patent. By law, officers and employees of the Patent Office are prohibited from applying for patents or acquiring, directly or indirectly (except by inheritance or bequest), any patent or any rights in one.

WHAT IS IT GOING TO COST?

This is usually the fifth question you will ask after:

1. "Why hasn't this been invented before now?" (Most likely something like it has already been patented.)
2. "Is my invention patentable?" (Most likely it is. Others like it probably were.)
3. "How much money am I going to make from it?" (Unfortunately, but typically, little or none.)

4. "What will I do with my new-found wealth?" (See the answer to question 3.)

The financial investment required is invariably a critical factor in an individual inventor's decision to apply for a patent. The total amount of that financial commitment will depend on the type of patent, and whether or not the applicant is a "small entity" (individual inventor, nonprofit organization, or a small business concern) or a corporation. Several other factors are also involved.

A patent on even the most basic invention can require a financial commitment of $3,000 to $5,000. An absolute minimum and realistic cost is $2,500 to $3,000 for a relatively simple invention and the application and documentation it will require. For a Utility patent, the basic filing fee, attorney's fees, and the issue fee might total approximately $5,000 for a small entity. The final cost can escalate from there. You must be prepared to spend up to $10,000 or more for a Utility patent. Expenditures for Design and Plant patents may be slightly lower.

If your invention is highly complex, and or involves a high degree of technology, your total cost will be accordingly higher. In July 1998, the Patent Office revised its fee schedule for fiscal year 1999. The new schedule is available on the USPTO website. This website, and all others cited in this book, are shown in the appended list.

Your search for patents will be a search for "prior art." The amount and nature of the prior art that will be found in the formal patent search will also be a determining factor. The more prior art and the closer it is to the subject invention, the more descriptive and explanatory content required in the application. The more time in preparation, the greater the expense. Prior art will be defined and discussed in detail in chapter 6.

Any assistance the inventor can provide to his or her attorney will mitigate legal fees. The number of succeeding drafts, revisions, and changes that are usually required during the course of preparation and prosecution will be significant cost factors. If changes and revisions can be minimized, expenses can be minimized. The estimate of the attorney's fees must be discussed before the application is prepared. These will be the major component of the final cost of prosecuting your patent. They can vary significantly from invention to invention, application to application, and attorney to attorney.

If the inventor is very careful in defining all of the "embodiments" of the invention (the description and depiction of its construction and methods of use–its "best mode") and if the required drawings are adequate, the application should progress more expediently and less expensively. The broadest number of claims will be allowed by an examiner if the application adequately describes as reasonable a number of conceivable and practical embodiments as possible. A discussion of claims and their critical importance in the application and, ultimately, in the patent, is beyond the scope of this book. The format and language of claims are best left to a patent attorney. The need for an attorney will be discussed further in chapter 5. For examples of claims, examine the sample patent in Appendix 1. Pay very close attention to the claims in each patent you identify in your search to determine if any are relevant, and potentially problematic for your invention.

HOW LONG WILL I HAVE TO WAIT FOR MY PATENT TO ISSUE?

This is another question every inventor will ask before the filing of the application. After the filing, you will constantly ask: "Will my patent *ever* issue?" The waiting time from the date of your application to the date of issue of the patent can seem interminable. The wait can be a very stressful and frustrating experience for an inventor who anticipates immediate and large profits. The patent process takes a long time. Much of it will be waiting for a final decision by the patent examiner assigned to your application. In the seemingly endless interim, there will be a varying amount of back and forth communication dealing with objections, revisions, clarifications, errors, and many other technical or procedural problems. You must be prepared to wait—and resign yourself to it.

The Typical Waiting Time

Expect to wait up to a year or more for the Patent Office to respond to your application. For a regular Utility patent to issue once an application is filed, the time usually varies from 18 to 24 months—or longer. It could be three years. As shown in the sample patent in Appendix 1, the application was filed on February 23, 1996, and the patent issued on August 4, 1998. The waiting period will vary according to the nature and complexity of the invention, and the adequacy of the application itself. A major determinant will be the workload of the examiner to whom your application is assigned.

If, on initial examination of the application, or at a later stage, it is found to be "allowable," a "Notice of Allowance" will be sent to the applicant, or to the applicant's attorney or agent. A fee for issuing the patent is due within three months from the date of the written notice. If timely payment is not made, the application will be regarded as having been abandoned. The PTO may accept a late payment if the delay can be shown to have been unavoidable.

When the issue fee is paid, the patent will issue as soon as possible after the date of payment. This will depend on the workload of the issuing Office. New patents are issued weekly and always on Tuesday. The formal patent grant (the "Letters Patent") is sent out on the day of its issue or as soon thereafter as possible. It will be sent to the inventor's attorney or agent if there is one of record; otherwise, directly to the inventor. On the date of issue ("publication") the entire patent file becomes open to the public, and a copy of it becomes available to anyone. The documentation will be entered into the Patent Office's databases and become available for online search. These databases, and the online search process–the focus of this book–will be described in chapter 8.

SPEEDING UP THE PROCESS: THE PETITION TO MAKE SPECIAL

There are provisions in the patent law that enable the application process to be accelerated—under certain conditions. This can be effected by the filing of a "Petition to Make Special." The various criteria of the petition are shown below. A supporting declaration, certain other supporting materials, and the prescribed fees must accompany the petition. Complete information on this topic is available from the Office or online at the PTO website. If you qualify under any of the criteria, an attorney can assist you in preparing a persuasive and effective petition.

Criteria for a Petition to Make Special

The PTO has several criteria that must be met to grant a Petition to Make Special:

- The individual applicant is in poor health or is terminally ill.
- The applicant is 65 years of age or older.
- A manufacturer for the product is immediately available.
- There is a case of infringement.
- The invention can be shown to have direct and immediate benefits to the overall quality of the environment.
- The invention will produce significant benefits in efficiency and cost of energy production.
- The invention facilitates the diagnosis, treatment, or cure of a major illness or medical condition (for example: cancer, HIV/AIDS).
- Recombinant DNA is involved.
- Superconductivity is advanced.

THE ESSENTIAL REQUIREMENTS OF A FILING

A patent is granted to an inventor in return for which the inventor provides in his or her patent application a clear and concise description of the invention, and the best mode known to the inventor for using it at the time it was made. Every patent application must demonstrate the three required elements discussed previously: (1) novelty, (2) utility, and (3) nonobvious. Necessity may be the "mother of invention," but prosecution is the father of a patent.

A patent will be issued only:

- When a complete and accurate application has been filed;
- after all applicable fees have been paid;
- after an *official* search of the prior art has been conducted by the Patent and Trademark Office; and
- when, and only when, the Patent and Trademark Examining Attorney "allows" any or all of the claims stated in the application.

5. The Need for a Patent Attorney

WILL YOU NEED A PATENT ATTORNEY?

You will not need an attorney (or agent) to do a preliminary search for patents. As you will see, this is the one part of the process that you can quite easily do yourself using the Internet. Eventually, after you have completed your search, and when the decision is made to file for a patent, you will ask: "Do I really need a patent attorney, or can I file the application and obtain a patent myself?" Patent law does *not* require that an inventor be represented by an attorney. You may prosecute the patent yourself. This is referred to as a *pro se* application. "Prosecute" is the legal term for filing and following through on the application. (Without a thorough understanding of the patent process and patent law, it can become "persecute.")

The patent application process is extremely complex. The language is arcane and very technical. It is one of the most difficult and challenging areas of legal writing. The required format is very specific. The protocols are strict. Do not look to the Patent and Trademark Office to assist you in the preparation of your application. This is not allowed. Office publications offer this sound advice: "We strongly advise prospective applicants to engage the services of a patent attorney." An attorney in civil or criminal practice, or your "family lawyer," is likely to be of no great value in the patent process.

The anticipated cost of prosecuting and obtaining a patent can be a major incentive for an inventor to attempt to do it on their own. He or she should understand that the cost of retaining a patent attorney more than justifies the expertise that the attorney can provide. Unless the inventor has a thorough knowledge of the highly complicated patent process, and the requirements of patent law—and also has the time, writing ability, drafting skills, persistence, and patience required—he or she is advised not to attempt to patent the invention themselves. His or her misguided efforts in an attempt to save money could ultimately cost them all legal rights to their invention, and in the long-run involve expenditures far in excess of those that might have been required if a patent attorney had been retained at the outset of the application process.

Your efforts to file your own application could be rewarded with a patent; however, if its language and your claims do not provide your invention with maximum protection from infringement, or from others' efforts to design around it, you have wasted your time and money and most likely forfeited many, if not all, of your patent rights. You can attempt a draft of the application in an effort to reduce expenses, but it should be reviewed by an attorney before it is filed. The attorney's time spent in reviewing and correcting your deficient draft will be billable. If it cannot be salvaged, you will also be charged for the attorney's time in preparing a new application.

Although the Office cannot recommend any particular attorney, and does not establish or control their fees, it does maintain a roster of approximately 17,000 patent attorneys and agents registered to practice before the U.S. Patent and Trademark Office. These are listed alphabetically by geographic region. This roster is available for review at any Patent and Trademark Depository Library (PTDL). (See Appendix 2 for a list of PTDLs.) It is also online at the USPTO website. Telephone directories of most major cities list the names of patent attorneys. You can contact the PTO's Office of Enrollment and Discipline; the staff can verify the credentials and professional standing of any registered patent attorney you are considering to represent you.

INFORMATION A PATENT ATTORNEY WILL REQUIRE FROM YOU

Before you meet with the patent attorney, you should have prepared:

- Usable drawings or sketches, digital images on a disk, or photographs of your invention;
- a model or prototype, if possible;
- the complete, accurate and precise description of the invention in all its possible modes and uses that you will have prepared prior to starting your search for patents;
- a recitation of any and all features, or essential and unique aspects that distinguish the invention from any other subject matter of the invention—also prepared before your search;
- a realistic statement of the problems or needs it addresses, and how it is intended to do so;
- any descriptive materials from other sources that may describe alternative approaches to the problems or needs addressed by the invention;
- any examples of such products, if obtainable;
- a list of any and all individuals who were directly involved in the conception and development of the invention; and
- any and all copies of patents, lists of patent numbers, and other materials that you may have derived in your preliminary search for patents.

You should retain the original copies of all such materials and provide duplicates to the attorney.

6. The Search for Prior Art

PRIOR ART DEFINED

A patent search is a search for "prior art." Prior art may be defined as any technology (structure or method) which predates the filing of a patent application for an invention that appears to incorporate the same or similar technology. Prior art includes:

- Any description or discussion of the primary and defining elements of the invention that has been revealed in any printed publication anywhere in the world; and which was available to the general public at any time prior to the date of conception of the subject invention;
- any description or discussion of the invention in a printed publication, or any public use or sale of the invention that occurred more than one year prior to the filing date of the application;
- any public knowledge of the invention in the United States that could be demonstrated to have existed at the time of the invention's conception;
- any relevant current or expired U.S. or foreign patents that had been issued at any time prior to the conception of the invention for which a patent is now applied for; and
- any relevant patent application that had already been filed (and is pending) in the U.S. Patent Office by another person prior to the filing of the subject application for the invention.

SIGNIFICANCE OF PRIOR
ART IN THE PATENT PROCESS

You will search for prior art to:

1. Ascertain whether or not your invention is patentable—that is, it is truly new; and that nothing exactly like it has *ever* been patented;
2. to determine your invention's relevance and similarity to others in the same field; and
3. should you elect to search for patents personally, to familiarize you with patents and the patent process.

The search for, and discovery of, any prior art is the most critical procedure in the patent process. Prior art comprises any and every disclosure presented in any printed description or graphic representation of an article, procedure, method, or device of any kind that is similar to the invention for which the patent application is being made. It includes prior use of something similar to the invention, of which there could be any kind of record or recollection. If there appears to be nothing similar to the invention, then prior art would be that which could be considered the closest thing to the invention that might be found anywhere in the world.

This search for prior art is sometimes referred to as a "Novelty Search." Even if the invention for which a patent is applied is not exactly that shown in any prior art, and may incorporate a number of distinct features that make it different from the most similar inventions known, a patent could still be denied if the differences claimed would be obvious. This is often a very contentious point. What might appear nonobvious to the inventor could be asserted to be patently obvious by an examining attorney. The subject matter for which a patent is sought must demonstrate such differences from what has been used or described previously, that it may be shown to be nonobvious to any person having ordinary knowledge and skill in the field of the invention. If the prior art demonstrates that your invention would be obvious to any person skilled in the relevant technology ("skilled in the art"), either you will not obtain a patent, or if a patent were issued to you by mistake, it would be invalid.

Disclosures of prior art will be presented by the PTO examiner, or another inventor (as an adverse party) in an effort to show obviousness of your invention. The deciding factor will be whether anyone skilled in the art would have or could have been likely to derive and integrate the same elements in such a way as to produce the same or a very similar result as represented by the invention you now claim.

There is no legal obligation to perform a prior art search before a patent application is filed. Prior art searches are not always done. However, a preliminary search for prior art can at least determine whether or not an inventor should even consider filing a patent application. Even when the findings of their search indicate the futility of proceeding any further, many inventors—determined, disillusioned, or desperate—will press on at any cost. The necessity of searching for prior art will be discussed further in chapter 7.

PRIOR ART IN THE EXAMINATION PROCESS

In reviewing and evaluating an application, patent examiners will endeavor to search all identifiable prior art. Your patent application will undergo "Substantive Examination" by a Patent and Trademark Office examining attorney. His or her search will be an exhaustive and comprehensive examination of all of the material in the Patent Office library and files to locate anything relevant to the subject invention. This will provide the basis for a determination ("allowance") of patentability. The examiner who is assigned the review of your application for patent has a legal obligation to conduct as thorough a search as possible. Any and all references from his or her findings will be cited as the basis for a rejection of your application.

The examining attorney will evaluate your invention for the definitive element of innovation. In order for the invention to be considered patentable it must provide a new function or a new manner of achieving an old function with regard to what has been disclosed previously in the field relating to the invention (the prior art). Any art which will be located and cited by the examiner will be derived from published materials, most of which would not be readily accessible to a searcher unless he or she goes to the Patent Office library.

Even though prior uses of an invention, or public verbal disclosures of an invention, can also constitute prior art, it would be highly unlikely if not impossible that the examiner could have any knowledge of such information. A PTO examiner has immediate access to a library (or other database) which can be exhaustively searched for prior art. This, of course, includes the documentation of every U.S. patent ever issued, and of those pending issue.

Filed and pending patent applications are considered to be prior art even though they have not yet been published. Neither you nor your attorney will have any way of discovering the existence of an unpublished, prior application. The PTO maintains all files for pending applications in strictest secrecy. They are not available for perusal by anyone outside of the Office, and the Office will not respond to inquiries about these—of any kind—from anyone. The examiner of your patent application will review any and all pending applications and consider the relevance of these to your invention.

Based on his or her findings, the examiner will make the decision (not necessarily final) as to whether or not your invention is patentable in view of the prior art he or she has uncovered during the course of their examination. In that event, the burden of proof is placed upon the applicant, who in order to achieve allowance must now demonstrate that the claimed invention was not "anticipated" or "suggested" by the prior art cited.

OBLIGATION TO CITE RELEVANT PRIOR ART

As previously noted, there is no legal obligation to perform a prior art search before a patent application is filed. However, once such a search is performed the applicant should be aware of the "affirmative obligation" to cite to the examiner in charge of the patent application the prior art the applicant has uncovered in his or her search (and any other prior art of which they or their attorney is aware).

The U.S. Patent and Trademark Office imposes the obligation to bring all relevant prior art to the attention of the examining attorney. Usually this would be in the form of a list of cited patents, including the patent numbers, dates of issue, and the names of the patentees. You should note this information on your worksheet as you conduct your search. It will be needed when, and if, you decide to file. This list should accompany the application, or it can supplement it within a reasonable time.

7. The Search for Patents and the Patent Search

THE NEED TO SEARCH FOR PATENTS

You will inevitably ask: "Do I need to conduct a search before I file my patent application?" The answer is "yes." The second question will be: "Can I do it myself?" The answer is "yes." You can search for patents. You cannot do a patent search. The examining attorney who will be assigned to your application will do the formal, definitive search—the true "patent search."

As thorough a preliminary search as might be possible can be an important determinant for the successful prosecution of an application for a patent. At least a cursory examination is recommended before committing to the considerable expense of retaining an attorney and filing an application. This an *absolute must*.

If you do not do a search, or contract to have it done, you are very likely to waste a great deal of your time and money in applying for a patent for your invention when someone may have been there ahead of you. Any inventor who believes that no one else could have possibly thought of his or her invention before them could be seriously and expensively disappointed. A patent for an invention like yours that is current, or one that has long expired, or had been abandoned, may exist in the files of the Patent Office. The patent search will find it; your search may not. Therefore, it is strongly advised that at least a preliminary search of previously issued patents—current and expired—be conducted to confirm whether or not your idea might already have been patented at anytime in the past. As you will see, your online search will allow you to go back only so far in the past—to 1971. But any patents issued before that date could scuttle your application. The examiner's patent search will resurrect these.

You may find, as have many inventors before you, that your "new" idea, or something virtually identical to it, may have already been patented—just last week, or on any date in the last century. Just because you have never seen an invention or product like yours on the market does not necessarily mean that it has never been patented. A logical question is: "Why have I never seen the product in stores, in catalogues, or on TV?" The logical answer might be that it was not particularly useful in the first place, and, therefore, there was no market for it. Obtaining a patent and marketing its subject invention are two entirely different processes. There are innumerable products for which patents have been issued and which have never been manufactured and marketed. These are never "as seen on TV" and really "not available in any stores"—never have been and never will be. There are several sites included in the list of websites that picture and describe patents of dubious merit. Most of the inventions represented are patently absurd. All are amusing. Very few were profitable.

Before you spend time and money filing for a patent—even before you develop a prototype—conduct a search. It is a critical investment. It may help you avoid inadvertently infringing on someone else's patent and incurring legal liability. Or, you may be confronted with the decision to abandon your idea if you determine that it will not be patentable, thus obviating the commitment to the expensive process of prosecuting a patent.

OTHER BENEFITS OF A PRELIMINARY SEARCH

The patents you locate and review can provide a wealth of information for you in the development stages of your invention and in the preparation of your filing. All or any one of the cited references you locate could reveal aspects that you had not previously recognized and addressed. In those instances where the prior art of the subject patent is found to have been previously disclosed, it may be useful to learn exactly how this had been done, and in what way these inventions may have anticipated yours. You may also gain valuable technical insight into your own invention that you may be able to use to your advantage to refine your invention, and effectively design around those that are problematic.

Any of these discoveries could be suggestive of new approaches, design changes, and legitimate, definable innovations that may enhance your application, or provide the basis for a new and successful application in the event that the first one would be denied. Even though your application may, eventually, not be allowed, there may be benefits to be derived from the rejection. The examining attorney may cite any number of references that he or she has found in the prior art that are similar to your invention, and which, individually or collectively, might render the particular innovation you claim unpatentable. In this event the PTO search will have proven informative and useful in any revision of your invention and resubmission of a new application. If you determine that your invention is flawed in some way, perhaps an effort to remedy the flaw will provide the basis for a patentable invention.

Learning from Others

The search and all references cited may help you to assess your invention's possible commercial potential. You might wish to contact the inventors cited in relevant patents to determine if they had any commercial success with their inventions. There could be an invaluable lesson in their experiences (if they will share them). It has been estimated that only one in every thousand patents granted ever realizes commercial success for the individual, amateur inventor.

Some patents identify an assignee or licensee who had been identified in their applications. Should you decide to contact inventors who have received patents, ask if they licensed or assigned their inventions *after* their patents issued, and if they would tell you to whom they licensed or assigned them. These assignees or licensees might eventually prove to be companies that might be interested in acquiring the rights to your patent—when, and if, it issues. Make a note of them for future contact possibilities. You might consider contacting these firms after your application has been filed, or after your patent issues. Prior to that, be careful in disclosing your invention without having signed confidentiality agreements. With rare exceptions, large companies will not cooperate with you on such an agreement (or in considering your invention at all). Never reveal your claims before your patent issues.

WHO WILL DO THE SEARCH?

As affirmed previously, before you make a final decision to file an application for a patent, you should conduct a preliminary search personally, or hire a professional to do it for you. It is quite possible that the findings of either search could preclude the filing of an application if the prior art uncovered indicates that the technology of your subject invention does not appear to be particularly innovative. This book was written for the inventor who intends to attempt the search for patents (or trademarks) himself or herself.

DOING IT YOURSELF

Should you elect to do the preliminary search yourself, the procedures will familiarize you with the basics of patents and the patent process. As noted, you may uncover a great deal of useful information, tips, and guidelines, and gain valuable insights. You may also realize your worst fear—someone beat you to it!

Therefore, you will be required to make a decision. Will you spend the time and money to do the recommended, if not obligatory, preliminary search yourself, or will you hire a patent attorney or agent to conduct it? If your personal search suggests that your idea may have already been patented, do not give up. You may, at the least, wish to discuss your findings with an attorney or agent. He or she may propose other search tactics that may produce the results needed to prepare an adequate application. Your search may simply not have been adequate.

The extent and effectiveness of your personal effort will be determined by your time and budgetary constraints, and also your patience, ingenuity, and diligence. It is not an impossible task. If you have a computer, or access to one, and basic computer skills, patience, and are good with details, you should be quite successful in an online search. The guidelines presented in chapter 8 will help you considerably.

You may reduce your filing expenses by conducting the search on your own prior to retaining an attorney. If your efforts are reasonably successful, you may be able to assist the attorney in the preparation of an effective patent application on your behalf. However, as part of the application process, a patent attorney will usually propose conducting a search personally or contracting for it. He or she is likely to insist on this—even if you have already done one yourself. You have the right to refuse. Much of your search effort, and most, if not all, of your results will likely be duplicated by a patent attorney or his or her agent in the pre-application process, and, eventually, by an examining attorney in the exhaustive formal search during the examination process. This may, to a great degree, replicate your previous research. (The more replication, the more successful your search has been.)

In fact, you do not have to do a search at all or have one done for you. The Patent Office does not require the applicant to do a preliminary patent search. You can file your application and let the Patent Office do it for you; they are required by law to conduct one for each application. However, as discussed in chapter 6, you must conform with the legal obligation to cite to the Patent Office any relevant prior art of which you are aware.

RETAINING AN ATTORNEY OR AGENT TO DO THE SEARCH

It is hoped that the guidelines presented in this book may make it unnecessary for you to hire an attorney or agent until you are ready to file. However, if you decide not to undertake the task yourself, you can readily contract for the services of either a registered professional or a lay searcher. You are cautioned in the use of a lay searcher; they are usually not registered with the Patent Office. It is always best to use a patent attorney or agent who is registered with the PTO. These professionals must meet specific legal, technical, and ethical qualifications, and pass a credentialing examination to be registered. They are bound by a professional code of conduct to maintain the invention's confidentiality, and not make use of it for personal gain.

Be aware that the PTO has no control over, or involvement in, the business practices or advertising of patent practitioners or organizations. That is the Federal Trade Commission's responsibility. The PTO website provides information on the inquiry procedure regarding locating registered attorneys or agents and confirming their credentials.

You are especially cautioned in contracting for the services of the so-called "invention promotion," "patent development," or "patent search" firms. These operators are discussed in detail in chapter 10. Be particularly wary of promises of "free" or low-cost patent searches. If done at all, they are likely to be a slapdash effort that will provide you with an expensive "research report" containing virtually worthless information. These "free" services are a come-on for an array of expensive "development" and "promotion" contracts—equally worthless. Hire a qualified expert if you cannot do it yourself.

WHAT WILL BE SEARCHED

As of July 27, 1999, there were nearly 6 million U.S. patents issued and on file—not including any duplications and cross-references. This, together with the system of classification, and frequently the lack of integrity of the files available in the PTO's public search room and library, may be a serious impediment to the lay searcher. These files contain only existing and expired patents. The collection is very well organized and classified. Much of the prior art can be found in the PTO files and nowhere else—usually because it was for some reason never used, or not used sufficiently to appear in any other records.

The files at the PTO library contain over 29 million documents. In addition, there is an incalculable amount of other possible prior art represented by the holdings of worldwide libraries—in textbooks, technical journals, and magazines—in any language, or shown in the patent files of any foreign nation. There are countless other possible sources. The inventor must remember that any such information, found anywhere in the world, and which antecedes his or her invention, will be as relevant and problematic as any ancient patent found in the files of the PTO. It would be inconceivably expensive, and physically impossible, to search for, locate, and obtain each and every possible extant citation of prior art. An extensive search in other sites for non-patented prior art or foreign-patented prior art is considerably more expensive than searching the PTO files.

There is also an extensive collection of documents in the Examining Group's libraries. These are not available anywhere else. These materials are known as "foreign art," and include technical articles, and any other relevant items that examiners have accumulated for any particular class and or subclass of patent. This collection is comprised principally of foreign patents; English abstracts are usually included. All of the notations made by many examiners over the years are included in the documents. As discussed in chapter 6, successful prosecution of a patent may rely heavily upon knowledge of the prior art known to the examiners in the Office. Therefore, professional searchers generally consider it prudent to search all the material available to these examiners, in the form that is available to them. A layperson simply cannot do all of this.

For the professional, and certainly for the lay searcher, it is simply not possible to identify every relevant patent. Relatively little of all this information is now online. What you may need may not be searchable on the Internet. You will not find it anywhere except the Patent and Trademark Office, or at a Patent and Trademark Depository Library.

SEARCHING OUTSIDE OF CYBERSPACE

As you can see, what you will be confronted with will depend on where you search, and where you search will be determined by what you want to confront—how far you wish to go—in miles or effort. The focus of this part of the book is searching for patents on the Internet. Because of the limitations presented by the present technology, and the limitations imposed by available databases, there must also be a discussion of searching at the PTO or at a PTDL. For those who may be computer illiterate, these may be the only viable alternatives.

SEARCHING AT THE PTO

Unless an inventor lives within a reasonable driving distance of the PTO, the cost of long distance travel, accommodations, and other expenses could easily equal or exceed the fee of a professional, experienced, and efficient searcher who works with the files constantly. Most of them have offices in Arlington, Virginia, and go to the PTO library daily. A search by a professional should cost between $300 and $500. Weigh this against your costs of travel, lodging, meals, and incidental expenses. If you fly to the Ronald Reagan Airport in Virginia, the good news is that you can walk to the PTO offices from the airport. The bad news is that it will be a very expensive stroll.

The PTO library is no place for the amateur. You will waste hours, days, weeks in what may well be a futile and frustrating effort. For the money you will spend, you can hire a professional. The results will be worth the cost.

SEARCHING AT A PTDL

Before the Internet, the most convenient and least expensive way to conduct a personal, preliminary search had always been at a Patent and Trademark Depository Library. Now, however, if you have access to the WWW and have just basic computer skills you can do a limited search online. If not, one or more visits to the nearest PTDL will be required. Not every PTDL has a complete record of PTO information, but there will be more than enough to get you started (or finished as the case may be). A list of all PTDLs is shown in Appendix 2; it is also online at the USPTO website (check the link on the PTO's Home page).

At the PTO, and at every PTDL, there is a highly trained professional staff who are required to assist in your search efforts. They are there to provide references, resources, instructions, and guidelines. They cannot do a search for you. They cannot advise you on the patentability of your invention. They cannot offer legal advice of any kind.

THE PROCESS OF SEARCHING FOR PATENTS ONLINE OR OFFLINE

There are no shortcuts to doing a complete, thorough search for patents—even your preliminary search. The process is not terribly difficult, but it is very time consuming. Expect to spend 30 to 40 hours or more—often much more. It requires a great deal of concentration, patience, and attention to detail. If you are not detail oriented—particularly with the inevitable task of checking and cross-checking hundreds of seven digit numbers—it may prove to be a stressful, confusing, and futile experience. This will be a painstaking process, and if it is your first effort you are very likely to achieve far less comprehensive and useful results than those of an experienced, professional searcher.

Your objective will not simply be to determine if your invention is now patented; it will be to confirm that you invention has *never* been patented. It is a process of elimination that will require you to examine each patent in your subject area (class/subclass) to determine if there is any prior claim to your idea—as far back in time as the subject of your invention has been technologically possible.

As confirmed in chapter 2, anything that has previously been patented cannot be repatented, even though its patent expired many years ago. Once a patent expires, the invention described in it becomes part of the public domain. Anyone may manufacture and sell the invention for which it had been issued. So, if you find such an invention that is identical to yours you will neither need nor get a patent. Your search is over—unless you can design around it.

THE 7-STEP STRATEGY FOR A PATENT SEARCH AT THE PTO OR AT A PTDL

The Patent Office suggests *The 7-Step Strategy* as a do-it-yourself search plan that the inventor can implement at the either the PTO library or any PTDL. These same guidelines will be used in the Internet search that will be discussed in chapter 8. There are minor differences in the online search strategy. You might wish to review Appendix 3, which shows the PTO's detailed description of each of the steps, and particularly the references utilized. This will assist you to some degree in identifying and following them as you proceed through the sample online search, and the search exercises presented in the next chapter.

PREPARING FOR YOUR PATENT SEARCH

This could prove to be the most critical element in your undertaking. How thoroughly you prepare will be the key to a successful search. You must define precisely what it is you are looking for *before* you start looking.

Your immediate challenge will be to "classify" your invention. You must first place your invention in the Patent Office's scheme of things. Every patent that has ever been issued has been classified within the PTO's hierarchy of classes and subclasses. (Locating and utilizing these will be discussed further in chapter 8.) Determining tentative relevant classes and subclasses will be the starting point and ongoing map of your search. You are likely to assemble a bewildering array as you proceed.

Your first, and most important, task is to define precisely what your invention is. You need not give it its final title at this time, although you should keep this in mind. Patents are issued on how the claimed invention works, not on its application or use. You must define the essence of your invention, the essential elements of its subject matter. You should describe it as concisely but in as many specific terms and "keywords" as possible. These will be the search "terms" you will enter for each query. The more specific and precise your search terms, the more efficient it will be for you to assign classes and subclasses, and to search the patent databases most efficiently and effectively. The invention must be refined to its essence, and that essence must be articulated.

Every significant feature should be identified and noted. Use a standard dictionary, thesaurus, and a crossword puzzle dictionary. There are a number of these online. These will be very useful, and will make your efforts of classification and subclassification easier and more accurate. Eventually, the search itself may provide additional descriptive terms and classes that can be used to expand your list of keywords. These can suggest new classes and subclasses to explore. Once you have assembled a concise and accurate list of search terms, you can begin. But first, prepare a search worksheet.

THE PATENT SEARCH WORKSHEET

A patent search worksheet is essential to assist you in keeping track of the vast array of patent numbers, classes, subclasses, names, and dates you will encounter and record. The worksheet can be in paper format, or maintained as a database on your computer. In an online search, a PC or laptop will be invaluable. A laptop will also be of great assistance at a PTDL. Set up a worksheet and or database with a separate file for each class and subclass you search.

You must examine each patent in each potential class/subclass you have assigned to your patent. Only one primary class/subclass will eventually be assigned by an examining attorney, although the patents you examine will list others that are relevant—note these carefully.

When you note patent numbers that are referenced in any relevant patent you examine, include the essential details of these for later examination. Note at least the number, last name of the patentee, and date of issue. These data could prove very useful in refining your search. If you have selected your keywords carefully, you may be fortunate enough to narrow the selection of classes and subclasses to only a very few. One class/subclass is your goal.

Format of the Worksheet

There is no fixed format for a worksheet. The database or hardcopy form you design should include several headings to make the process as efficient, comprehensive, and meaningful as possible. For each possibly relevant patent you locate note:

- Dates searched, checked, cross-checked
- Class/subclass
- U.S. patent number
- Name of patentee
- Date issued
- Expiration date
- Title and or brief description
- Abstract reviewed
- Retrieved and reviewed full documentation of patent
- Patent numbers referenced
- Classes/subclasses referenced
- Notes: for example, follow up, recheck, locate, leads, tips
- Comments: for example, similarities, differences, improvements
- Name(s) of assignees or licensees, if any

Above all, incorporate in your worksheet some method of keeping track of precisely where you are in your search at any given time. This will assist you in determining where you have looked, where you might look next, and where not to bother looking. This will help you avoid duplicating your efforts, chasing down rabbit holes, and going off in all directions at the same time.

Whatever system works for you is fine, so long as it works. Experiment. Copies of your disks and or worksheets, and all the other materials you had generated in your search, should be given to your attorney when the time comes to file your patent application.

YOUR SEARCH RESULTS

A successful search will yield one of two results: either there is at least one reference that could deny patentability, or a basis for patent may be defined with respect to the pertinent prior art. In either case the field of the search was defined by the invention's class and subclass, and the pertinent references identified and discussed in relation to the innovation searched.

In the first case, only the references that deny patentability would be noted, and the summary of your findings will likely be relatively brief. In the second case, documentation of the most pertinent references are assembled and presented. These are offered as the basis for your obtaining a patent over these references and the prior art represented in any and all of them.

A number of patents might describe inventions with the same purpose as the subject of your invention, but may be significantly different in several ways. You should evaluate these very critically and objectively, and, only after having done so, make a decision to file. If there appears to be no reasonable chance of you getting a patent, an application may be futile. This is why it is strongly recommended that you consult a patent attorney when your final decision on a patent application is to be made. The attorney, from extensive experience, might be able to derive features of the invention that could make it significantly different from prior art and or provide significant or new advantages over it. With a properly worded and persuasive application, a patent might be obtained based on these features. A competent attorney can usually get at least one claim accepted.

Should your search discover an expired patent for a device that is virtually identical to your invention in form and function, you would, of course, not file a patent application. It would be a complete waste of time and money. Since such an expired patent is now in the public domain, you would be free to manufacture and sell "your" invention—as would anyone else!

A preliminary search and or a follow-up search, regardless of who conducts it, or how thoroughly it is done, is absolutely no guarantee of patentability. If a search by the inventor (or his or her attorney or agent) does not reveal any relevant prior art, and if the inventor believes his or her invention has definite commercial potential, he or she can then elect to file a patent application. At best, there will be no undiscovered prior art that could preclude a patent issuing from his or her application. At worst, their search has missed it.

LIMITATIONS OF YOUR SEARCH

When you do your search, you will likely locate some relevant prior art. You may find a great deal, or you may find virtually nothing of use. Regardless, there is a reasonable chance that every one of the most relevant (and most problematic) examples will not be found. Whether a search is done manually, or with the aid of a computer, the process and techniques are subject to human frailty. No search can be absolutely comprehensive, complete, or all-encompassing. It is a process that cannot be perfect. The human searcher is not perfect. Even with the aid of vast computer databases, the searcher must define, and present to the computer, the keywords, the search terms for which its electronic brain must hunt. The thoroughness and scope of the search will be limited by the exactitude of a human's (your) choice of words. It is a painstaking, complex process in which useful results will come only from patience and persistence, or at times, serendipity.

THE SEARCH GOES ON

After you have filed an application, use the online search steps that will be outlined in chapter 8 to do a periodic review of your class/subclass to determine if any new patents have been issued that appear to be similar to yours. If a very similar, if not identical, patent issues before yours, you will likely not be granted one for your invention.

At any time after your patent search has been done and your application has been filed—and up until the day your patent issues—another that had been pending and undiscoverable could issue, and it will obviate a patent for you. The patent examination process would eventually disclose this pending application, and a notice of denial would be sent to your attorney. In the interim, it could be an expensive wait for confirmation of a development that you could not have discovered or anticipated, and that could require you to reconsider, redesign, reapply—or rescind and forget the whole thing. In such instances, consult your patent attorney, and discuss your choices in light of this drastic (but unlikely) occurrence.

Even after your patent has issued, you may want to do a periodic search to determine if any subsequent patents have issued for inventions that are similar to yours in form and or function. You might be surprised to find that someone has successfully designed around your invention. A lawsuit for infringement may be in order.

8. Searching for Patents on the Internet

SEARCHING FOR PATENTS ON THE INTERNET

In the preceding chapters, the terms "patent search" and "search for patents" have been used somewhat interchangeably; however, there is a significant difference, particularly as they relate to the successful prosecution of a patent. It is much more than a semantic distinction.

An online search for patents is *not* a patent search. Although it is now possible to conduct a limited search for patents on the Internet, it is not possible to do a true patent search; and the one that you, or your attorney or agent, may conduct online will *not* qualify as such. None of the databases now available online can be so thoroughly and effectively searched as to accomplish a true patent search.

As you have read, a complete patentability search must include *all* prior art, including all earlier patents, foreign patents, and non-patent literature. The available databases cannot replace the array and extent of the research tools and materials available at the Patent Office library, or even the relatively limited resources available at a PTDL. The fact that a patent for an invention like yours may not be located by searching the online databases which will be discussed in this chapter does not mean that your invention will be patentable.

The PTO files contain every U.S. patent ever issued (a number approaching 6 million in July of 1999) and every one that is relevant must be located and reviewed. In scope and magnitude, that is a patent search. And that is what the examining attorney will do before your application is allowed, and your patent issues. The websites that will be cited in this chapter, and several others included in the appended list, will prove very useful in conducting a preliminary search only.

U.S. PATENT OFFICE RESOURCES FOR ONLINE PATENT SEARCHING

The U.S. Patent and Trademark Office Home Page (Appendix 4) will be your starting point for both patent and trademark searching as well as your resource for virtually all information and guidelines on each of these topics. The content of the Home Page changes frequently, but these changes are usually in the section titled "New on the PTO site," which primarily consists of current official announcements. Once you have bookmarked the various pages suggested in the six search steps and exercises in this chapter, you should not have to access the PTO Home Page very often—if at all. However, at this time, you may wish to quickly review the PTO Website for the wealth of patent information you can link to in the future. As previously noted, many of these publications are must reading for the amateur inventor and aspiring patent applicant. Note particularly the link "Inventor Resources."

URL
    USPTO Home Page
    http://www.uspto.gov

For now, the side bar on page [139] will be your focus for patent searching. Click on the "Patents" bar. On the next screen, "Patent Information" (Appendix 5), you will see a number of links to the very useful information previously discussed: e.g., "General Information Concerning Patents." Click on the "Search US Patent Databases" link at the top of the page. This will take you to the USPTO Web Patent Databases page (Appendix 6).

URLS
    Patent Information
    http://www.uspto.gov/web/menu/pats.html

Web Patent Databases
    http://www.uspto.gov/patft/index.html
    Bookmark these URLs.

This Web Patent Databases page shows the links to the various search options available in the databases. As shown in Appendix 6, these include: Boolean Search; Manual Search; Patent Number Search; and Help.

In your patent searching, you will utilize the Boolean Search and the Patent Number Search options primarily. At this time, you are advised to click on the link to each of these two sites and bookmark them for quick access and use in the search exercises to follow in this chapter. You will not likely use the Manual Search option.

When necessary, go to the "Help" link in each database for instructions on how to use these search options. Before entering data at the various Web pages you will access, read the data entry instructions or help text. Note carefully whether or not embedded spaces, slashes, hyphens, quotation marks, or commas are allowed—or required—in the query format.

The United States Patent Office Full-Text Database

The United States Patent Office Full-Text Database—which became available online on March 26, 1999—contains approximately 2 million patents—over 20 million pages. It consists of 2 terabytes (TB), or, 2 trillion bytes. The Full-Text Database includes only those United States patents issued from January 1, 1976, up to the most recent weekly Tuesday issues. As previously noted, all relevant patents issued prior to that date must also be searched. (You will find many of these cross-referenced in the patents you will locate and examine.)

THE IBM INTELLECTUAL PROPERTY NETWORK

An additional resource for online searching is the IBM Intellectual Property Network (IPN) which was formerly known as the IBM Patent Server. The IPN Home page is shown in Appendix 7. Prior to March 1999, the IBM site had been the only free source for online patent drawings. This database includes only patents issued since January 5, 1971. The IBM site also allows you to retrieve, examine, and print each page of the drawings, in addition to the full text, the bibliographic data, and the abstract of a patent—all of which are now also available at the PTO's Full-Text site. It also presents the two options of a Boolean Search and a Patent Number Search. For example, if you search by patent number, the first page you receive will be basically identical in content to the page you would receive in response to a patent number query at the PTO site. The images on page 1 will be virtually the same content as the patent's *Official Gazette* entry (see Appendix 16).

The IBM site does provide more options in printing images. Should you elect to use it in a search, experiment with the "magnify" and "demagnify" options to determine which best suits your print output needs. You can do your initial review of the text and drawings at the size or resolution they present with on the screen, then demagnify as needed. The smaller the magnification, the fewer number of pages printed, but the less the clarity of drawings and legibility of text. Also, the maximum magnification option might result in individual drawing pages being split into two or three separate pages, with fragments of text and or graphics on each. Reduction by a factor of one will usually give adequate results for printed text and drawings. This will depend on the size of the drawings and the number shown on each page.

URL
IBM Intellectual Property Network
http://www.patents.ibm.com

Note: You will not need any special software to use the IBM IPN. The patent images from this site are in regular bitmap format (.bmp). The PTO Full-Text Database images format can be problematic, as discussed next.

RETRIEVING PATENT IMAGES
FROM THE PTO FULL-TEXT DATABASE

Return to the USPTO Web Patent Databases page (Appendix 6) which you had bookmarked. Note the statement/link: "How to access full-page images." Click on this link. This will take you to the Patent Full-Page Images page (Appendix 8) regarding retrieving patent images. These comments and instructions are highly relevant in the six patent search steps to be presented later.

Note particularly the statement that the: "Full-page images can be accessed from each patent's full-text display by clicking on the 'Images' button at the top of the patent full-text display page." The images can be accessed from this page only. You will do this in search step 6.

Also note the statements:

- "Patent images must be retrieved one page at a time."
- "Patent images are only accessible from the full-text display of each patent."
- "The 'Images' button links are valid only for a fixed period from the time each search is conducted and the hit list generated. This period is currently set at two hours. If this time period expires, the user must execute another search to generate a hit list which will lead to valid image links."
- "Successful printing of patent images is entirely dependent on the user's browser and image viewer software. With most image viewers (including AlternaTIFF) images may best be printed using the plug-in's print button rather that the browser's print function."

This page—Patent Full-Page Images—also discusses the file format of the images and the software required to access them.

REQUIRED PLUG-IN SOFTWARE TO VIEW
PATENT IMAGES IN THE PTO FULL-TEXT DATABASE

Before you successfully attempt to access and print the PTO database images, you must first determine if your computer browser is configured to retrieve and print them in the file format in which they are provided. If it is not, you will get various messages regarding the file format, or stating that the patent cannot be found. You will *not* get any patent drawings.

In search step 6, you will determine your browser's capacity to retrieve and view patent images from the PTO database. At that time you can download the free plug-in software should you find that you will need it. It is available online. It is free. It is relatively easy to download and install. If you use Netscape Navigator as your browser, you may not need to download it. If you use Internet Explorer, you likely will need it.

Review the Patent Full-Page Images page (Appendix 8). Note particularly the statement: "They [the images] are not directly viewable using most Web browsers." This page explains in detail the file format of the PTO database images—Tagged Image Format (TIFF;. tiff)—and the plug-in software you may need to view and print them.

Follow the link on the Patent Full-Page Images page to the Medical Informatics Engineering's "AlternaTIFF" Home Page (Appendix 9). This will describe the browser plug-in that MIE offers free and the procedure for downloading it. After you have confirmed whether or not you will need this type of software—as you will do later in search step 6—you can return to this site and download the AlternaTIFF plug-in. At that time also download the 11-page "Documentation" file from the link shown. Save and or print it. It will be invaluable in installing, using, and troubleshooting the plug-in software.

As stated at the top of the AlternaTIFF Home Page: "AlternaTIFF is a free Netscape-style browser plug-in that displays most of the common types of TIFF image files. It is compatible with ... Internet Explorer 3.0 and higher." You must have IE 5.0 for this software. Install a free upgrade to IE 5.0 before you install the AlternaTIFF plug-in. You can download the upgrade from: http://www.microsoft.com/ms.html.

PRINTING PATENT IMAGES FROM THE ALTERNATIFF PLUG-IN TOOLBAR

The AlternaTIFF plug-in will install its own tool bar. Its functions are explained in detail in the documentation file you download. Print the patent images from this tool bar only. This will print out the pages of the patent documents as they would be in the original file. If you use your browser's tool bar print function, it will print the entire page as shown on the screen—including the graphics and links in the sidebar—you will see an example after search step 6 has been completed.

In addition to magnification—very large to astronomical—the toolbar also allows images to be manipulated in a number of other ways—none of which are particularly useful. These options are not available on the IBM IPN site whose magnification (and demagnification) functions are far superior. You may wish to experiment with the image magnification/manipulation tools using this software versus those available on the IBM IPN site.

THE U.S. PATENT CLASSIFICATION SYSTEM

In order to conduct an actual search for patents efficiently and effectively, you *must* understand the U.S. Patent Classification System (USPCS). The seven-page PTO publication *How to Use the Patent Classification System* is free and online. It is included in this book as Appendix 10. It explains the System—as "clearly" as a government document can—and provides examples of its structure and use.

Unless you have a basic understanding of the USPCS you will *not* be able to begin a patent search let alone carry out a successful one. The reader is strongly advised to read Appendix 10! If you are not clear about some of the content, do not be concerned. The USPCS is not difficult to use, but does take some patience and persistence. It can be confusing and appear to have no logical order. As you conduct the search exercises presented later in this book, you will come to better understand the System and utilize it effectively in any future searches for which it will serve as your guide. You will encounter the USPCS in step 2 of a patent search.

URL
  http://www.uspto.gov/web/offices/pac/dapp/sir/co/overvw.htm

THE STEPS IN CONDUCTING A
SEARCH FOR PATENTS ON THE INTERNET

As discussed in chapter 7, the Patent Office suggests *The 7-Step Strategy* for conducting a patent search at a Patent and Trademark Depository Library (see Appendix 3 for the full text). This strategy changes somewhat when a search is done on the Internet. The PTO's step 6—a search of the *Official Gazette of the United States Patent and Trademark Office*—cannot be done online. This reduces the number of online search steps to six. You will use all six steps primarily in your first search attempt of any given invention. Once you have determined the class/subclass of the invention (step 1), you will utilize principally steps 4, 5, and 6 as your search progresses.

Appendixes 11 through 15d are generally arranged to follow the search exercise included in the description of each of the six steps. Use the URLs listed in each step to retrieve the sample pages/sites shown in the appendixes. I encourage you to do each of six search exercises as a means of familiarizing yourself with the various references and resources cited, and the methodology of searching in a logical order.

SEARCHING FOR PATENTS FOR AN INVENTION LIKE YOURS

For the purpose of the following search exercises, we will assume that you have invented a device that consists of a bracket assembly which is designed to be mounted on a ladder and provide a means to attach a shelf or other devices to the ladder. A rough sketch of your invention is shown below.

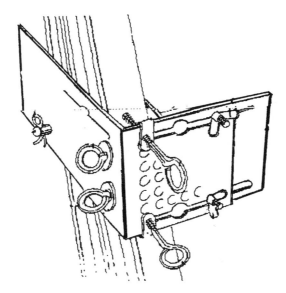

The objective of your search exercise will be to determine if anyone else has already patented an invention very similar, or identical, to yours. In the next section of this chapter are the six steps you will take to confirm that—unfortunately—someone has already been issued a patent for "your" idea as you will discover when your search exercises eventually locate U.S. Patent Number 5,788,198. This is the patent shown in Appendix 1 as a sample of a patent's full text documentation, including drawings. It will be your reference for several of the patent search exercises. It will also be utilized in Part II of the book in a trademark search exercise.

To avoid "cheating" in the patent search exercises to come later in this chapter, you are asked not to examine any of the documentation of this patent at this time. Doing so now could negate the learning objectives of the search exercises in each step to follow. For now, focus only on the above sketch and defining the purpose and function of your invention—what it does rather than how it does it. Your challenge will be to reduce it to its essence—to *classify* it. You will do this in the first of the six steps of a patent search.

THE SIX STEPS IN A PATENT SEARCH

STEP 1: FIND THE PRIMARY CLASS FOR THE INVENTION IN THE INDEX TO THE MANUAL OF CLASSIFICATION

As confirmed in the USPCS (Appendix 10), the entire patent classification system is based on the class/subclass pair assigned to each and every patent by the PTO. As you will see in examining patents, the primary class/subclass pair will be indicated as the "U.S. Cl." and any number of relevant pairs will be listed in the "Field of Search."

In the absence of any other data, this class/subclass designation is the starting point for each patent search. If there is a patented invention that is the same as or very similar to yours, it will have been assigned the same class/subclass pairing that would likely be applicable to yours. You will search these class/subclass fields as the logical place to find all such patents. To do this, you must first classify your invention; that is, identify the primary class(es) under which the invention could be grouped. You will do this using the *Manual of U.S Patent Classification* (MOC). The MOC became available on the USPTO Website for online searching on June 28, 1999. This was a major innovation in facilitating searching for patents online.

The *Manual of Classification* is a collection of the class schedules, a list of the class titles in numerical order by class number and in alphabetical order, a list of classes by Examining Groups, and a theoretical organization of classes into major groups.

Using your bookmark, return to the Patent Information page—URL http://www.uspto.gov/web/menu/pats.html. Click on the link at the bottom center: *Manual of Classification*. This will take you to the *Manual of U.S Patent Classification* page(s) as shown in Appendix 11.

URL
  http://www.uspto.gov/web/offices/ac/ido/oeip/taf/moc/index.html

This is an essential search resource. Bookmark this site and download the 14-page index and save it in a directory or folder as a file: e.g., C:\patserch\moc\index. You can then retrieve and review the index off-line in any future searches.

From the alphabetical list which begins at the bottom of page 1 of 14, you will attempt to identify the primary class number for your invention—one of the two key fields for your search—the subclass number is the second.

Identifying the Class.

What keyword(s) will you use to find the primary class of your invention? Your first task is to list every conceivable term you can think of to describe every aspect of your invention. Include any possible synonyms or variants of each term. Define the essentials of the subject matter of your invention. (Online PTO publications may be of help in this effort.) When you are satisfied that your list of keywords is as exhaustive and definitive as possible, you can begin your search.

Step 1 Search Exercise

Your search begins by looking in the MOC for your most relevant subject terms—the keywords you had listed that best describe the subject of your invention. Depending on the complexity of your invention, this list could include a relatively large number of words. You may be required to check each and every one of the terms on your list. We will simplify this process in this search exercise.

Your sketch shows a bracket assembly attached to a ladder. Its purpose is to allow the user to attach a shelf or other items to the ladder. Focus on what it is rather than what is does—its form, rather than its function. Start with the keyword "bracket." The word "ladder" is secondary. The word "shelf" is not relevant.

URL (Bookmarked.)

http://www.uspto.gov/web/offices/ac/ido/oeip/taf/moc/index.html.

Or, search the file of the MOC index you had previously created for the term "BRACKET." (This will be the most expedient method in all searches.)

As you will see, the specific term "BRACKET" is not listed. Using your keywords list, you would search the index further. As you review the entire list, try to identify any other terms in the class titles that could describe your invention in any way. As you do this, note in your worksheet/database the class number assigned to each title. You may be eventually required to search several of these; some could lead you in new directions—many will be dead-ends.

Reviewing the index, you may find that your invention could be classified under any number of titles: e.g., 016: MISCELLANEOUS HARDWARE. (Step 3 will help you to eliminate the contenders.) Your objective is to find *the* keyword that will lead you to *the* primary class number for your invention.

To expedite your initial attempt in this search exercise, ask: Does the invention "support" anything? Yes, it supports a shelf and other attachments. Search the list for the term, "SUPPORTS." Click on Class 248, Title SUPPORTS.

Unknown to you at this point, you have now identified 248 as the primary class number for your invention. You have also retrieved the first of 21 pages from the MOC showing the list of subclasses and titles under Class 248: SUPPORTS as shown in Appendix 12. You will search these in step 2.

Bookmark this site. Download and save these 21 pages in a directory/folder as a file: e.g., C:\patserch\moc\class#\248. You will use these pages in step 2, and again in step 3. In an actual search, you would download and save each such MOC listing of each Class and Title you retrieve in step 1. There could be a relatively large number of pages for each. You can then search these more expediently off-line. You are not advised to routinely print out each such file you will set up. This is a waste of time and materials. Having obtained the list of subclasses for the invention, you are now ready to proceed to step 2.

Step 2: Find the Subclass for the Invention in the Manual of Classification

You will do this by using the appropriate Class/Title listing in the MOC which you located in step 1.

This will be your first encounter with the USPCS. As you proceed, note the "dot-indent" system used to further subdivide the *Manual*'s subclass listings, and to identify these more precisely. These dots will be your markers as you proceed through the MOC. This is explained in *How to Use the Patent Classification System* which you had been advised to review.

Step 2 Search Exercise

Review or search the 21-page list of Class 248: SUPPORTS until you locate a subclass number and title that most accurately describes your invention.

You will eventually come to the primary subclass "BRACKETS" as shown in Appendix 13. (Note that this word is in capital letters—the USPCS format.) As you had determined previously in step 1, this term was *not* the title of a *primary* class. But it is the title of a *primary subclass*. The number of this primary subclass is: 200. (It is not necessarily the subclass number that will be assigned to your invention.)

Go down the list for primary subclass 200: BRACKETS shown in Appendix 13 and locate the specific subclass: 210. . Ladder. (Note the use of upper case and lower case in "Ladder"—USPCS.) Note also that this subentry has two leading dot indents, whereas others have one to four.

You have now identified 248/210 as the most likely class/subclass pairing for your invention. This pair will be the basis for your first search attempt. You will undertake this in step 4. But first, a quick review of the PTO Classification Definition of "SUPPORTS"—step 3.

STEP 3: REVIEW THE PATENT CLASSIFICATION DEFINITIONS

The *Classification Definitions* are statements of the scope embraced by each of the official classes and subclasses. Also included is an archive of PTO examiners' search notes and tips that direct the searcher to related subject matter in other classes and subclasses. These notes can be very helpful in defining the limits of a particular class or subclass. They can also be very confusing to a lay searcher. In an actual search, they must be reviewed in detail.

In an actual search, you should review the definition of each relevant class title that you retrieved in step 1. You are advised to download and save each as a file for detailed review off-line.

Step 3 Search Exercise

Return to you bookmarked page of the *Manual of U.S. Patent Classification*—Class 248 SUPPORTS (Appendix 12).

URL

http://www.uspto.gov/web.offices/ac/ido/oeip/taf/moc/detai179.html.

Under the title "Class *248 SUPPORTS*" note the statement: "class definitions may be accessed by clicking on the class title, above [sic]." Click on the title link. This will take you to the 40 pages of the CLASS DEFINITION of CLASS 248, SUPPORTS—page 1 of which is shown in Appendix 14. Save the 40-page definition as a file: e.g., C:\patserch\classdef\248.

Off-line, search the 40-page definition until you find the reference to the primary subclass: 200+, "for brackets of general utility" also listed "for other brackets," and the second entry from the end of the list on page 40: "for small brackets having an outwardly extending article for support." Search the list further, locate the reference for the more specific subclass of 200+: 210+, that refers to "for other ladder secured brackets."

Tip

In future searches for Classification Definitions, you can access the PTO list directly, and quickly locate class-specific definitions.

URL

http://www.uspto.gov.web/offices/pac/clasdefs/

Enter the class number as requested. In this search exercise, you could have entered the following URL:
http://www.uspto.gov.web/offices/pac/clasdefs/0248
You would have then have retrieved the classification definition.

Note the need here to include the required number of leading zeros before any class number to make it a four-digit number.

STEP 4: DERIVE A LIST OF PATENTS FOR EACH CLASS/SUBCLASS PAIR THAT YOU HAVE IDENTIFIED

Once you have identified the class/subclass pair which appears to be most relevant to your invention, you must now search the PTO database to locate any and all patents that have been issued under that pair, and which could be problematic for your invention.

In steps 1 to 3, you may have obtained any number of such pairs. You will have to derive a list of patents for each relevant pair. After you have reviewed the patent titles in each list you derive and noted any that appear most relevant to your invention, your next task will be to check the text for each of these. You will do this in step 5. In step 6, you will examine the images of each relevant patent as determined by the text in its documentation.

Be aware that in your review of a patent's full-text documentation—step 5—you will find any number of other class/subclass pairs listed in the "Field of Search" and cross-referenced in each patent you examine. You will have to derive a list of patents for each of these pairs and—again using step 5—review the documentation of each one that appears relevant. It can get complicated and sometimes appears to have no end. It is here that your worksheet or database will prevent duplication of effort in identifying, locating, and examining the same patent class/subclass pair more than once.

If step 4 does not yield satisfactory results, you will be required go back and repeat steps 1 to 4 using another set of keywords.

Step 4 Search Exercise

Retrieve the bookmarked U.S. Patent Full-Text Database Boolean Search page as shown in Appendix 15.

URL

http://patents.uspto.gov/access/search-bool.html

As shown in the appendix, enter the class/subclass number you want to search in the Query window—Term 1. Leave the window for Query Term 2 empty. The Boolean operator "AND" is the default setting, as is "All fields" in both Field windows. Do not change this at this time. You can refine your searches as you become more advanced in the use of the databases. Select the years you want to search. For this exercise enter 1998-1999 as shown. In an actual search, you would start from the earliest date. Click on "Search."

The next screen will be similar to the list shown in appendix 15a. The search results you will you receive will include the patent numbers, and titles for each class/subclass pair you had specified as Query Term 1 at the Boolean Search page. The length of the list will vary as the parameter of inclusive dates is changed in the "Select years" box.

At this time you have several options. You can print out the list; you can save the list as a file in a directory (C:\patserch\listpats\clsubcl#\248-210); or you can now begin to retrieve the documentation of each relevant patent online by clicking on its link.

The last option is not advised—you will loose track very quickly. You are strongly advised to save each list by its class/subclass pair number. You can retrieve the file of an entire list at any time, edit it, print all or part of it, and examine only the most relevant patents—as you will do in step 5. These lists will, in effect, be adjunct worksheets. As created, they will not be as versatile as a database per se, but you will use them to create one as you examine the patents catalogued on them.

By the process of elimination, you will eventually narrow the class/subclass designations to the most definitive and appropriate. The lists for these will be your focus. Eventually, you should save and print these out for reference, and to aid in checking and cross-checking.

Tip

Here in step 4, you can also search for lists of patent numbers and titles using the keywords you had previously defined for your invention as Boolean query terms. A list similar to that shown in Appendix 15a could have been obtained by using the query terms "bracket" AND "ladder" as Query Terms 1 and 2 respectively. Try this brief exercise: Enter "bracket" in Term 1. Enter "ladder" in Term 2. Select "Search." The list of search results shown will contain several of the same entries shown in the first list you obtained using the class/subclass pair. (If you had entered "ladder" as Term 1, and "bracket" as Term 2, you would have retrieved a different array and number of patents; but otherwise, this list would include many of those on the other lists.) Always compare the lists derived from a search of keywords or terms to those you obtain by searching various classes/subclasses.

STEP 5: REVIEW THE FULL
TEXT OF EACH RELEVANT PATENT

From the lists of patent numbers and titles you have obtained in steps 1 to 4, you will now begin to examine all or part of the documentation of each patent that appears relevant to your invention. You will retrieve, examine, and reproduce the drawings in step 6. As previously recommended, do not attempt step 5 online. You will quickly lose track of where you have been, and where you want to go next. Work only from your printed list and make notes on it as you go.

From your files, select the class/subclass list you intend to search. Print all or a part of it. Then review the content carefully to identify those patent titles or descriptions that appear to most closely describe you invention. Highlight these. These will be the sub-list you will search initially.

If you elect to work from a *short* on-screen list, click on the number or title link of each patent whose title you have noted as appearing to be most descriptive of your invention. Otherwise using the Full-Text Database: Number Search (Appendix 15c), you will enter each of the patent numbers on your lists to locate the documentation for each patent.

At this point, when you retrieve the documentation, you are advised to read only the abstract, and not examine the full text and or drawings of the selected patents. Focus on the abstract and proceed from there. If the wording of the abstract of any patent appears to recite any elements of your invention, then review the full documentation and make appropriate notes on your worksheet or database. You can return to it later for further review; you can save it as a text file and print out all or parts of it later; or you can print it out at that time if it appears to be problematic. (Do not print out the claims; they will be of no great use to you. Leave these for your patent attorney.)

If the abstract does not appear to describe your invention in any way, note that fact (and the patent number) on your list and or in your worksheet or database. You are done with that particular patent and should not have to look at it when you encounter its number again—and you will—possibly many times in cross-references.

If the abstract does not seem to describe an invention that is even remotely similar to yours, there is no point in wasting your time reading, let alone printing a great deal of material that is likely to be of no great use to you—the "claims" for example. There is certainly no point in retrieving that patent's images.

Tip

Step 5 can also be done to a limited degree by a search of the *Official Gazette of the United States Patent and Trademark Office* (OG). See Appendix 16 for an example of the limited content of an OG announcement. Note that only the bibliographic data, one drawing, and one claim are shown in each announcement. The *Gazette* is *not* online; you will be required to go to a library which shelves the OG to use this search resource. The *Official Gazette* is discussed further in chapter 9. There really should be no need to use the OG if the searcher has Internet access and follows the online search steps outlined in this chapter. One possible but dubious advantage is that the OG will allow you to examine one image and the abstract for any patent issued prior to the chronological limits of the online databases—1971 (IBM) or 1976 (PTO). Let the PTO examiner do this; it is a tedious and time consuming process for the amateur.

Step 5 Search Exercise

From the list of patent numbers and titles for class 248/210 you retrieved in step 4 (Appendix 15a), note patent number 5,788,198, and its title: "Bracket for mounting ladder shelf." Two of the keywords from your list are in this title.

For this exercise, if your list is on-screen, click on this patent number. Otherwise, using the Full-Text Database: Number Search page which you may have bookmarked earlier, enter the patent number as shown in Appendix 15b and click on "Search." (Note: Commas in the number are optional here; they are required at the IBM patent search site.)

URL

US Patent Full-Text Database: Number Search
http://164.195.100.11/netahtml/srchnum.html

The next screen—Results of [number] Search—you will see is shown in Appendix 15c. This intervening page appears to serve no purpose other than as a superfluous link to the Full-Text page which you will derive next. Click on the Patent Number/Title link shown. This will take you to the first critical point in your search.

On the next screen, you will see the full-text documentation for patent number 5,788,198 as shown in Appendix 15d. At this time in an actual search, you would proceed as described previously regarding reading, saving, and or printing the documentation.

At the top center of this page is the box showing the "Images" link. This takes you to step 6.

STEP 6: RETRIEVE AND EXAMINE PATENT IMAGES

In step 5, you located the "Images" link at the top of each Full-Text page This link will take you to the drawings of each patent. As confirmed previously it is the only way you can access the drawings.

Here in step 6, you will retrieve, examine, and print out all, or selected, drawings of each patent you have determined to be most relevant to yours. The number of drawings can vary from none to many pages. You may also see photographs.

It is recommended that you print out only the most relevant images. Examine all of the drawings and select only those that clearly depict any features similar to your invention.

The quality of patent documentation and images printed from online sites will not match that of copies purchased from the PTO; it will be comparable to copies made at a PTDL. Regardless, it will be adequate for your needs. The PTO (TIFF) images (discussed earlier in this chapter) are of a higher quality than IBM's, although both are basically BMP,. bmp file format. In any case, copies of patents retrieved online will be far less expensive and quicker to obtain than ordering them from the PTO.

Should a search reveal that a patent has already been issued on an invention similar or identical to yours, this is not necessarily the end. Review the literature available from the Patent Office. You will find many suggestions on how you might be able to "design around" a conflicting invention. And, your search efforts may yield very valuable insights which, when incorporated into your design, could make your invention patentable.

Lastly, consult a reputable and competent patent attorney. He or she will likely be successful in getting a patent to issue for your invention.

Printing copies for the patent attorney.

In printing out the documentation and drawings of each patent, you may wish to print two copies of only the most relevant ones; your patent attorney will need a copy of these. Or you can copy your lists of patent numbers/titles to disks, and give the attorney these; he or she can then review these, and view and print those they consider most relevant. He or she can also print out the drawings—following the steps presented in this chapter. You are advised *not* to attempt to save the drawings themselves as individual files. This is completely unnecessary and simply not worth the time or disk space their size will require.

Step 6 Search Exercise

Return to the Full-Text patent documentation page for patent number 5,788,198 that you obtained in step 5. Click on the "Images" link at the top of the page. On you screen, you should see page 1 of the patent images as shown in Appendix 1. If so, your search has been a success. Your browser needs no further configuration. That's the good news. The bad news is that you can immediately see that the drawing of the patented invention shown on page 1 is virtually identical to the sketch of "your" invention. *Its class/subclass is 248/210.*

If you do not see page 1 as shown in Appendix 1, and receive a message indicating that the "patent cannot be found," or a similar "error" statement, you must now download and install the plug-in software discussed previously in this chapter.

When you have reconfigured, your browser as directed, repeat the step 6 search exercise. You should then be able to retrieve and print the patent images. Remember: Print them from the plug-in toolbar only.

Summary of the Six Patent Search Steps

Step 1: *Find the Primary Class for the Invention in the Index to the Manual of Classification*

URL
http://www.uspto.gov/web/offices/ac/ido/oeip/taf/moc/index.html

Step 2: *Find the Subclass for the Invention in the Manual of Classi fication*

URL
http://www.uspto.gov/web/offices/ac/ido/oeip/taf/moc/index.html

Step 3: *Review the Patent Classification Definitions*

URL
http://www.uspto.gov/web/offices/pac/clasdefs/index.html
(Or link directly from Manual of Classification URL)
http://www.uspto.gov/web/offices/ac/ido/oeip/taf/moc/index.html

Step 4: *Derive a List of Patents for Each Class/Subclass Pair That You Have Identified*

URL
http://patents.uspto.gov/access/search-bool.html

Step 5: *Review the Full Text of Each Relevant Patent*

URL
http://164.195.100.11/netahtml/srchnum.htm

Step 6: *Retrieve, Examine, and Print the Patent Images*

9. The *Official Gazette* of the United States Patent and Trademark Office

THE *OFFICIAL GAZETTE* AS A PATENT SEARCH RESOURCE

You should have no need to access and review the *Official Gazette*—step 6 of the *7-Step Strategy* for conducting a patent search at a PTDL. All of the information that you might need should be obtainable from an online search. As confirmed, the *Official Gazette* is not online.

If you elect to do so, searching the OG is a relatively quick and easy way to locate prior art. If you have accumulated a very long list of patent numbers you must review, a trip to a library that shelves the *Gazette* and a quick check of each number on your list might save a great deal of computer search time. This will depend on how close and accessible the library is.

The *Official Gazette* is a weekly publication that lists all patents issued on Tuesday of that particular week. Each volume of the OG will contain patents that issued on that date only. It will be shelved in bound volumes with a different color cover for each year. The listing of patents in each volume is arranged according to the ascending class and subclass number of each. The spine of each volume shows the date and the inclusive patent numbers in that volume.

Before you go to the library, use your database to sort all of the patent numbers into descending numerical order. At the library, start with the highest number and work down your list—this will proceed much more quickly than a random check of the numbers in scattered volumes. There may be many entries showing only a number, and stating that: "No patent was issued for this number." The patent documentation you will likely be examining will be found in the first section of each issue: "GENERAL AND MECHANICAL."

If it is more convenient for you than using the Internet, you may elect to continue checking appropriate class/subclass numbers in succeeding and current issues of the OG—up to and after the date of your filing, and throughout the time you will be waiting for your patent to issue. This could reveal patents that had issued after the date of your filing, and which could be problematic.

Content of an OG Announcement

As shown in Appendix 16, the entry for each patent number listed will include:

- The patent number;
- title of the invention;
- name and address of the inventor(s);
- date on which the application was filed;
- serial number of the application;
- international class;
- U.S. classification as class—subclass (not class/subclass);
- a *single* drawing, or a photograph of the invention showing its best mode;
- the number of claims; and
- the text of one claim.

Look at the example of the OG page for patent number 5,788,198 shown in Appendix 16, and compare it with the documentation of the patent included in Appendix 1 that contains the bibliographic information, abstract, referenced patents, one of seven drawing sheets, and the full text of the six claims.

LOCATING A LIBRARY

Should you decide to utilize the *Official Gazette* at any point in your search, it is shelved at the PTO library and at every PTDL shown on the list in Appendix 2. It may also be found in major metropolitan libraries and many university libraries—especially those with large science and engineering departments. A local librarian can usually locate a regional library that shelves the *Official Gazette*.

You can also locate a library on the Internet through the Federal Depository Library Program. To locate a Depository Library in your area, retrieve the Program's Web pages as shown in Appendix 17. To locate the *Official Gazette*, the search procedure for this—*and every GPO publication*—is shown below. Use appendixes 17 through 17e to review the Web page you should retrieve at each search step.

Steps in Locating a Federal Depository Library

There are over 1,400 Federal Depository Libraries throughout the United States and its territories. There is at least one located in every congressional district. Every library provides free public access to a wide variety of federal government information in both print and electronic media. Each has an expert staff that is available to assist users.

Using the Internet, you can easily locate a Federal Depository Library anywhere in the United States and its territories.

Step 1

Go to: "GPO Access," the Superintendent of Documents Home Page (Appendix 17).
Website: http://www.access.gpo.gov/su_docs/index.html
Select: "Locator Tools."
(Note the many other useful links on this website.)

Step 2

At "Locator Tools" (Appendix 17a) select under Search "Catalog of U.S. Government Publications (MOCAT)."

Step 3

At the next screen: "Catalog of U.S. Government Publications (MOCAT)" (Appendix 17b), enter the search term: "Official Gazette of the United States Patent and Trademark Office." (*Note:* For this particular query, quotation marks are optional. In certain others, they are required.) Click on "Submit."

Step 4

At the next screen: "Catalog ... Search Results" (Appendix 17c) scroll down until you locate the publication you had selected in the preceding step. (*Note:* An *Official Gazette* is published for both trademarks and patents. A Depository Library will shelve both.) At the entry "*Official Gazette .... Patents,*" click on the "Locate Libraries" link.

Step 5

At the next screen: "Locate Federal Depository Libraries by State or Area Code" (Appendix 17d) enter the two-letter abbreviation of your state. Click on "Submit."

Step 6

At the final screen: "Federal Depository Libraries in Selected States" (Appendix 17e) review the list of libraries in your state that shelve the publication you had selected—the *Official Gazette.*

BEFORE YOU GO

Decide which library is closest to you, and whether or not it will be worth the trip. It is suggested that before you go call the library to confirm its operating hours. Do not forget to take your list of patent numbers, your laptop computer, and or your worksheets with you. Take several rolls of dimes for the copying machine.

10. Patent Search and Invention Promotion Services

INVENTION AND PATENT
PROMOTION ORGANIZATIONS

Having read this far, and realized what you could be getting into, you may be tempted to turn your chore of searching over to one of the many operations that advertise their services on the WWW, in strident TV pitches, or in glowing advertisements in the print media. These are usually called an invention or patent "promotion" firm, "broker," or "developer." Some of these outfits may actually help you get a patent. But beware, many inventors pay thousands of dollars to firms that promise to do patent searches, and to evaluate, develop, patent, and market their inventions. Unfortunately, many of them then do little or nothing in return for their fees. Before you sign up and pay out, consider the facts and warnings presented in this chapter.

There can be a great deal of personal satisfaction and excitement in developing an invention and getting a patent for it. But be extremely cautious. Your enthusiasm for your idea may make you highly vulnerable to unscrupulous promoters who can easily take advantage of an inventor's unbounded confidence in his or her own idea or product—of their hopes and dreams—of their greed! They will not only urge every client to patent his or her idea, but they will also make false and exaggerated claims about the fantastic market potential for their invention—and any and all ideas that are presented to them. Invention promoters invariably promise more than they can deliver. The hard facts are:

- If the criteria of patentability are met, you can get a patent on just about anything, no matter how wacky or useless it is.
- Relatively few patented inventions ever make it to the marketplace.
- Getting a patent does not necessarily increase the chances of commercial success.

PROMOTION FIRMS' ADVERTISING AND SALES TECHNIQUES

Their advertisements target the independent, amateur inventor with enticing offers of "free" information on how to patent and or market his or her invention. They always include a toll free telephone number that inventors can call for this "invaluable" information. Most often, however, the free information sent consists only of brochures that freely promote their costly services. If you respond to these advertisements, you will encounter a "consultant," "professional" (fill in a title), "associate" something-or-other, or "expert"— or any other euphemism for a well-coached telemarketer.

The pitch begins with a request that the inventor provide information about himself or herself, and send a description and sketch of the invention. And all this must be done "immediately" so that you can "begin making a great deal of money as soon as possible."

As an inducement, they might offer to do a free patent search and or "preliminary review" of your invention. After confirming that they have conducted this "extensive, in-depth evaluation," and based on their (invariably) positive findings, they will likely tell you there is a need to conduct a "market study" for your idea. This will not be free. The usual fee for this will vary from several hundred to several thousand dollars. The questionable firms do neither a review of the invention, nor a market study. Such reports from questionable firms often make vague and general statements, and provide no hard evidence that there is a consumer market for your invention. The "research" is bogus, and the glowing (and predictably positive) reports of their findings are boilerplate. The objective is to sell the client on additional promotional and marketing services—for additional fees, of course. Fraudulent promotion firms never offer an honest or realistic appraisal of the merits, technical feasibility, or market potential of an invention. The reports of reputable companies will present realistic, qualified specifics. Before you pay for a so-called research report on your idea, ask what information you can expect to receive.

Some invention promotion firms may claim to have been retained by, to know, to have special access to, or to have business relationships with any number of manufacturers who are "sure to be interested in licensing your invention," and who are "actively looking for new product ideas just like yours." These kinds of claims are usually false or exaggerated. Therefore, before signing a contract with an invention promotion firm that claims special relationships with potential manufacturers, ask for some written, verifiable proof. Contact the manufacturers—if the promoter will give you names.

Some of these firms may also proffer a contract in which they agree to act as your "exclusive" agent in helping you find a licensee or assignee for your invention. In return for this service they will invariably require you to pay a fee of several thousand dollars *in advance*, and to commit to them a percentage of the royalties your invention may earn.

The request for an upfront fee is another distinguishing characteristic of a questionable operation. Reputable licensing agents usually do not rely on large advances. Rather, they routinely depend on royalties from the successful licensing of clients' inventions. How can they make money when so few inventions achieve commercial success? They are very selective about the inventions to which they commit. If a firm purports to be as enthusiastic about the commercial potential for your idea as you are, but demands a large fee in advance—look for another promoter.

The Federal Trade Commission (FTC) has found that many invention promotion firms make outrageous claims that they can turn ideas into cash— "guaranteed." The FTC cautions smart inventors to try to spot the sweet-sounding promises of a fraudulent promotion firm. Often it is difficult to distinguish between a dubious operation and a legitimate one. This may be because both unscrupulous and honest firms often use many similar advertising and sales techniques, fee schedules, and offer the same services under similar contract arrangements. Many of the legitimate providers are registered patent attorneys or agents—as are many of the shysters.

High-Pressured Sales Pitches

Here are just some of the many sales pitches suspect firms and pushy promoters will attempt to use on the unwary inventor.

> "Congratulations! We have done a patent search on your idea, and we have some great news! There is nothing like it out there!"

They may have not looked far enough—or not looked at all!

Many invention promotion firms claim to perform patent searches for ideas brought to them. Purported searches by fraudulent invention promotion firms are typically incomplete, conducted in the wrong class/subclass, or not accompanied by a legal opinion, by a patent attorney, on the results of the search.

Require the provider of this service to conduct a patent search based specifically on your idea for an invention, and provide you with a full, verifiable report of their findings. Because unscrupulous firms are willing to promote virtually any idea or invention without regard to its patentability, they will strongly encourage you to apply for a patent for an idea for which someone already has a valid, unexpired patent, or for one that is the subject matter of a patent that has long expired. You will eventually have either of these facts confirmed to you—by a PTO examining attorney when your application is disallowed.

> "We think your idea has great market potential!"

Few ideas, however great in the inventor's estimation, become commercial successes. Beware if a company fails to disclose that your investment in your idea is a high risk venture, and that most ideas never make money for the inventor.

"Our company has successfully licensed/assigned many inventions!"

If they tell you that they have a "proven track record" in any area of the patent process, and in the development and marketing of ideas, insist that they prove it to you. Ask for a list of their satisfied clients. Contact several; confirm that they actually had obtained patents and to what degree their inventions have been a commercial success. Ask the service provider for a list of the numbers of the patents issued to their previous clients. Using the procedures outlined in chapter 8, spot check these numbers to determine the merits and types of inventions they have promoted for these clients. If the company refuses to give you such lists, it is very likely because they do not have any to give.

"You must hurry to patent your idea before someone else does!"

There always seems to be an intense sense of urgency—of imperative— in their advice. "We want to get started on your idea [and your bank account] immediately! Send us your money now, or all will be lost!" All will be lost eventually; they just want you to expedite your fleecing.

"Our professional staff, research department, engineers, and patent attorneys have evaluated your idea. We definitely want to move forward on it!"

This is a standard sales pitch. Questionable firms do not perform any such evaluations. Their "professional" staff and "engineers" are telemarketers. The urgency to "move forward" is to move in on you as quickly and effectively as possible.

"Our company has evaluated your idea, and now wants to prepare a more in depth research report."

If their initial evaluation is so positive, ask why they are not willing to cover the expense of researching the idea further. Their proposal of "in depth research" is most likely to be an effort to determine the depth of the potential victim's pockets.

"Our company makes most of its profits from the royalties it receives from licensing our clients' ideas. Of course, we will require the advancement of certain fees from you before we can begin providing our services."

This is the "good faith" appeal to the inventor to share the risk. If a firm tells you this but asks for a large fee upfront, ask why they are not willing to assist you on a contingency basis. Unscrupulous firms make virtually all of their profits from such large upfront fees for which they take absolutely no risks (except for possible criminal prosecution). The inventor usually makes nothing, and may eventually have to file a lawsuit in a futile attempt to recover his or her investment. Simply refuse to pay large upfront fees. If the promoter is not willing to assist you on a contingency basis, look elsewhere.

HOW TO PROTECT YOURSELF: CAUTIONS FOR THE INVENTOR

Should you decide to work with an invention promotion firm, consider taking certain precautions before you sign a contract and pay significant amounts of money.

- Consult an attorney.
- Be aware of all of those high pressure sales tactics. Ignore them. You must, above all, be absolutely objective, coldly realistic, and unflinchingly skeptical in the face of the barrage.
- Do not hold out pie in the sky expectations for what may well be an "ingenius" halfbaked, flaky idea. Your family and friends may marvel at your idea (sincerely or politely), but that does not guarantee that everyone else will. No one wants to tell you your invention is as useful as teats on a bull.
- Avoid being taken in by flashy promotional brochures and claims of affiliation with a list of impressive-sounding organizations. Either they do not exist, or they have had their name and reputation appropriated without their consent or knowledge.
- Be very cynical of their rave reviews of your invention. They are telling you what they know you want to hear. Scam artists tell *everyone* that their idea is a "surefire money maker," a "winner." Their evaluations are always flattering, but never realistic. They pander to the inventor's ego and avarice.
- Be suspicious of claims and assurances that your invention will certainly make money—that it "will make you rich." No one can guarantee your invention's success. Unscrupulous invention promotion firms tell *all* inventors that their ideas are among the relatively few that they have ever seen that have surefire patentability and or market potential. The truth is that most inventions never make money. More than 99 percent of new ideas and products never make a dime for their inventors. No one but the fickle consumer in the competitive marketplace can decide an invention's success or failure. Just because your idea is patentable does not mean it is going to make you wealthy. Question any and all claims and assertions that your invention will make you rich beyond your dreams.

- There may be a promise to exhibit your invention at trade shows or similar venues. In all likelihood, the promoter never attends such shows, let alone presents their clients' inventions.
- If the inventor has not filed a patent application and or received a patent, fraudulent promotion firms may offer to "register" his or her idea with the PTO's Disclosure Document Program. They will charge a high fee for this additional "professional service." The actual cost of such a filing is $10; you can do it yourself very easily. Complete information about the Program is available online at the PTO website.
- Fraudulent invention promotion firms offer inventors two types of service in a two-step process. One involves a research report or market evaluation of your idea that could cost you hundreds, if not thousands, of dollars. The other involves patenting or marketing and licensing services that could cost several thousand dollars. At the outset, request a written statement of the total cost of these "services." If the sales representative is unwilling or hesitates to provide an estimate in writing, consider it a warning. Walk away.
- Be careful of the firm that offers to "review" or "evaluate" your invention but refuses to disclose the details concerning its criteria or system of review, and the qualifications of those who will conduct it. Without this information, you cannot assess the integrity of that firm, or make meaningful comparisons with others. And you certainly will not be able to evaluate the veracity or worth of the so-called review "report." Reputable firms should provide you with an objective evaluation of their findings, *regardless* of the merits, feasibility, and commercial potential of your invention—if it has any.
- Be wary of an invention promotion firm that will not disclose its success and rejection rates. Success rates show the number of clients who made more money from their invention than they paid the firm. Rejection rates reflect the percentage of all ideas or inventions that were found unacceptable by the invention promotion company. The legitimate firm generally has a high rejection rate. Check with your state and local consumer protection officials to determine if invention promotion firms are required to disclose their success and rejection rates in your locality. In several states, disclosure is required by law. According to experts retained in Federal Trade Commission cases, an invention promotion firm that does not reject most of the inventions it reviews may be unduly optimistic, if not blatantly dishonest in its evaluations.

- If you do not get satisfactory answers to all of your questions, consider whether you want to sign a contract. Once a dishonest company has your money, it is unlikely you will ever get it back. It will vanish with the promises. At worst, they will sell your unpatented idea to someone else, who can then file ahead of you and steal your invention.
- Make sure that any contract you intend to sign contains all agreed upon terms—written and verbal—before you sign and that you fully understand every detail of the contract. Consult an attorney before signing any contract. You would be foolish and reckless not to do so.
- Thoroughly investigate the company before making a commitment. Contact the Better Business Bureau, consumer protection agencies, and the attorney general in the state in which the firm has its principal offices. Determine whether or not there have ever been any consumer complaints about the firm; what was the nature of the complaints; and if, and how, these charges were resolved. Be aware that these operations can change their names, locations, and advertising pitches at the drop of a summons. Review the website of Ronald J. Riley for the names and convoluted business connections on his list of firms with shady histories.
- Remember, the Patent and Trademark Office has no control over, and does not maintain information about, patent promotion organizations. The Federal Trade Commission monitors their activities. If you are thinking of using one of these organizations, it is advisable to check on the reputation of any firm before making any commitments. Investigate first!!

For More Information

A number of government agencies and private organizations offer publications and assistance to independent inventors. You can call the U.S. Patent and Trademark Office at (703) 557-4636, or the U.S. Small Business Administration (SBA) at 800-827-5722, for publications about inventions. You also may want to call your SBA district office to learn about services available through the Small Business Development Centers program.

Inventor's clubs and associations can be valuable sources of information and services. For their locations, search the Internet, and or contact the following organizations:

United Inventors Association of the United States of America
P.O. Box 50305
St. Louis, Missouri 63105
(A stamped, self-addressed envelope is required.)

National Congress of Inventor Organizations
727 North 600 West
Logan, Utah 84321
801-753-0888

Websites and Links

Federal Trade Commission: "Project Mousetrap"
http://www.ftc.gov

Inventors Awareness Group, Inc.
http://www.fplc.edu/iag/
"Red Flags"
http://www.fplc.edu/iag/iag3.htm#red

National Inventor Fraud Center
http://www.inventorfraud.com

Ronald J. Riley's Caution List
He posts a long list of attorneys and firms of questionable merit.
http://www.rjriley.com/caution

WHAT TO DO IF YOU ARE A VICTIM

If you believe you have been a victim of a fraudulent invention promotion company, first contact the firm and try to get your money back. If you are unsuccessful, report your problem to your local Better Business Bureau, state consumer protection agency, and the attorney general of your state and of the state(s) where the company is located. (Many have offices in one or more states and or foreign countries.) Your information may help in any ongoing investigation, or demonstrate the need for one.

You may also file a complaint with the FTC by writing to the address shown below: The FTC generally does not intervene in individual disputes. However the information you provide may indicate a pattern of possible law violations that the Commission might pursue.

General inquiries:
Federal Trade Commission
6th & Pennsylvania Avenue, N.W.
Washington, DC, 20580
202-326-2222

Complaints:
Correspondence Branch
Federal Trade Commission
6th & Pennsylvania Avenue, N.W.
Washington, DC, 20580

Part II

Searching for Trademarks on the Internet

11. Trademarks

USPTO ONLINE RESOURCES
FOR TRADEMARK INFORMATION

This chapter will present a very brief overview of trademarks. For detailed information on the many other aspects of trademarks, including the registration process and frequently asked questions, see the sample pages of the U.S. Patent and Trademark Office websites shown in Appendixes 18, 19, and 20 (the latter has a total of 38 pages; only two shown here). The various links shown on these pages will provide you with online access to an array of PTO publications on several of the subjects discussed in this part of the book, and many other related topics which could not be covered. A list of the PTO's most relevant publications is shown in the bibliography. These links will lead you to anything you might need to know about trademarks—except *how to search* for them online, which will be discussed in chapters 15 and 16.

WHAT IS A TRADEMARK?

You will be searching the USPTO Web Trademark Database (Appendixes 21 and 21a) to determine if the trademark you have decided on may have already been registered. Before you begin a search, you should have a basic understanding of what a trademark is, the various types of trademarks, and what you will be looking for—and at—in your search.

Throughout our discussion, the terms "trademark" and "mark" will be used to refer to any of the classifications of trademarks, or to the type of mark. Your search will likely focus on trademarks, or service marks. A term can serve either as a trademark or service mark, and a trade name at the same time.

Definition of "Trademark"

The Trademark Act of 1946 defines a trademark as any word, name, symbol, or device—or any combination of these—used, or intended to be used, in commerce to identify and distinguish the goods of one manufacturer or seller from goods manufactured or sold by others. A trademark is a brand name. It can be the name of the inventor, or any other person's name. A trademark can be a neologism—a made-up word—such as "Intel" and "Pentium." Or it can be any word or phrase, including those in a foreign language, that describes a product. The words may have no direct descriptive relationship to the product per se. It may be a combination of letters (IBM, AOL), numbers, a combination of letters and numbers (WD-40), a sound, a scent, a color, or a combination of colors. The name "Coca-Cola" is a trademark whose distinctive colors, script, and overall design are recognized worldwide—in any language. It may be a distinctive architectural design—the McDonalds arches for example. "Microsoft Windows" is a registered trademark. "Microsoft" is the tradename for a company that is neither "micro" nor "soft."

A trademark is different from a copyright or a patent. A copyright protects an original artistic or literary work. A patent, as noted in chapter 2, protects rights in an invention. Many patented goods are also covered by trademarks. Maintaining a trademark in perpetuity may effectively extend a patent term.

A well-chosen mark may mean the difference between success or failure in the marketing of a product or service. If an inventor maintains all rights in a trademark that is applied to his successful invention, the mark could be extremely valuable in and of itself, and could provide opportunities for further marketing under license for other products.

TRADE NAME

A trade name is the name under which an individual or a company conducts its business, its trade. It is any word or phrase that identifies an individual proprietorship, corporation, or partnership as a business entity, as distinct from the goods or services it produces and offers. On December 1, 1997, an industrial era came to an end in the United States when Westinghouse was merged into CBS, and its name was obliterated. Since 1886, the trade name Westinghouse Electric Corporation, and its trademark motto: "You can be sure if it's Westinghouse," appeared on a vast array of products that made significant and long-lasting changes in people's lives—turbines, refrigerators, locomotives and so on.

As with patents, trademarks and trade names can also infringe. Therefore, before you start using a mark, a search should be conducted to determine the possibility of infringement and any possible legal liability. This issue will be discussed further in chapter 14.

In a recent court case in Pennsylvania, WAWA Food Markets, a large chain of minimarkets, sued a one-shop husband-and-wife operation doing business as "HAHA." WAWA claimed infringement. The court ruled in favor of WAWA. The case was appealed to see who would have the first—and perhaps last—HAHA.

Trade names (and service marks) include the legal names of individuals or business establishments that they use in the course of their business, as well as any fictitious or assumed names. Before using a fictitious trade name in commerce, it is advisable to check the requirements for the registration and legal notification of a such a name. State and local laws vary on this requirement, but usually the fictitious name and certain relevant information must be published in a mass-circulation daily newspaper under "Legal Notices"—"Notice of Fictitious Name." If it is not a fictitious name, registration and advertisement may not be necessary.

Individuals may use their own names (not assumed names). A person can legally call themselves any name they wish—provided it is not for an illicit purpose (such as an alias). To make your trade name or service mark sound more impressive, append "and Associates," or "and Company"—even if it is just you alone, operating from your kitchen table. Who will know? But be careful using "Incorporated," "Inc.," "PC" (Professional Corporation), or the affectation of the British "Limited," or "Ltd." The law has different regulatory implications for a corporation and a sole proprietorship. Corporate entities are also "persons" and have certain unique standing under law. Designating yourself as any of these could have legal connotations that might involve misrepresentation, false advertising, or even fraud. In addition to the trademark and trade name, there is also the service mark.

SERVICE MARK

A service mark is any word, name, symbol, device, or any combination of these used, or intended to be used, in commerce to identify and distinguish the services of one provider from those of others, and to indicate the source of the services.

A service mark is much the same as a trademark and trade name except that it identifies and distinguishes the source of a service provided rather than a product. Normally, a mark for goods appears on a product or on its packaging, while a service mark appears in advertisements for the service. A business card usually includes some form of service mark; it may also include a trade name.

CERTIFICATION MARK

A certification mark is any word, name, symbol, or device—or any combination of these—used or intended to be used in commerce (with the owner's permission) by someone other than the owner to certify regional or other geographic origin, material, mode of manufacture, quality, accuracy, or other characteristics of someone's goods or services, or that the work or labor on the goods or services was performed by members of a union or other organization.

COLLECTIVE MARK

A collective mark is a trademark or service mark used, or intended to be used, in commerce by the members of a cooperative, an association, or other collective group or organization, including a mark that indicates membership in a union, an association, or other organization.

TRADE SECRET

A trade secret is anything that gives the owner of it a competitive advantage over another manufacturer of a similar product. It can be a list of a company's clients, a single exotic ingredient, or a combination of components. An example is the highly guarded formula for the alloy of tin, copper, and a trace of silver from which Zildjian cymbals are made. The formula was discovered in 1623 in Constantinople by an alchemist named Avedis, and has been used by the Zildjian family for 375 years (including a member who appropriated the secret, and set up a competing business in New Jersey).

Trade secrets do not fall under the laws of trademark. Protection of trade secrets is an area of law outside the scope of this book. It more properly relates to the general area of obtaining patents—or in this case foregoing a patent to avoid divulging the secret. Trade secrets have become the newest and most lucrative target of international espionage in the economic wars between competing nations.

THE PRINCIPAL AND SUPPLEMENTAL REGISTERS

In your search for trademarks, you will see that they will be shown as being on either the Principal Register or the Supplemental Register. The Principal Register is where most marks are registered. The Supplemental Register exists to allow registration of marks that are not distinctive but are "capable" of becoming distinctive. Registration on the Supplemental Register does not bar later registration on the Principal Register once the mark has become capable of distinguishing the owner's goods or services from those of others.

REQUIREMENTS OF A MARK

A mark cannot simply describe a quality, function, feature, or component of the goods or services. However, such a mark could be accepted for registration if, through widespread usage, it has become distinct and recognizable to the general public to such a degree as to clearly identify the source of the goods or services.

Drawing of the Mark

In your search for trademarks, you will retrieve a "drawing" for every mark. The drawing is the page that depicts the mark that is pending or registered, and as it is actually used—or intended to be used. An applicant cannot register more than one mark in a single application. The drawing will display only one mark and only one representation of it on the page. Every trademark application must include a single, separate, drawing page.

A drawing must be in accordance with all PTO specifications. The drawing must be in black and white only. No color or gray shading is allowed. The mark can be a "Typed Drawing" or "Special Form Drawing." If the mark includes words, numbers, or letters, the applicant can usually elect to submit either type.

Typed Drawing

A "Word Mark" that consists only of words, letters, or numbers, without indicating any particular style or design, is classified as a "Typed Drawing." In this form, the typewritten mark must be entirely in CAPITAL LETTERS, even if the mark, as used, includes lower-case letters. Only standard fonts and sizes are acceptable. (See the example in Appendix 22.)

Special Form Drawing

To register a word mark in the *particular form* in which it is actually used or intended to be used in commerce, or any mark that includes a design of any kind, a Special Form drawing must be submitted. (See the example in Appendix 23.) The drawing must appear in black and white only. No color or gray shading is allowed. To indicate colors in a drawing, the PTO provides a color code guide using various black and white patterns (available online). If your intended mark incorporates a specific color scheme, you must take this into account in your search.

SERVICES OF THE TRADEMARK OFFICE

The Trademark Office is a subdivision of the U.S. Patent and Trademark Office, which is a division of the U.S. Department of Commerce. In order to provide improved service to trademark applicants, registrants, and the general public, the Office has implemented a program called the "Trademark Assistance Center." The Center provides basic trademark information, including general information about the registration process, and responds to inquiries pertaining to the status of specific trademark applications and registrations. To obtain more information about the Center, click on its link on the USPTO Home page: (http://www.uspto.gov).

12. Trademark Law

THE TRADEMARK ACT

Since filing for a trademark is a relatively easy and uncomplicated procedure, and one that the average person can do without the need for an attorney (discussed further in chapter 13) there is no need to digress on the relevant statutes, rules, regulations that govern trademarks. Suffice to say that trademark law is set forth in: 15 United States Code, Section 1051 *et sequitur*. This is the 1946 Trademark Act—also known as the "Lanham Act." It is online at any number of websites should you feel the need to peruse it.

ESTABLISHING TRADEMARK RIGHTS

Under the law, your trademark rights will arise from either the filing of a proper application to register a mark in the United States Patent and Trademark Office, stating that the you have a bona fide intention of using the mark in commerce regulated by the United States Congress; or your actual use of the mark—known as "common law rights." (The search for such marks present particular challenges that will be discussed in chapter 14.)

THE TYPES OF RIGHTS IN A MARK

There are two related but distinct types of rights in a mark: the right to *register*, and the right to *use*. Generally the first party who either uses a mark in commerce, or files an application in the PTO, has the ultimate right to register that mark. The PTO's authority is limited to determining the right to register. The right to use the mark can be more complicated to determine. This is especially true when two parties have begun use of the same or similar marks without knowledge of one another, and neither has a federal registration. Only a court can render a decision about the right to use—such as issuing an injunction or awarding damages for infringement. As you will see, a federal registration can provide significant advantages to a party involved in any court proceedings. The PTO cannot provide advice to the public concerning rights in a mark. Only an attorney can provide such legal advice.

CONFLICTING MARKS

To determine whether there is a conflict between two marks, the PTO decides whether there would be any likelihood of confusion; that is, whether the average consumer would be likely to associate or confuse the goods or services of one party with those of the other party as a result of the mark each uses. The principal factors that will be considered in making a decision will be the degree of similarity between the marks, and of any commercial association between the goods or services identified by them. To generate a conflict, the marks need not be identical, and the goods or services need not be the same. Your online search will be conducted to determine the degree of similarity or difference between your proposed mark and any of those that may be pending or already have federal registration. You will be searching for registered marks which could conflict with yours.

FEDERAL REGISTRATION OF A MARK

There is no need or legal requirement for you to register your mark in order to establish exclusive rights to it. However federal registration has several advantages, including notice to the public of the registrant's claim of ownership of the mark, a legal presumption of ownership nationwide, and the exclusive right to use the mark on or in connection with the goods or services set forth in the registration. Registration confirms the recognition by the government only of the right to use the mark in trade and commerce in such a way as to distinguish the registrant's goods or services from those of another.

As noted previously, the first person either to use a mark in commerce or file an "Intent to Use" application with the PTO has the ultimate right to use and register the mark—provided there is no conflicting prior use of the mark. A registered mark will give the owner national priority in its use as of the filing date of the application—subject to common law rights of others that may have been established prior to the application and registration of that particular mark. As you will see, common law marks cannot be searched in any database now online.

LEGAL ADVANTAGES OF FEDERAL REGISTRATION OF A MARK

Although federal registration is *not required* to establish your rights in a mark, or to begin use of it, it can secure benefits beyond the rights acquired by mere use of a mark.

Registration has a number of advantages.

- Evinces ownership of the mark.
- Provides constructive notice nationwide of the trademark owner's

claim. The owner of a federal registration is presumed to be the owner of the mark for the goods or services specified in the registration, and to be entitled to use the mark nationwide. (Federal registration is advised if goods or services will be involved in interstate commerce.)

- Conveys broader rights in a mark that will be used in interstate commerce or international commerce; there is no need to register the mark in each state.
- Establishes the constructive date of first usage of a mark in commerce.
- Grants broader rights over and above the common law rights obtained by merely using a mark. Registration will prevent anyone from claiming new rights that supersede those provided by the registration.
- The application and the registration will be readily discoverable in trademark searches conducted by others.
- It will be *prima facie* evidence of the validity of the registration, the registrant's ownership of the mark, and of the registrant's exclusive right to use the mark in commerce in connection with the goods and services specified in the certificate of registration.
- Offers the possibility of incontestability, in which case the registration constitutes conclusive evidence of the registrant's exclusive right (with certain exceptions) to use the mark in commerce.
- Presents constructive notice of a claim of ownership and of prior rights. This effectively eliminates a "good faith" defense for a party adopting the trademark subsequent to the registrant's date of registration.
- Provides that the jurisdiction of a *federal* court may be invoked— the right to sue in a federal court for trademark infringement.
- Allows recovery of profits, damages and costs in a federal court infringement action, and the possibility of triple damages and reimbursement of attorneys' fees.
- Limits grounds for attacking a registration once it is five years old.
- Provides for criminal penalties in an action for counterfeiting a registered trademark under the anti-counterfeiting provisions of the Federal Trademark Act.
- Grants the right to deposit the registration with United States Customs in order to stop the importation of goods bearing an infringing mark.
- Establishes a basis for filing trademark applications in foreign countries.
- Grants the right to use symbol ® or the statements: "Registered in the U.S. Patent and Trademark office" or "Reg. U.S. Pat. & Tm. Off."

STATUTORY GROUNDS FOR
REFUSAL OF REGISTRATION

In deciding on a mark, you should be aware that it must conform to certain legal criteria in order to be registered. The Office will refuse to register matter if it does not function as a trademark. Not all words, names, symbols, or devices can function as trademarks. Section 2 of the Trademark Act (15 United States Code, Section 1052) contains several of the most common—although not the only—grounds for refusal of a registration. These are summarized below.

A Trademark Examining Attorney may refuse registration if the mark:

- does not function as a trademark to identify the goods or services as coming from a particular source; for example, the mark is merely ornamental;
- is merely a surname;
- so resembles an active mark that is already registered with the PTO as to be likely to cause confusion, mistake, or deception;
- is merely descriptive or deceptively mis-descriptive of the applicant's goods or services;
- the proposed mark consists of, or comprises immoral, deceptive, or scandalous matter;
- may disparage or falsely suggest a connection with any person, (living or dead) or any institutions, religions, cultural beliefs, or national symbols, or may bring any of these into contempt or disrepute;
- is primarily geographically descriptive—that is, it merely indicates that the products or services are from a particular geographical area;
- consists of, or simulates the flag, coat of arms, or any other official insignia of the United States, or of any of its political subdivisions, or those of any foreign nation;
- is the name, image, or signature of a particular identifiable living person, unless it can be shown that the person has given their written consent for such use;
- is the name, image, or signature of a deceased president of the United States that is used during the lifetime of his or her surviving spouse, without the consent of the spouse.

PROPER USE OF A TRADEMARK

In order to protect and advance your rights in a mark it is necessary that you utilize it properly. Otherwise your rights in the mark could be significantly diminished, or possibly lost entirely. The federal registration, if any, may not be sustainable in a situation of improper usage.

As a general rule, the mark should never be used as a noun or as a generic name of goods or services. It should be used as an *adjective only*. To assure this, a noun or a generic term should be placed after the mark. It should be readily distinguishable from other text or graphics with which it is displayed. This distinction can be made by varying the size or the type of font used for the mark. The proper trademark notice or symbol should be placed immediately after the word, phrase, or logo that serves as the mark.

To protect a mark as it relates to particular goods or services, it must be properly applied to those goods or services. This includes the direct placement of the mark on the goods, their packaging or containers, on a label that is affixed to these, or on any means of display for the goods. The use of a mark for advertising purposes only may not be considered sufficient to establish use of it in connection with the goods. For services, proper use would be demonstrated by displaying the service mark on signs, business cards and stationery, but not on certain other business forms as specified in PTO publications (see Appendix 20).

USE OF THE SYMBOLS "TM," "SM," AND "®"

There are no federal regulations governing the use of the designations "TM" or "SM" with a mark. Anyone who claims rights in a mark may use the TM or SM designation with it to alert the public to their claim. The user's claim may or may not be a valid one. These symbols are frequently used before a federal registration is issued. It is not necessary to have the mark registered, or have a pending application, in order to use either of these designations.

However, the registration symbol ® may be used only when the mark is actually registered with the PTO. It is unlawful to use this particular symbol at any time prior to the issuance of a registration—including a pending registration. Likewise, the statements "Registered in the U.S. Patent and Trademark Office," or "Reg. U.S. Pat. & Tm. Off." may not be used until the mark is actually registered.

The federal registration symbol ® should be used only on goods or services that are the subject of the federal trademark registration. (Note: Several foreign countries use the letter R enclosed within a circle to indicate that a mark is registered in that country. Use of the symbol in the United States by the holder of a foreign registration may be proper.)

Use of these symbols may also be regulated by state, local, or foreign laws. The laws of the particular jurisdiction should be consulted before any of them are used. Of course, federal law always takes precedence in the United States.

All such symbols, phrases, or terms must be omitted from a mark in any drawing of it submitted with a registration application. These are not considered part of the mark.

13. Applying for a Trademark Registration

WHO MAY FILE AN
APPLICATION TO REGISTER A MARK?

Only the owner of the mark can file an application for its registration. This is usually an individual, a corporation, or a partnership. The owner of the mark controls the nature and quality of the goods to which it is affixed, and which are identified by it, or the services for which it is used. He or she may submit and prosecute their own application for registration (*pro se*), or they may elect to be represented by an attorney—particularly if international trade and foreign rights are involved. An application filed by a person who is not the owner of the mark could be declared void.

Whether or not a minor can file a trademark application will depend on the laws of the state in which he or she maintains their legal residence. If, under state law, the individual can enter into a contract or any other legally binding obligation, then he or she is permitted to file a trademark application. Otherwise, a parent or legal guardian must sign the application and clearly set forth their status as the parent or legal guardian of the minor who is the owner of the mark.

The rights of survivors of a deceased owner of a mark also vary according to state laws. In the event that such a question is raised, the survivor or the administrator of a decedent's estate is advised to consult an attorney. The PTO cannot provide advice on such matters.

An individual does not have to be a United States citizen to obtain a federal registration. However, the applicant's citizenship must be set forth in the record. If an applicant has dual citizenship, then the applicant must choose which citizenship will be printed in the *Official Gazette* of the United States Patent and Trademark Office and on the certificate of registration.

Information Required

In applying for federal registration, the applicant must:

1. Clearly identify the mark; and
2. the goods or services with which it will be used; and
3. the manner in which it will be used; and,
4. if the mark is already in use, identify the date of first use; and
5. the date of first use in interstate and or foreign commerce.

INTERNATIONAL SCHEDULE OF CLASSES OF GOODS AND SERVICES

The application form (PTO Form 1478) shown in Appendix 25 has a block in the upper right corner labeled "CLASS NO. (if known)." The applicant is asked to identify the appropriate "International Class" of the goods and or services covered by the mark—if known. The applicant is not required to indicate a class number. A trademark examiner will ultimately assign the class number for the mark. In fact, the PTO prefers to do this. In my personal experience, an examiner telephoned, and she suggested a more specific and descriptive class designation than that which I had indicated, and which was finally used.

Identifying the proper class number from an online search of the PTO database will be discussed further in chapter 15. See Appendix 24 for the International Schedule of Classes of Goods and Services. A detailed description of each of the classes of goods and services is given in Frequently Asked Questions About Trademarks (pages 11–30 of the document). This document is online; see Appendix 20 for the website.

NEED FOR AN ATTORNEY IN FILING AN APPLICATION

You should not have to use an attorney to file your application. As a general rule, the services of an attorney should not be required for either a trademark search or filing. In chapter 16, you will learn how to search the Internet for registered trademarks. You can complete and file the relatively simple application form on your own. You can now also do this on the Internet. For more information on electronic filing, click on the "Trademark Electronic Application System" (TEAS) link on the Trademark Information website (Appendix 18).

However, in some circumstances it may be advisable to retain an attorney who is experienced in trademark matters. As stated in Appendix 21a, page 1: "If you have any questions regarding adoption or use of a trademark, the PTO strongly recommends that you consult with an attorney. The PTO cannot recommend attorneys." The Office will not directly assist an applicant in locating and retaining an attorney. The PTO does maintain an online roster of attorneys and agents registered to practice before the United States Patent and Trademark Office. This list is accessible through a link on the USPTO Home page.

The applicant is ultimately responsible for compliance with all substantive and procedural issues and requirements, whether or not he or she is represented by an attorney.

14. Searching for Trademarks

THE NEED FOR A TRADEMARK SEARCH

A trademark search is an attempt to discover if there are any actual or potential conflicts between the mark you are using, or intend to use, and any mark that is already in use as either a "common law" mark or a federally registered mark. The objective will be to determine if a particular mark is already in use by someone else. If it is, this could preclude you from using and or registering the same mark, or one that is so similar that it could cause confusion.

You are not required to conduct a search for conflicting marks prior to applying to register your own. You can file and let an examining attorney do the search. However, in the long run a personal search prior to filing, or any use of the mark, could prove very useful and cost effective. The cost of a basic search could prove far less than the expense of changing a mark in use, and refiling an application. It could also help you to avoid a lawsuit for infringement, and the expense of defending against such litigation.

If the mark you have been using has already been used and registered by another party, and that party initiates a civil lawsuit against you for infringement, the court may presume that you were aware or should have been aware that the mark was registered to the other party. Under the law, you could be held liable as a "willful infringer." As such, you could be liable for a substantial monetary award in damages (possibly triple), for your attorney's fees, and also for the plaintiff's legal costs in bringing the suit against you. The court would also enjoin you from any further use of the mark under penalty of criminal law. You could go to jail for failure to desist in using it.

A potential applicant—or anyone who intends to begin use of a mark—is advised that a basic, preliminary search should be conducted of all federal registrations, and as many unregistered or common law marks as can be found.

The PTO does not conduct searches for the general public to confirm if a conflicting mark might already be registered, or is the subject of a pending application. An official search will be done only after an application has been filed. When that has been done, the PTO will conduct a search of Office records as part of the official examination process. The official search is not done for the convenience of the applicant, but rather to determine whether the mark that has been applied for can be lawfully registered.

The PTO will not provide preliminary advice or respond to advance queries about possible conflicts between marks. The Office can advise an applicant of a conflict only after an application has been filed and reviewed. A conflict will be confirmed when the notice that the application for registration has been rejected is sent. In that event, the application fee that covers processing and search costs will not be refunded.

SEARCHING FOR REGISTERED TRADEMARKS

Regardless of how you might elect to do it, the search for *registered* marks is rather easy and uncomplicated. Up until September 1998, there were several ways that you could have determined if your intended trademark had already been registered. As with patents, you would have been required to visit the PTO public search library in Arlington, Virginia, or any PTDL. Or you could have contracted for the services of a professional or lay searcher, or an attorney. As of September 1998, you can now conduct an online search of the USPTO Web Trademark Database of registered trademarks.

SEARCHING REGISTERED TRADEMARKS ON THE INTERNET

The USPTO Web Trademark Database includes the full bibliographic text of pending and registered trademarks. The database contains the bibliographic data and the full text of all registered trademarks (January 1, 1999: over 800,000) and pending trademark applications (January 1, 1999: over 300,000). As shown at its website (Appendix 21) the Web Trademark Database allows a Combined Marks Search, a Number Search, a Boolean Search, or a Manual Search. There is also a "Help" menu. Searching the database will be discussed in detail in chapters 15 and 16.

SEARCHING THE *OFFICIAL GAZETTE*

The OG does not list all marks that are in pending applications. It contains only registered marks and those published for opposition. It is not a practical way of searching for marks. It may be helpful in locating special form drawings for marks when these might not be found in the database.

SEARCHING FOR COMMON LAW MARKS

Common law rights to a mark arise from actual use of the mark. Generally, the first party to either use a mark in commerce, or file an "Intent to Use" application with the PTO has the ultimate right to use and register that mark.

A common law search involves examining an array of records other than the USPTO's database of registered and pending trademarks. If a mark is already listed in the PTO's database, it is, of course, no longer a common law mark.

Searching for common law marks will require you to check local and national telephone directories, white and yellow pages, industrial and commercial directories, individual state trademark registers, any number of other publications, and the Internet.

SEARCHING ON THE INTERNET

The Internet may also be a resource in searching for unregistered marks. There are several search engines that can locate businesses by name in a given geographical area, or nationwide. These can also search the Internet to determine if the mark is being used at any WWW site. No search engine, even a so-called "metasearch" engine, is 100 percent comprehensive in its search scope or results. Therefore, you should repeat the search with a variety of engines until you are satisfied that the mark does not appear in any retrievable website.

You can also search "domain" names—the unique combination of words or phrases in its URL which identifies each website. Many entrepreneurs now use their trademark or service mark, or some variation of it, as the domain name for their website. This facilitates consumer recognition and more rapid access to the products and services advertised on their web pages. Try entering: "http://www.(yourmark).com" as a URL. You may get a "hit." Try variations of your mark (pseudo marks) also.

SEARCHING INDIVIDUAL STATE RECORDS

Each state maintains records of trademarks that have been registered with the appropriate offices in that particular state. This is usually the office of the Secretary of State. You may call or write to the office and request confirmation of the status of the mark in question. Should their search be inadequate, and the mark missed, the consequences would not be as severe as they would be had it involved the federal register. Unlike federal registration, a state registration does not create the presumption in law that the user of such a mark is a "willful" infringer. In the event of a civil lawsuit, the infringer could still be found liable, but the damages may be mitigated by the circumstances.

A complete search of all state and foreign registrations (if the mark is to be used in international trade) and any and all other sources that list common law trademarks would be beyond the abilities of the average person. Let the PTO do a search of this scope.

USING THE SERVICES OF A SEARCH FIRM

As it is with patents, there are many search firms that offer trademark search services for a fee. These can be found in metropolitan telephone directories and on the Internet. Search such headings as "Trademark Consultant," "Patent Attorneys/Agents," or "Information Brokers." Legal journals and other publications may also carry advertisements for such services offered to attorneys and or the public. These are available at any law library.

Many of these services are provided by attorneys who practice in the area of intellectual property law. An attorney can also provide you with a legal opinion on the merits of using your mark, given the findings of his or her trademark search. This legal opinion could offer you some protection in the event that you would be sued for infringement. As previously discussed, the services of an attorney are not necessary in filing an application to register a trademark. However, should you have any concerns regarding a situation of possible infringement that you may have identified in your search, you should consult an attorney before filing.

15. Searching the USPTO Web Trademark Database

THE WEB TRADEMARK DATABASE

As shown in Appendix 21, the PTO advises that: "Understanding the limitations of this Web database can help you avoid significant problems. It is critical that you review [the information on the Important Notice page, Appendix 21a] before interpreting the results of searches of the PTO's Web Trademark Database." This notice confirms that the U.S. Patent and Trademark Office now offers World Wide Web access to selected trademark information obtained from its internal trademark database. The purpose of this chapter is to assist you in understanding those limitations and utilizing the database to its maximum potential.

CONTENT AND LIMITATIONS OF THE DATABASE

As we have discussed previously, the Web Trademark Database includes the full bibliographic text of both pending and registered trademarks. The fact that a mark is not present in the database does not necessarily mean the mark is not currently being used as a common law mark. The database contains only those trademarks that are federally registered, or that are pending (applications undergoing examination at the PTO). Images will be added as they become available.

The database does not include information on inactive applications and registrations such as abandoned applications, or canceled or expired registrations. Since it is possible for inactive applications or registrations to be "revived" or reinstated, active marks that may present possible conflicts with your mark will not be retrieved if they have temporarily fallen into an inactive status.

Pending trademark applications are usually entered in the database one to two months after filing. The database is updated on a two-month cycle. Coupled with the time required for data production, this means that particular trademarks could be as much as four months out of sequence with the PTO's internal trademark database.

TIPS ON FIELDED SEARCHING OF THE DATABASE

For a complete description of fielded searching, review the 17 pages of the PTO's publication *Tips on Fielded Searching*. Appendix 26 shows the links to each item in its contents. The document's URL is shown at the bottom of the page: http://www.uspto.gov/tmdb/helpflds.html. This online brochure contains the abbreviated field name or code, a definition of each of the many search fields listed, and provides examples and tips on how to do field searching for trademarks. By narrowing your search to terms in a field that you specify, you can greatly decrease the likelihood of retrieving extraneous material. Your search will likely be limited to only a few of the search fields listed. Those you could be using have been extracted and summarized below.

Description of Mark (DE)

This field contains words contained in the written description of the mark. Example: For the three musical notes that make up the sound mark registered to NBC, this field states: "The mark comprises a sequence of chime-like musical notes .... "

Design Search Code (DC)

This field contains a six-digit code (which must include the periods) used to identify design elements that comprise a mark that contains a design (special form drawing). A mark may have more than one design code associated with it. Design search codes are defined in the *Design Search Code Manual*. (This manual is available at the Trademark Search Library in Arlington, Virginia, and at all Patent and Trademark Depository Libraries.) An example of a search using the three design codes shown in Appendix 23 will be given in chapter 16.

Disclaimer (DS)

This field contains words in a statement waiving exclusive rights to specific words or elements of a mark. Without this disclaimer, the PTO would not register the mark. Example: The trademark for Ladder Witch (Appendix 23) states: "NO CLAIM IS MADE TO THE EXCLUSIVE RIGHT TO USE 'LADDER' APART FROM THE MARK AS SHOWN."

Filing Date (FD)

This field contains the date when a complete application was received by the U.S. Patent and Trademark Office, following receipt of all filing material requirements. Contingent upon registration, it constitutes the date of constructive use (the legal equivalent of actual use) of the mark.

Goods and Services (GS)

This field contains a written description that clearly identifies the nature of the goods and or services as set forth in the application or registration. The various goods and services are described in detail in the PTO publication *Acceptable Identification of Goods and Services Manual*. This manual is online. (See Appendix 27 for the website, and Appendix 27a for the first page of its table of contents.) Note that the *Manual* has 34 pages, and as a download file contains 754KB. Select "Search."

International Class (IC)

This field identifies the class assigned to a mark under the International Classification of Goods and Services. This is based upon the goods or services on which the mark is used. The International Classification has been the primary classification for marks in the United States since September 1, 1973. Determining the class number for your mark will be discussed in detail in chapter 16. The concise schedule is shown in Appendix 24. It is also listed below with the appropriate database search number and title. Note the leading zeroes; you must include these in entering your query.

International Trademark Class Numbers and Short Titles

GOODS

001 Chemicals
002 Paints
003 Cosmetics and Cleaning Preparations
004 Lubricants and Fuels
005 Pharmaceuticals
006 Metal Goods
007 Machinery
008 Hand Tools
009 Electrical and Scientific Apparatus
010 Medical Apparatus
011 Environmental Control Apparatus
012 Vehicles
013 Firearms
014 Jewelry
015 Musical Instruments
016 Paper Goods and Printed Matter
017 Rubber Goods
018 Leather Goods
019 Non-metallic Building Materials
020 Furniture and Articles Not Otherwise Classified
021 Housewares and Glass

022 Cordage and Fibers
023 Yarns and Threads
024 Fabrics
025 Clothing
026 Fancy Goods
027 Floor Coverings
028 Toys and Sporting Goods
029 Meats and Processed Foods
030 Staple Foods
031 Natural Agricultural Products
032 Light Beverages
033 Wines and Spirits
034 Smokers' Articles

SERVICES

035 Advertising and Business
036 Insurance and Financial
037 Construction and Repair
038 Communication
039 Transportation and Storage
040 Material Treatment
041 Education and Entertainment
042 Miscellaneous Services

Mark Drawing Code (MD)

This field provides a code to indicate the type of mark drawing. There are six codes to indicate the types of mark drawings. Your search will most likely utilize code 1.

1. Typed drawing (words, letters, or numbers not depicted in special form). An example is shown in Appendix 22.
2. Design only.
3. Design plus words, letters and or numbers. An example is shown in Appendix 23.
4. Words, letters and or numbers in block form.
5. Words, letters and or numbers in stylized form.
6. No drawing (sensory marks, such as sound and fragrance marks).

Mark Search (MS)

This field includes entries in Word Mark, Pseudo Mark, and Translation. That is, the Word Mark, the Pseudo Mark, and the Translation have been combined into a single index. It is important to search for similar marks in all three of these fields since they are all considered by the PTO when making a determination as to whether to refuse an application based on a likelihood of confusion with a registered mark or prior-filed application. Using this field allows you to search all fields simultaneously. See Appendix 28 for an example of a Combined Marks Search page.

Owner Address (OA)

This field contains the address of the owner or applicant for a mark, including street, city, state or country, and zip code. It also indicates if the owner is an individual, corporation, partnership, association, or other entity. It will also show the state or country of citizenship or incorporation.

Owner Name (ON)

This field contains the name of the individual, corporation, partnership, association, or other entity having controlling interest in the use of the mark.

Pseudo Mark (PM

This field provides an additional search tool for locating documents whose Word Mark may contain an alternative or intentionally corrupted spelling for a normal English word. The Pseudo Mark field often contains spellings that are very similar or phonetically equivalent to the Word Mark. An example of a pseudo mark is shown in Appendix 22.

Published for Opposition (PU)

This field contains the date that the application was published for opposition in the *Official Gazette.*

Register (RG)

This field identifies the mark as being either on the Principal Register, or on the Supplemental Register. This field applies to registered marks only.

Registration Date (RD)

This field contains the date on which a mark was registered by the U.S. Patent and Trademark Office.

Registration Number (RN)

This field contains the unique number assigned to applications that have received approval for registration. To search this field use the seven-digit registration number. If the registration number does not contain seven digits, pad it with leading zeros. Any commas included in a registration number will be ignored. This field applies to registered marks only.

Renewals (RE)

This field contains the date on which a renewal for a trademark was registered by the U.S. Patent and Trademark Office. Trademarks may be renewed indefinitely for ten-year periods provided certain conditions are met. This field applies to registered marks only.

Translation (TL)

This field contains other language equivalents of English language Word Marks or English language equivalents of other language Word Marks. Example: Enter "wolf" to retrieve documents containing the words "lupo," "ookami," "lobo," and other language equivalents in the Word Mark field. Marks containing other language equivalents may prevent the registration of a mark containing the English word. As the Italian equivalent to wolf, "lupo," and other foreign language words, may or may not be registerable based upon other criteria.

Type of Mark (TM)

This field indicates the type of mark: trademark, service mark, collective mark, collective membership mark, or certification mark.

Trademark. Any word, name, symbol or device, or any combination thereof, used or intended to be used by a person to identify and distinguish his or her goods from those manufactured or sold by others and to indicate the source of those goods.

Service Mark. Any word, name, symbol or device or any combination thereof, used or intended to be used by a person to identify and distinguish his or her services from the services of others, to indicate the source of the services (i.e., banking activities).

Collective Mark. Any trademark or service mark used or intended to be used by the members of an association, cooperative, or other collective group to identify and distinguish their goods or services. For example, the FTD mark is used by members of the Florists' Transworld Delivery Association.

Collective Membership Mark. A mark adopted or intended to be adopted for the purpose of indicating membership in an organized group. For example, the letters AAA inside an oval indicates membership with the American Automobile Association.

Certification Mark. A mark that is used or intended to be used to certify that goods or services of others meet certain standards established by the owner. The most common types of certification marks are those which:

1. Originate from a specific geographic region, such as "Roquefort" cheese; or
2. meet standards in relation to the quality, materials, or mode of manufacture, such as "Underwriters Laboratory" approval; or
3. were performed by an individual who has met certain standards or belongs to a certain organization or union. An example would be a union label in clothing.

Word Mark (WM)
This field contains a mark, or portion of a mark, that contains words, letters or numbers. This field cannot be used to search marks using only a design, fragrance, sound, and so forth.

(Adapted from *Tips on Fielded Searching.*)

16. Trademark Search Exercise

HAS SOMEONE ELSE
REGISTERED "YOUR" MARK?

You have decided on a possible trademark for your product, or a service mark for your new business, but do not know if someone else may have already claimed the mark you would like to use, and has registered it with the PTO. How will you be able to confirm if your mark, or one very similar to it has, or has not been registered? You will search the USPTO Web Trademark Database using the search steps presented in this chapter.

For this trademark search exercise, refer to the patent shown in Appendix 1. The descriptive title of the invention is: "Bracket for Mounting Ladder Shelf." Assume for the moment that you are the inventor, and you would like to give the product an appropriate trademark. Considering its intended purpose and many uses, the trademark you have decided on is: "Ladder Lackey." You will not include a graphic of any kind, or any other decorative design elements in your mark. The PTO will classify "Ladder Lackey" as a Word Mark, and you will prepare a Typed Drawing. For a description of the drawings of a mark, and Office requirements, review the PTO's online publication "Some Basic Facts About Registering a Trademark" (link at the website shown in Appendix 19).

SEARCH STEPS FOR A
WORD MARK-TYPED DRAWING

Step 1

Locate the "Welcome to the USPTO Web Trademark Database" index page shown in Appendix 21. Bookmark this page.

Website

http://www1.uspto.gov/tmdb/index

Step 2

Search for the phrase "ladder lackey."

In the "Access the Trademark Database" box select: "Combined Marks Search." This will take you to the U.S. Trademark Combined Mark Search Page shown in Appendix 28. Bookmark this page.

Website

http://trademarks.uspto.gov/access/search-mark.html

At the "Select Database" option select "Both."

In the box: "Words in the Marks," enter: "ladder lackey."

In the box: "Results must contain," select: "This exact phrase." (As a general rule, you need not include quotation marks in a query; and queries are not case sensitive in any of the search options.)

Click on "Search."

This will produce the "Results of Search in ALL db...."page shown in Appendix 28a. This confirms: "No trademarks have matched your query." The Search Summary confirms that there are "0 occurrences in 0 trademarks," and also confirms that the search time was 0.01 seconds, demonstrating that this database is very fast.

You can also carry out Step 2 in another way.

In the "Access the Trademark Database" box (Appendix 21) select "Manual Search."

This will take you to the Manual Search Page shown in Appendix 29. At "Select Database" option select: "Both."

In the "Query" box enter: "ladder lackey."

Note: In this query format you *must include the quotation marks*, or you will be curtly advised you that your query is "unparsable."

You will receive the "Results of Search in REG db... ." page shown in Appendix 29a.

As you can see, the Search Summary is more detailed than that retrieved in the Combined Marks Search. But both search approaches confirm that there is no pending or registered trademark for the phrase "ladder AND lackey." That does *not* mean that the mark is not in use as a *common law* mark–a possibility that the database cannot confirm. This search took only 0.02 seconds.

Step 3

Search the terms "ladder" and "lackey" individually.

Although you have already confirmed in the first two steps that the exact wording of the trademark you intend to use is not pending registration, or has been registered, you should search for those trademarks that incorporate either of the terms "ladder" or "lackey." The incidence of each term in registered trademarks was shown in your manual search results (Appendix 29a) which you obtained in step 2.

Searching each term separately will show you all marks that may be similar to the one you propose, and that could possibly conflict with yours, and cause your application to be rejected.

Return to the Combined Marks Search page that you had bookmarked. Website

http://trademarks.uspto.gov/access/search-mark.html

In the box: "Words in the Mark" enter "ladder" as shown in Appendix 30. (You need not include the quotation marks.) Since there is only one term in the query, you may use any option in the "Results must contain" box.

Click on: "Search."

This will give the search results shown in Appendix 30a. Only the first 25 of 81 hits are shown here. Bookmark this page; you will be using it again in this trademark search exercise.

Repeat step 3 using the second term: "lackey."

In the lists of trademarks shown in the search results for either term, note any trademarks that are very similar to "Ladder Lackey" and that could possibly confuse the consumer. These could be problematic.

Step 4

Determine the class number for the mark "ladder lackey." This is *the* step that could save you a great deal of time and effort.

Return to your bookmarked page for the search results of the term "ladder" that you retrieved in step 3.

On the list, locate the trademark "LADDERMASTER" (number 12 on the list shown in the appendix).

Click on this trademark link.

This will retrieve the data field page for this trademark which is shown in Appendix 22. Among other things note that "LADDERMASTER" is a Word Mark; that a Pseudo Mark is shown; that the Mark Drawing Code is: (1) TYPED DRAWING; and the Type of Mark is: TRADE-MARK.

As you retrieve marks from this, and any other search, note that all are rendered in CAPITAL LETTERS. This format is required by the PTO in completing Form 1478, and in preparing the drawing page for the mark.

At the bottom of the page, note the "International Class" as 006. In filing for a trademark for "Ladder Lackey," this will be the class number that would be entered in the block in the top right corner of Form 1478–the application for trademark registration (Appendix 25).

Had you taken the time to search through the 34 pages of the *Trademark Acceptable Identification of Goods and Services Manual* (sample page 1 in Appendix 27) you would have found "Ladders–Metal" classified as 006. Had you searched for "ladder brackets," or just "bracket" you would have found no listings for either. There is also none for "shelf," or "hardware." It is a very long list that may not be of much help in deciding on the correct class number for any given product or service.

If you had reviewed the International Schedule of Classes of Goods and Services (Appendix 24) you would have seen that class "6" (006) for Goods includes just about any metal hardware, such as a ladder or a bracket. (Plastic ladders are 007.)

In the end, you can leave the Class Number box on the application form empty, and the PTO examiner will fill in the blank—or possibly change the number you had inserted. It does say "if known." Skip step 4. Leave it blank.

SEARCHING FOR A SPECIAL FORM MARK

In the event that the mark you intend to register incorporates a design element such as a specific decorative script or an element of graphic art, it is considered a Special Form drawing. In selecting trademarks from your search results, you will frequently retrieve those that include such elements, and these will be shown at the top of the page that details the data in the various field codes. The PTO is adding drawings to the database as they become available.

If your proposed mark will be a Special Form, you may wish to determine if the depiction of your design is already registered. In preparing your trademark, you can easily confirm whether or not the specific word or words embodied in it have been used in a pending or registered mark. Confirming whether or not a particular design or drawing of the mark has been used is another matter, and not quite so easy to accomplish as the following discussion will show.

Special Form Search Online

Return to the Combined Marks Search bookmarked page showing the results for the query "ladder" (Appendix 30a). Locate the trademark: "LADDER WITCH." Click on this link.

You will retrieve the page summarizing the data in all the search fields for the registered trademark "LADDER WITCH" (Appendix 23).

Compare the information in the data fields with that for "LADDER-MASTER" (Appendix 22), particularly the Mark Drawing Codes. The drawing of the mark for "LADDER WITCH" is shown; "LADDERMASTER" does not show a drawing. It is a Word Mark with a Mark Drawing Code of: (1) TYPED DRAWING. "LADDER WITCH" is also a Word Mark but its Mark Drawing Code is: (3) DESIGN PLUS WORDS, LETTERS, AND/OR NUMBERS.

For "LADDER WITCH," the Design Search Code (Description of Mark, DE) indicates three code numbers. If you would return to the Combined Marks Search Page, and enter each of these code numbers separately you would retrieve a list of trademarks incorporating a feature that the DE describes. Number 14.09.02 relates to the term "ladder," and your list for this code number would include all trademarks featuring a depiction of a ladder in one form or another–including the one for "LADDER WITCH."

You could then search each of these marks to determine if the drawing shown in any of them is in any way similar to the one that you intend to use for "Ladder Lackey." But that would be an utterly futile endeavor.

ALTERNATIVES TO A SPECIAL FORM SEARCH ONLINE

An online search for specific trademark drawings is pointless. However, you could go to the PTO trademark files in Arlington, Virginia, and manually search the drawers of trademarks to examine the drawings. Before the Internet, I had done it twice. It is a tedious process, so do not bother.

Do not vex yourself with either approach to searching for drawings. Each would be a tiresome and fruitless effort. The likelihood that your trademark drawing would be identical, or very similar, to another is extremely remote (unless the similarity is intended).

Let the PTO do the search for conflicts in Special Form drawings in your mark. The conflict, if any, will arise in a Typed Drawing—in the words you use—the same words you used to search the database. If you found no conflict in the wording, your mark should register. If there is a common law conflict, it will find you.

SUMMARY

As you have seen, an online search for a Word Mark can confirm whether the mark you would like to use is already taken—either pending registration, or already registered. If this would be the case, you would have to change your mark. The search will satisfy your curiosity and could save you the expense of filing an application for a mark that will not be accepted. And determining that no one else has been clever enough to think of your mark does boost one's ego.

You can save time and money by letting the Patent and Trademark Office conduct your trademark search. An examiner will do one regardless of what you have or have not found. (You may attach your findings to your application.) Unlike a search for patents that could preclude expenditure of large sums for a patent application, a trademark application is a simple form requiring a modest fee. And a very critical block may be left empty.

Part III

Searching
for Copyrights
on the Internet

17. Searching for Copyright Information on the Internet

COPYRIGHT INFORMATION AVAILABLE ON THE INTERNET

Part three of this book discusses the subject of copyright, which is the third principal area of intellectual property law. It is a topic that often engenders some confusion vis-à-vis trademark. The title of this part of the book is "Searching for Copyrights on the Internet." It is more accurately described as Searching for Copyright Information on the Internet—the title of this chapter.

At the present time, the Library of Congress (LOC) has not made a database available that would facilitate an online search for registered copyrights. There is very little likelihood that such a search capability will ever exist because of the nature, number, and variety of registered copyrights. The emphasis in this discussion is on where the reader can find *information* and resources online to assist him or her in preparing and filing a copyright application. There is a great deal of information available online regarding copyrights and the criteria and procedures for registering them—if you know where and how to look.

Appendix 31, the United States Copyright Office Home Page (http://lcweb.loc.gov/copyright/), is the starting point in your search for information and resources regarding copyright. On that page is a link to Copyright Basics (http://lcweb.loc.gov/copyright/circs/circ1.html). This chapter is basically a summary and review of this LOC publication (*Circular 1*). It is included as Appendix 32 for the reader's convenience. A second link on the LOC home page is "Copyright Office FAQ": Questions Frequently Asked in the Copyright Office Public Information Section (http://www.loc.gov/copyright/faq.html). This document has been included as Appendix 33. Appendix 34 is a current list of all Copyright Information Circulars and Form Letters (FL.) cited in this chapter and or available free from the Copyright Office. This list can be retrieved from the link on the LOC Home Page, or at: http://www.loc.gov/copyright/circs/index.htm/ circ1.

A review of these various publications and of the material presented in this chapter should provide the reader with virtually everything he or she might need to know about copyright. It should also explain why copyrights per se are not searchable on the Internet—now or likely never.

THE INTERNET AND THE WORLD WIDE WEB: IMPLICATIONS FOR COPYRIGHT

An entirely new area of law is developing with the unrestrained growth of the Internet and the World Wide Web. The amount of information now in cyberspace is incalculable, as is any estimate of what may become available in the future. The questions of copyright raised are equally incalculable. These are beyond the scope of this book. They have been, and will continue to be, addressed by legal scholars and those technology phantoms who maintain the Web. You are advised to exercise the same caution and discretion in retrieving and utilizing the content of websites and webpages in the "public" domain of cyberspace as you would any other document with a copyright notice affixed to it. Webpages and websites usually display a copyright notice. The effectiveness of such notices is dubious at the very least. Efforts to confirm infringement and prevent the distribution of copyrighted material in cyberspace could be futile.

WHAT IS COPYRIGHT?

Copyright is a form of protection, an array of property rights, for "intellectual" property provided by the laws of the United States to the authors of "original works of authorship," including literary, dramatic, musical, and artistic works such as poetry, motion pictures, songs, computer software and architecture, and certain other intellectual works. Under the law, the creator of the original expression in a work is its "author." The author is also the owner of the copyright unless he or she has transferred ownership in some way. Like any other form of personal property, the owner can transfer all or any part of the rights in a work to another.

Copyright does not protect facts, ideas, systems, or methods of operation, although it may protect the way these things are expressed. (See Appendix 32, section "What Works Are Protected," on page 196.) Copyright is one form of intellectual property law. Patents and trademarks, also the intangible products of the human intellect, are also protected by the laws of intellectual property. In copyright law this protection is available to both published and unpublished works. The discussion in this chapter will focus primarily on literary works for which authors will seek copyrights.

Most persons understand that the works of living authors, painters, sculptors, photographers, and composers are covered under copyright law. But the law extends far beyond these traditional forms of creative art—and even beyond the grave of the artists. The creative efforts of scientists, engineers, architects, and many other professionals are protected. The writings of the student and the aspiring poet or author are protected. As recently as 1980, computer programs were included as protected works. In a related but separate statute, the "mask work" of semiconductor chips was given protection in 1984.

COPYRIGHT LAW

The Constitution of the United States, Article 1, Section 8 states: "The Congress shall have Power To ... promote the Progress of Science and useful Arts, by securing for limited Times to Authors and Inventors the exclusive Right to their respective Writings and Discoveries." In succeeding years, Congress enacted various laws, and courts handed down various decisions that expanded the definition of "Authors" and "Writings" to mean creators and works created, respectively. It is from this Constitutional provision that our present copyright laws derive.

Present-day copyright law had its statutory beginnings in an English law of 1710, known as the "Statute of Anne." For the first time, there was statutory recognition of an author's right to protect his or her work and an established duration of time for that protection, after which the work entered the public domain.

The first federal copyright law in the United States, modeled on the English statute, was enacted in 1790. Throughout the nineteenth century, the law was expanded to protect existing art forms such as painting, prints, music, and sculpture, and newly created art forms such as photography. In the twentieth century, further expansion of the law covered motion pictures, phonograph recordings, videotaped material, and—today—computer programs. The position of Register of Copyrights was created in 1897, and the Copyright Office (the Office) became a part of the Library of Congress.

At the present time, the copyright law in the United States is the result of a recodification of the federal statutes in 1909, and again in 1976, and another less extensive revision in 1988. The intent of the 1909 and 1976 revisions was to provide copyright to new technologies. The primary purpose in 1988 was to bring United States law further in line with the provisions of the Berne Convention, an international treaty that defines minimum standards for copyright in those nations that are parties to the treaty. This was necessary because of the growing importance of copyrighted works in international trade, and the need to cooperate in an effort to suppress the piracy of such works.

Most of the provisions of the Copyright Act of 1976, as Amended, 17, U.S.C.A. (the Act) that went into effect January 1, 1978, remain in force today. A 1988 provision eliminated the requirement that all works carry a copyright notice. However, significant advantages accrue to the owner of a copyright who affixes the notice to his or her work. Prosecution of copyright is not merely the filing of an application form. You should know those rights that registration conveys to you.

RIGHTS GRANTED UNDER THE LAW

Section 106 of the Act generally gives the owner of copyright the exclusive right to do, and to authorize others to do, and to prohibit others from doing, any of the following:

- To reproduce the copyrighted work in copies or phonorecords (the statutory definition of the term "phonorecord" is given below);
- to prepare derivative works based upon the copyrighted work;
- to distribute copies of phonorecords of the copyrighted work to the public by sale or other transfer of ownership, or by rental, lease, or lending;
- to perform the copyrighted work publicly in the case of literary, musical, dramatic, and choreographic works, pantomimes, and motion pictures, and other audiovisual works;
- to display the copyrighted work publicly in the case of literary, musical, dramatic, and choreographic works, pantomimes, and pictorial, graphic, or sculptural works, including the individual images of a motion picture or other audiovisual work; and
- in the case of sound recordings, to perform the work publicly by means of a digital audio transmission.

Phonorecord

"Phonorecords are material objects in which sounds, other than those accompanying a motion picture or other audiovisual work, are fixed by any method now known or later developed, and from which the sounds can be perceived, reproduced, or otherwise communicated, either directly or with the aid of a machine or device.... [The term phonorecords] includes the material object in which the sounds are first fixed." (Section 101.)

In addition, certain authors of works of visual art have the rights of attribution and integrity as described in Section 106A of the Act. For further information on this particular subject, *Copyright Information Circular 40* is available online from the Copyright Office: http://lcweb.loc.gov/copyright/circs/.

For further information about the statutory limitations of any of these rights, the reader is referred to the Copyright Code, or is advised to write to the Copyright Office. The Office is not permitted to give legal advice per se.

If information or guidance is needed on legal matters such as disputes over the ownership of a copyright, lawsuits against possible infringement, or procedures for getting a work published, or methods of obtaining royalty payments, an attorney should be consulted.

NEED FOR AN ATTORNEY IN APPLYING FOR A COPYRIGHT

Now that copyright law has been discussed, you can take comfort in the fact that only a very basic knowledge of it is required to register a copyright. It is when someone infringes on your rights and in certain other situations that you will need an attorney. There is no requirement that a copyright application be prepared and or filed by an attorney. The information and the assistance provided by the Office, and the relative simplicity of the procedures, are such that the average citizen can easily register a copyright on their own with little or no difficulty and at modest cost. In any matters of copyright other than registration and notice, particularly if any procedural requirement is not clear, or in the area of international copyright law, or in the event of infringement, a copyright attorney should be retained.

A registered copyright is an official, legal document. You must be accurate, complete, and careful in the application process. It is hoped that this chapter will facilitate this. Do not hesitate to avail yourself of the services of the Copyright Office. They have a staff of experts willing and able to help with any questions or problems you might have regarding your application.

WHO CAN CLAIM COPYRIGHT, AND WHEN?

An author's work is under copyright protection the moment it is created and fixed in tangible form so that it is perceptible either directly or with the aid of a machine or device. The copyright in the work of authorship immediately becomes the property of the author who created the work. Only the author or those deriving their rights through the author can rightfully claim copyright. Copyright protection, and immediate offensive rights, commence at the moment the work is created. A work is created when it is in "fixed form." You do not need permission from the Copyright Office to place a notice of copyright on your material. You can register your claim for a work fixed in tangible form anytime you choose—before, at the time of, or after publication, or even if you have no intent to publish. "Publication" and its precise meaning in copyright law will be defined and discussed later in the chapter.

You do not have to register your claim to copyright, nor do you have to receive a certificate of registration in order to publish, reproduce, sell, distribute, or license your work. Registration is voluntary. However, you must register if you wish to bring a lawsuit for infringement of a United States work.

You might ask: "Why should I register my work if copyright is automatic?" Registration is recommended for a number of reasons. Many individuals choose to register their works because they wish to have the facts of their copyright on the public record and hold a certificate of registration. In the event of infringement of their registered work they may be eligible to receive statutory damages and reimbursement of attorney's fees in a successful lawsuit. And, if registration occurs within five years of publication, it will be considered *prima facie* evidence in a court of law. (See *Copyright Information Circular 1*, section "Copyright Registration," and *Copyright Information Circular 38b on non–U.S. works.*)

WORKS MADE FOR HIRE

Although the general rule is that the person who creates the work is its author, there is an exception to that principle and that is a "work made for hire." This is a work prepared by an employee within the scope of his or her employment; or a work specially ordered or commissioned in certain specified circumstances. In the case of works made for hire, the employer or the party who commissioned it is considered to be the author. The employee can be identified as the author, but the employer must be identified as the owner of the copyright.

Under Section 101 of the Act a work made for hire is:

> 1. a work prepared by an employee within the scope of his or her employment; or
> 2. a work specially ordered or commissioned for use as a contribution to a collective work, as a part of a motion picture or other audiovisual work, as a translation, as a supplementary work, as a compilation, as an instructional text, as a test, as answer material for a test, or as an atlas, if the parties expressly agree in a written instrument signed by them that the work shall be considered a work made for hire.

In all cases, the author of a work for hire should have the specific terms of the arrangement in writing. This written agreement protects all parties in the event of any dispute over the legal ownership of the rights to the work produced and the claim for its copyright. *Copyright Information Circular 9: Work-Made-for-Hire Under the 1976 Copyright Act* is available online.

TWO GENERAL PRINCIPLES OF COPYRIGHT

1. Mere ownership of a book, manuscript, painting or any other copy or phonorecord does not give the possessor the copyright. The law provides that

a transfer of ownership of any material object that embodies a protected work does not, of itself, convey any rights in the copyright.

2. Minors may claim copyright, but individual state laws may regulate the business dealings involving copyrights owned by minors. For information on the relevant state law, the reader is advised to consult an attorney.

THE THREE CRITERIA FOR COPYRIGHT

There are three basic criteria that *must* be satisfied in a determination of whether or not a creative work ("work of authorship") may be protected by copyright: (1) the originality of the work, (2) the medium of expression of the work, and (3) its fixation in tangible form.

ORIGINALITY OF A WORK

The work must be original and not merely the result of extended effort; the author must have created it independently, not simply copied it. In claiming copyright, you are claiming that yours is an original work. Therefore, the work must have some element of originality and creativity; that is, it must have been the product of human intellect. (This gives rise to the question of the copyrightability of works "created" by computer graphic software—that was created by a human mind.) It does not have to be the product of a great intellect. It does not even have to be good writing or art. It can be obscene.

There are no art, literary, or morality critics on the Copyright Office staff. The Office does not pass on the merits of the subject matter for which copyright is claimed—that is the prerogative of the public, the critics, or the courts. In literature, art, and entertainment today, there are, arguably, no definitive rules regarding what constitutes creativity or the elements that demonstrate it. The Office does not evaluate a work for originality and requires no proof of a claim for such. There will be no comparisons made to confirm originality as is done in the patent examination and issuing process.

To be original, a work need not necessarily be "novel." A certificate of copyright will be issued without consideration of a work's novelty. Therefore, you can obtain copyright protection for a work that is very similar to a preexisting work, provided it is not merely a duplicate of it. A work may be a work of authorship if it is a compilation or a derivative of preexisting works.

Compilation
"A 'compilation' is a work formed by the collection and assembling of preexisting materials or of data that are selected, coordinated, or arranged in such a way that the resulting work as a whole constitutes

an original work of authorship. The term 'compilation' includes collective works." (Section 101.)

This is a semantic distinction since a "compilation," by definition, is a collection. However, in a compilation, the authors of the selected preexisting works may be merely approving their use rather than actively producing and contributing them for inclusion. If a work is prepared over a period of time, the part of the work that is fixed on a particular date constitutes the created work as of that date. The author of a compilation merely gathers and assembles the material and does not modify, adapt, or alter it in any significant way.

Derivative Work

"A 'derivative work' is a work based upon one or more preexisting works ... in which a work may be recast, transformed, or adapted." (Section 101.) This chapter is largely a derivative work.

The material is adapted or reworked in some way as to produce what can be considered a new work. It must contain at least some elements of new and original authorship and not consist of just minor changes or embellishments of the prior matter. The preexisting works can be in any number of forms that may have been rewritten, condensed, translated, or adapted in some way so that the final version is accepted as an original work of authorship. The implications for copyrightability will depend on the degree of modification or adaptation of the original elements.

The author of the original work can be the author of a derivative work, or it can be another person—provided he or she has received permission to use the original copyrighted work that underlies the derivation. Copyright law prohibits unauthorized derivatives. They are an infringement. The author of the derivative work can claim copyright for it. *Copyright Information Circular 14: Copyright Registration for Derivative Works* is online.

Collective Work

"A 'collective work' is a work, such as a periodical issue, anthology, or encyclopedia, in which a number of contributions, constituting separate and independent works in themselves, are assembled into a collective whole." (Section 101.)

In such a work any number of individuals have actively made contributions that, in and of themselves, are considered separate and independent, and that are intended to be assembled into a unitary work. The authors of a joint work are coowners of the copyright in the work, unless there is an agreement to the contrary. Copyright in each separate contribution to a periodical or other collective work is distinct from copyright in the collective work as a whole and vests initially with the author of the contribution.

MEDIUM OF EXPRESSION OF THE WORK

Copyrightable works include the following categories when they are fixed in tangible form. This list is representative, not exhaustive.

- Literary works—other than audiovisual works—that are expressed in words, numbers, or other symbols; these include *any* part of manuscripts, books, magazines, pamphlets, newsletters, catalogs, directories, compilations. Also databases, phonorecords, film, tapes, and disks.
- Musical works, including any lyrics or arrangements.
- Dramatic works, including operas, stage plays, skits, sketches, and pantomime no matter where performed.
- Choreographic works.
- Pictorial, graphic, and sculptural works; including works created in any of the fine, graphic, or applied arts. These include paintings, drawings, photographs, prints, cartoons, sculpture, art reproductions, models, and technical drawings; also jewelry, dolls, designs for fabrics or paper, greeting cards. Such technical and scientific works as architectural or engineering drawings, models, charts, and maps are also covered.
- Audiovisual works, such as motion pictures, that consist of a series of images shown by such devices as projectors, viewers, or computer monitors, regardless of the medium in which they are embodied.
- Sound recordings that are works that result from the fixation and embodiment of verbal, musical, natural, or any other sounds in some material object; these do not include soundtracks of motion pictures or other audiovisual works.
- Architectural works, including a design for a structure that is embodied in any tangible medium of expression—the structure itself, or any plans or drawings of it. Architectural works became subject to copyright protection on December 1, 1990. The copyright law defines "architectural work" as "the design of a building embodied in any tangible medium of expression, including a building, architectural plans, or drawings." Architectural works embodied in buildings constructed prior to December 1, 1990, are not eligible for copyright protection.

These categories should be viewed very broadly. For example, computer programs and most compilations may be registered as literary works; maps and architectural plans and models may be registered as pictorial, graphic, and sculptural works.

The Idea and the Expression of the Idea in Copyright

To understand copyright law, and the concept of copyright, it essential to understand the difference between an *idea* and the *expression* of that idea. A copyright goes to the "form of literary expression" embodied in the work rather than the subject matter of the work. It will not protect the idea or concept that underlies an expressive work. It protects only the literal form that the work takes—the expression of the idea fixed in tangible form. Whenever an idea and expression are inseparable, the expression cannot be copyrighted.

As an aspiring writer, you may be discouraged to know that the plot, setting, concept, and most likely the characters and title—indeed, the very inspiration for your masterpiece—*will not belong to you ... and never will.* Only the *form*, the context, the shape you give them—the expression—will remain yours. No one can "steal" your idea, because it is, effectively, not yours to begin with. Anyone is free to copy, adapt, and use your idea in any way they choose. You can "own" only your secret, unspoken, thoughts. Once these leave the cloister of your imagination they belong to the vulgar masses. The law will not protect your revealed secrets and dreams. Only the cloak of silence and anonymity can do this.

An explanation or description of anything can be copyrighted. For example, a detailed description of a machine, its components, how it is assembled, and how it is used can be copyrighted, but this would prohibit others from copying the *description only*. It would not preclude anyone else from writing their own version of the description, and it would not prevent anyone from constructing, using, and selling the machine described—unless it were protected by a patent, or trade secret law. Patents and copyrights are usually mutually exclusive, as are trademarks and copyrights.

FIXATION OF THE WORK IN TANGIBLE FORM

Copyright protects "original works of authorship" that are "fixed in a tangible form of expression." To satisfy this requirement, the work must be embodied in a form that is sufficiently permanent and stable to permit it to be perceived, reproduced, or otherwise communicated over an indefinite period of time. The fixation need not be directly perceptible so long as it may be communicated with the aid of a machine or device.

WHAT IS NOT PROTECTED BY COPYRIGHT

Several categories of material are generally not eligible for federal copyright protection. These include:

- Works that have *not* been fixed in a tangible form of expression. For example: choreographic works that have not been noted or recorded, or improvisational speeches or performances that have not been written or recorded.
- Names of products, services, businesses, or organizations.
- Names of persons—legal or assumed.
- Single words or short phrases, slogans, mottoes; familiar symbols or designs; mere variations of typographic ornamentation, lettering, or coloring; and mere listings of ingredients or contents. A symbol that incorporates certain artistic components may be copyrighted as a work of visual art. An example would be the logo of the International Olympic Committee.
- Titles of works are not copyrightable. When a work is registered with the Copyright Office, it must include a title. This will be used only to identify the work. No copyright is imparted to the title. Use of the title of another, copyrighted, work where the intent is to capitalize on the success or notoriety of the work itself by confusing the public could be subject to legal challenge. You are referred to *Copyright Information Circular 34: Copyright Protection NOT Available for Names, Titles*, available online.
- Ideas, plans, procedures, methods, systems, processes, concepts, principles, discoveries, or devices, as distinguished from a description, explanation, or illustration of any of these. The work of authorship—the *manner* of expression—is copyrightable, but not the matter expressed.
- Works consisting *entirely* of information that is common property and containing no original authorship. For example: standard calendars, height and weight charts, tape measures and rulers, and lists or tables taken from public documents or other common sources. Any creative artwork incorporated in any of these could make them copyrightable.
- Certain blank forms that do not communicate information but require only that data be entered in designated places. Creative artwork on such a form may be copyrightable. See *Copyright Information Circular 32: Blank Forms/Other Works Not Protected by Copyright*.

- Lists of components or ingredients, unless they include creative art-work. A recipe may be copyrightable (*FL122*).
- The idea for games or the names of games. Appendix 35, *FL108* provides information on what aspects or components of a game may be copyrightable, e.g., a game board.

PUBLICATIONS INCORPORATING UNITED STATES GOVERNMENT WORKS AND OTHER WORKS IN THE PUBLIC DOMAIN

Works published by the U.S. government are, by law, not eligible for U.S. copyright protection. Virtually all such material is free to be copied, rewritten, and sold or resold. (Works published by state or local governments could be copyrightable—to avoid infringing, check before using these.)

For works published on and after March 1, 1989, the previous notice requirement for works consisting primarily of one or more U.S. government works has been eliminated. However, use of a notice on such a work will defeat a claim of "innocent" infringement (discussed shortly) *provided* the notice also includes a statement that identifies either those portions of the work in which copyright is claimed or those portions that constitute U.S. government material.

> Example: © 1999 Charles C. Sharpe. Copyright claimed in Chapters 1–17, exclusive of United States Government materials.

Other works in the public domain are considered to be any materials that any citizen can freely access and retrieve in repositories of public records, copy, distribute or otherwise utilize without permission or license from anyone. This would include any works that are unpublished uncopyrighted works, any that are inherently not copyrightable, and works for which a copyright has expired. There are thousands of books now available online at various websites for which copyrights have expired, and which anyone may retrieve, reproduce, and sell. Once a copyright has expired, it can never be reclaimed. Also included are any works that an author has endowed to the public domain. Any such works can be reproduced in whole or in part and distributed in any quantity and in any manner, including sale for profit.

Public domain materials must not bear a copyright notice. They belong to the public-at-large, and no individual citizen can lay claim to them. No one really owns them; they are the communal property of world society—everyone owns them. You cannot claim copyright for any such materials, but you can claim copyright for anything you personally create and incorporate into the final derivative or compiled work that includes art or literature in the public domain.

Materials in the public domain include most of the greatest masterpieces in classical literature, music, painting, and sculpture. Any of these can be reproduced and sold as "reproductions." Selling them as "originals" is forgery, piracy, theft-by-deception, scam—or whatever the law may call it.

The absence of a copyright notice on a published work does not necessarily indicate that it is in the public domain. Under the Act, unpublished works do not require a notice. Do not assume that in the absence of a notice you are free to use the material as you choose. If there could be any uncertainty as to what material is truly in the public domain, consult an attorney.

UNPUBLISHED WORKS

The 1976 Copyright Act attempted to ameliorate the strict consequences of failure to include a notice under prior law. It contained provisions that set out specific corrective steps to cure omissions or certain errors in notice. Under these provisions, an applicant had five years after publication to cure an omission of notice or certain errors. Although these provisions are technically still in the law, their impact has been limited by the amendment making notice optional for all works published on or after March 1, 1989.

DURATION OF COPYRIGHT PROTECTION

WORKS ORIGINALLY CREATED ON OR AFTER JANUARY 1, 1978

The Copyright Term Extension and Music Licensing Act which was signed into law on October 28, 1998, extend the duration of copyright protection. Under the new statutes, a work that is created (fixed in tangible form for the first time) on or after January 1, 1978, is automatically protected from the moment of its creation and is ordinarily given a term enduring for the author's life plus an additional 70 years after the author's death. In the case of "a joint work prepared by two or more authors who did not work for hire," the term lasts for 70 years after the last surviving author's death. For works made for hire, and for anonymous and pseudonymous works (unless the author's identity is revealed in Copyright Office records), the duration of copyright will be 95 years. The full text of the act is available at the Copyright Office Website at http://lcweb.loc.gov/copyright/. Click on: "The Copyright Term Extension and Music Learning Act."

INFRINGEMENT OF COPYRIGHT

It is illegal for anyone to infringe any of the rights provided by the copyright code to the owner of copyright. These rights, however, are not unlimited in scope. Sections 107 through 120 of the Act establish limitations on these rights. In some cases, these are specified by exemptions from copyright liability. One major limitation is the "Doctrine of Fair Use" that is given a statutory basis in Section 107. The Doctrine of Fair Use will be discussed in detail later in this chapter. In other instances, the limitation takes the form of a "compulsory license" under which certain limited uses of copyrighted works are permitted upon payment of specified royalties and compliance with statutory conditions.

A copyright can be infringed when another individual or entity personally and directly violates one of the exclusive rights of the copyright or imports any works into the United States that do so. To prove infringement, an author/plaintiff must show (1) that they own the copyright; (2) that the work infringed was copied without their authorization; and (3) that this was done after their claim of copyright. Direct evidence must be presented to establish these assertions. It may be difficult to prove direct copying; however, proof may come from circumstantial evidence by a demonstration that the works in question are substantially alike and that the accused infringer had access to the copyrighted work.

"Innocent infringement" occurs when the infringer did not realize that the work was protected. If you do not use another's work deliberately and knowingly, you are not infringing. You must actually knowingly copy to infringe. There is always the extremely unlikely possibility that one author's work will so closely resemble another's as to substantially replicate its concept and form of expression. Unless it can be proven to have been copied, it may not be considered infringement. If it can be shown that you had access to the earlier, original work that your own work so closely resembles, you will have to make a very good case for yourself in court.

Use of the copyright notice is important because it informs the public that the work is protected by copyright, identifies the copyright owner, and shows the year of first publication. Furthermore, in the event that a work is infringed, if a proper notice of copyright appears on the published copy or copies to which a defendant in a copyright infringement suit had access, "then no weight shall be given to such a defendant's interposition of a defense based on innocent infringement in mitigation of actual or statutory damages, except as provided in Section 504(c)(2) of the copyright code."

The Copyright Office does not become involved in claims of infringement. The office does not notify a claimant to a previously copyrighted work that it has or may have been infringed. Discovering that is the responsibility of the copyright owner who can then take whatever action he or she may wish to protect his or her claim. A party may seek to protect his or her copyright against unauthorized use by filing a civil lawsuit in a federal district court. An attorney must be retained in this instance. In cases of willful infringement for profit, a U.S. attorney may initiate a criminal investigation. If you copy and use the work of another, and that is discovered, you could be the subject of a lawsuit unless you can demonstrate what is known as the Doctrine of Fair Use.

THE DOCTRINE OF FAIR USE

It has often been said that stealing from a single author is plagiarism; stealing from several authors is "research." How much is stolen could make the difference between infamy and fame.

One of the rights accorded to the owner of copyright is the right to reproduce or to authorize others to reproduce the work in copies or phonorecords. This right is subject to certain limitations found in Sections 107 through 120 of the Copyright Act (Title 17, U.S. Code).

One of the more important limitations is the Doctrine of Fair Use. Although fair use was not mentioned in the previous copyright law, the doctrine has developed through a substantial number of court decisions over the years in an effort to mitigate the stringent, absolutist, limitations of copyright law. This doctrine has been codified in Section 107 of the copyright law that lists the various purposes for which the reproduction of a particular work may be considered "fair" and also four factors to be considered in determining whether or not a particular use is fair.

SECTION 107: LIMITATIONS ON EXCLUSIVE RIGHTS: FAIR USE

Notwithstanding the provisions of Sections 106 and 106A, the fair use of a copyrighted work, including such use by reproduction in copies or phonorecords or by any other means specified by that section, for purposes such as criticism, comment, news reporting, teaching (including multiple copies or classroom use), scholarship, or research is not an infringement of copyright. In determining whether the use made of a work in any particular case is fair use the factors to be considered shall include:

> 1. the purpose and character of the use, including whether such use is of a commercial nature or is for nonprofit educational purposes;
> 2. the nature of the copyrighted work;
> 3. the amount and substantiality of the portion used in relation to the copyrighted work as a whole; and
> 4. the effect of the use upon the potential market for or value of the copyrighted work.

DEFINING FAIR USE

Although incorporated into the Act, the doctrine does not attempt to define the precise limits of fair use of a copyrighted work. Therefore, any person or institution who reproduces copyrighted material could technically be in violation of a copyright, no matter the degree or purpose. Under Section 107, certain persons or organizations are allowed to reproduce copyrighted material for certain purposes without the permission or the copyright holder. The provision's guidelines are very broad. Usually it will be for the courts to decide, on a case-by-case basis, whether a particular use is fair. Essentially the doctrine permits copying that could otherwise constitute infringement. It refers to limited use of a work that is copyrighted, under certain conditions. (See *Copyright Information Circular 21*, and Appendix 36.)

The distinction between fair use and infringement may be unclear and not easily defined. There is no specific number of words, lines, or notes that may safely be taken without permission. Acknowledging the source of the copyrighted material does not substitute for obtaining permission.

The 1961 *Report of the Register of Copyrights on the General Revision of the U.S. Copyright Law* cites examples of activities that courts have regarded as fair use:

> [Examples are the] quotation of excerpts in a review or criticism for purposes of illustration or comment; quotation of short passages in a scholarly or technical or, for illustration or clarification of the author's observations; use in a parody of some of the content of the work parodied; summary of an address or article, with brief quotations, in a news report; reproduction by a library of a portion of a work to replace part of a damaged copy; reproduction by a teacher or student of a small part of a work to illustrate a lesson; reproduction of a work in legislative or judicial proceedings or reports; incidental and fortuitous reproduction, in a newsreel or broadcast, of a work located in the scene of an event being reported.

The fact that a work is unpublished will not in itself bar a finding of fair use if such finding is made upon consideration of all of the above factors. An author is allowed to quote from the work of another or to reproduce limited amounts of graphic material as part of a critique or to support a position taken. An author should quote all material accurately, in context, and cite the source. This is not required under the doctrine of fair use, but it will show the source that you are really trying to be fair and may obviate the need for permission.

Fair use is just what it says—use that is fair. What is "fair"? What is "reasonable"? These are just two of many words whose meanings are open to various interpretation and argument. Ultimately, a judge or jury may decide and impose a definition. It is generally accepted that use of any author's work in its entirety, from a chapter to an entire book, does not fit the definition. Selected use of material will be judged on its relative quantity in the user's work and its proportion to the whole of the original work. There is no fixed rule as to quantity; however, as a general rule, the least material used, the more likely it will be considered as fair use. Publishers typically define fair use as not to exceed 300 words, and will require an original source's written permission for any number over that. Obtaining this is usually the author's responsibility.

The courts have held that paraphrasing is copying. Long-standing copyright doctrine regards lengthy paraphrasing as nothing more than an attempt to disguise verbatim copying. An author who paraphrases very limited quantities of materials would not likely be liable for infringement of copyright. Extensive or limited—evaluating either for infringement will take into consideration the four factors defined in Section 107 of the statute and discussed previously.

INFRINGEMENT

Even though a plaintiff can show that they own the copyright and that the defendant infringed on it by copying their work, the infringer may avoid legal liability by claiming one of several defenses provided in the Act. The most widely used defense offered is that of fair use. In allowing this defense, a court will primarily consider the four factors cited in Section 107 in adjudicating a claim.

The court will ask what was the purpose or circumstance of the use; for example, was there a profit motive or was the use in a nonprofit or educational context? The nature of the work for which copyright infringement is claimed will be examined—was it a work of fiction, a derivative work, a widely known play, or musical composition? There will be an evaluation of the extent of the copying relative to the entire work—were only isolated passages used, or were whole pages or sections lifted? And lastly, was there any adverse economic impact of the claimed infringement on the owner of the copyright and on the value or marketability of his or her work—and what was the amount of damages? (If it benefits them economically, you can still be sued.)

The last factor is considered to be the most significant of the four. If a plaintiff is successful in a lawsuit for infringement, they may recover actual monetary damages plus any and all profits that the infringer may have derived as a result of their transgression. If the copyright of the work had been registered within three months of its publication, the claimant may also recover statutory damages and attorneys' fees. If the infringement occurred after March 1, 1989, the minimum statutory award is $500, the maximum is $20,000. If the court determines that the defendant's action of infringement was intentional, an award of up to $100,000 may be adjudicated.

Under the Act, a temporary or permanent injunction may be obtained, and or infringing copies of the work may be seized and destroyed. In some instances the government can file criminal charges against an infringer of any copyrighted work.

PERMISSION

If there is any doubt about using the work of another author, it is always best to request permission from the owner of the copyright before using copyrighted material. You can write to an author directly or to the permissions or copyright department/editor of the publisher who owns the copyright—not write to the author in this situation. Consult Bowker's *Literary Market Place* for the names and addresses of publishers. When it is impracticable to obtain permission, use of copyrighted material should be avoided unless the Doctrine of Fair Use would clearly apply to the situation.

As a general rule, an author is advised that if the use of the material in question appears to meet all the criteria of fair use, then no permission should be required or requested. The legal right to fair use should be exercised with the utmost integrity and not dissipated by unfounded fear or caution. The Copyright Office does not become involved in any way in determining fair use, obtaining permissions, or in matters of infringement. It could be necessary to consult an attorney in these matters.

LIBRARY COPYING AND FAIR USE

The language of the Act (Section 108) contains very specific guidelines for libraries. Unofficial guidelines have evolved for educational institutions. Under the law, it is not an infringement of copyright when a library or archive staff—acting within the scope of their employment—reproduce no more than one copy of a work under certain conditions. The single copy must include the original notice of copyright and must be made for one of the purposes defined in the statute. These include the following:

> If the copy is made for a library's own use, because the library's own copy of the work is damaged or missing and a replacement cannot be obtained at a fair price. If the copy is made for a patron's use and is limited to an article or small part of a larger work—or the whole of a larger work if a printed copy cannot be obtained at a fair price—and only if the copy is intended for use by the patron in private study, scholarship or research.

Copies made by libraries or archives cannot be made for profit—or in the language of the statute for "any purpose of direct or indirect commercial advantage." A reasonable fee may be charged to the patron, but this cannot be a business on the side. Generally, only one copy is permitted (Section 108). The exception is if the same item is copied in "isolated and unrelated" circumstances and "single" copies are made on "separate occasions." The original copyright notice must appear on any copy—this is to prevent the recipient from mistakenly assuming that the material is not copyrighted.

The Act prohibits indiscriminate, systematic reproduction by a library if this can be shown to be an effort to avoid purchase of the materials, or to provide library patrons with such materials without regard to their intended use of such materials. Unpublished works can be copied in order to preserve them. The repository must be a "public" library or archive—the law defines neither of these. It can also be any library that is accessible to anyone conducting research. The libraries of virtually every university, college, museum, and medical institution are open to legitimate research by a professional and layperson alike. Certain others would qualify, including private libraries or those maintained by business or professional organizations.

Libraries are allowed to copy materials for patrons. These materials must be in the form of text only plus any incorporated graphic material. Copyrighted fine or graphic art works cannot be copied for patrons but can be reproduced for the use of the library. Such copies should be provided only for use in research. If another use is intended, the individual requesting the copies should be directed to make them personally. The library cannot retain ownership of copies provided, or require their return unless they are made available as "circulating" material.

The law requires a notice or warning be prominently displayed in the library advising patrons of the implications of reproducing copyrighted material and the possibilities of infringement. This in effect relieves the library staff of responsibility and liability for unsupervised or unauthorized use of its materials and copying equipment by patrons. The patron can still be liable. Suggested language of the notice is shown below.

Warning of Copyright

> The copyright law of the United States (Title 17, United States Code) governs the making of photocopies or other reproductions of copyrighted material. Under certain conditions specified in the law, libraries and archives are authorized to furnish a photocopy or other reproduction. One of these specified conditions is that the photocopy or reproduction is not to be "used for any purpose other than private study, scholarship, or research." If a user makes a request for, or later uses, a photocopy or reproduction for purposes in excess of "fair use," that user may be liable for copyright infringement. This institution reserves the right to refuse to accept a copying order if, in its judgment, fulfillment of the order would involve violation of copyright law.

The ten cents-a-copy photocopy machine in virtually every library is an ubiquitous medium of infringement—for the general public and for the library staff. The exemptions in the Act are included for, and *only* for, the library and its staff carrying out their duties. They do not apply to the general patrons of the library (even if the staff does the copying). There must be fair use of the copy machine. Needless to say, a public library has no control over what or how much patrons themselves copy for their own use—legal or otherwise.

EDUCATIONAL, NONPROFIT, AND RELIGIOUS
INSTITUTION COPYING AND FAIR USE

The Act does not provide similar guidelines for these institutions. However fairly liberal allowances are made for them. Various rules and regulations have been developed and it is generally accepted that limited amounts of such copying is considered fair use. Copying for use in a classroom should be done only when there is inadequate time to obtain permission. The number of copies should not exceed the number of students in a class. They should not be a substitute for materials that could and should be purchased. Nor should the same material be copied and distributed repeatedly—semester after semester, year after year.

Each and every copy must include the copyright notice shown on the original. An anthology that a faculty member derives from a number of authors' works is an infringement under the law if expressed permission has not been received from *each* of the authors who own the copyrights. A commercial printing or copying service firm that reproduces any such material can be liable for a claim of infringement and a lawsuit.

The content of a lecture or seminar is the property of the presenter and cannot be recorded on tape or video without permission of the author of the material. Verbatim transcriptions cannot be reproduced and sold without expressed permission. *Copyright Information Circular 21: Reproductions of Copyrighted Works by Educators and Librarians* should answer most questions in these two areas.

HOW TO SECURE A COPYRIGHT

The way in which copyright protection is secured is frequently misunderstood. No publication or registration or other action in the Copyright Office is required to secure copyright under the law. There are, however, certain definite advantages to registration as discussed in the following section: Copyright Registration.

Copyright is secured automatically when the work is "created," and a work is created when it is fixed in tangible form in a copy or phonorecord for the first time. A "copy" is any material object (other than a phonorecord) in which a work is first fixed by any method now known or that might be developed at some later time, and from which the work can be reproduced, read, or visually perceived either directly or with the aid of a device or a machine.

PUBLICATION

Publication has a very technical meaning in copyright law. The Copyright Act of 1909 defined publication as follows and this definition remains the standard to the present time:

> Publication is the distribution of copies or phonorecords of a work to the public by sale or other transfer of ownership, or by rental, lease, or lending. The offering to distribute copies or phonorecords to a group of persons for purposes of further distribution, public performance, or public display constitutes publication. A public performance or display of a work does not of itself constitute publication.

Publication is no longer the key to obtaining federal copyright as it was under the Copyright Act of 1909. Under that act, if an author failed to place the proper copyright notice on a published work, the work forfeited to the public domain—irretrievably. Therefore, before 1978, federal copyright was generally secured by the act of publication with notice of copyright, assuming compliance with all other relevant statutory conditions. United States works in the public domain on January 1, 1978 (for example, works published without satisfying all conditions for securing federal copyright under the Copyright Act of 1909), remain in the public domain under the 1976 Copyright Act.

Federal copyright could also be secured before 1978 by the act of registration in the case of certain unpublished works, and works eligible for ad interim copyright. The 1976 Copyright Act automatically extends full-term copyright for all works including those subject to ad interim copyright if ad interim registration has been made on or before June 30, 1978.

Generally, publication occurs on the date on which copies of the work are first made available to the public. The legislative reports define "to the public" as distribution to persons under no explicit or implicit restrictions with respect to disclosure of the contents. The reports state that the definition makes it clear that the sale of phonorecords constitutes publication of the underlying work—for example, the musical, dramatic, or literary work embodied in a phonorecord. The reports also state that it is clear that any form of dissemination in which the material object does not change hands—for example, performances or displays on television—is *not* publication no matter how many people are exposed to the work. However, when copies or phonorecords are offered for sale or lease to a group of wholesalers, broadcasters, or motion picture theaters, publication does take place if the purpose is further distribution, public performance, or public display.

SIGNIFICANCE OF PUBLICATION

Publication continues to be very important to copyright owners. Although publication is not necessary for copyright protection, it is an extremely important concept in the copyright law for several reasons:

- Works that are published in the United States are subject to *mandatory* deposit with the Library of Congress. This will be discussed later in this chapter.

- Publication of a work can affect the limitations on the exclusive rights of the copyright owner that are set forth in Sections 107 through 120 of the Act.
- The year of publication may determine the duration of copyright protection for anonymous and pseudonymous works (when the author's identity is not revealed in the records of the Copyright Office) and for works made for hire.
- Deposit requirements for registration of published works differ from those for registration of unpublished works. A deposit is usually one copy of an unpublished work or two copies of a published work to be registered for copyright.
- When a work is published, it may bear a notice of copyright to identify the year of publication and the name of the copyright owner and to inform the public that the work is protected by copyright. Copies of works published before March 1, 1989, must bear the notice or risk loss of copyright protection.

The Copyright Office does not become involved in publication in any way. See *Copyright Information Circular 1*, section "Publication."

NOTICE OF COPYRIGHT

The purpose of this notice is to advise the public-at-large that the copyright owner claims exclusive rights to the work on which the notice appears. The use of the copyright notice is the responsibility of the copyright owner and does *not* require advance permission from, or registration with, the Copyright Office. The use of a notice is no longer required under United States law for works published after March 1, 1989. The Office does not take a position on whether copies of works first published with notice before March 1, 1989, and which are distributed on or after March 1, 1989, must bear the copyright notice. However, it is advisable to place a notice on each published copy of a work, and, although not required, it is also highly advisable to place a notice on all work before it is published, distributed, or shown publicly.

Should you omit the proper notice from copies of works published, your rights will expire within five years unless your register the copyright and place the proper form of notice on all copies subsequently published and distributed. Because prior law did not contain such a requirement, however, the use of notice is still relevant to the copyright status of older works.

Notice was required under the 1976 Act. This requirement was eliminated when the United States adhered to the Berne Convention, effective March 1, 1989. Although works published without notice before that date could have entered the public domain in the United States, the Uruguay Round

Agreements Act restores copyright in certain foreign works originally published without notice. The revisions of the copyright law in 1976 (Sections 401–406) have made the notice requirements much less stringent than they had previously been and have substantially reduced the risk to an author of losing their rights. It is still necessary for an author to place the proper copyright notice on his or her work.

FORM OF NOTICE FOR VISUALLY PERCEPTIBLE COPIES

There are certain technicalities that must be observed in proper form and placement of the notice. In the past, failure to observe these could have resulted in loss of copyright. This is no longer the case, but proper, statutory, wording and placement of the notice is still required. The notice for visually perceptible copies should contain *all* of the following three elements in the order given:

1. The symbol ©, or the word Copyright, or the abbreviation Copr.; and
2. The year of first publication of the work. In the case of compilations or derivative works incorporating previously published material, the year date of first publication of the compilation or derivative work is sufficient. The year date may be omitted where a pictorial, graphic, or sculptural work, with accompanying textual matter, if any, is reproduced in or on greeting cards, postcards, stationery, jewelry, dolls, toys, or any useful article; and
3. The name of the owner of the copyright in the work or an abbreviation by which the name can be recognized, or a generally known alternative designation of the owner.

Example: © 1999 Charles C. Sharpe

The C in a circle notice is used only on "visually perceptible copies." Certain kinds of words—for example, musical, dramatic, and literary works—may be fixed not in "copies" but by means of sound in an audio recording. Since audio recordings such as audio tapes and phonograph disks are "phonorecords" and not "copies," the "C in a circle notice" is not used to indicate protection of the underlying musical, dramatic, or literary work that is recorded.

FORM OF NOTICE FOR PHONORECORDS OR SOUND RECORDINGS

Sound recordings are defined in the law as: "works that result from the fixation of a series of musical, spoken, or other sounds, but not including the sounds accompanying a motion picture or other audiovisual work." Common examples include recordings of music, drama, or lectures. A sound recording is not the same as a phonorecord. A phonorecord is the physical object in which works of authorship are embodied. The term "phonorecord" includes cassette tapes, CDs, LP, as well as other formats.

The notice for phonorecords embodying a sound recording should contain *all* of the following three elements:

1. The symbol: ℗ (P in a circle) and
2. The year of first publication of the sound recording; and
3. The name of the owner of the copyright in the sound recording, or an abbreviation by which the name can be recognized, or a generally known alternative designation of the owner.

Since questions may arise from the use of variant forms of the notice, you may wish to seek legal advice before using any form of the notice other than those given here.

POSITION OF THE NOTICE

The appropriate copyright notice should be affixed to copies or phonorecords in such a way as to "give reasonable notice of the claim of copyright." The three elements of the notice should ordinarily appear together on the visually perceptible copies or a phonorecord label or container. The Copyright Office has issued regulations concerning the form and position of the copyright notice in the *Code of Federal Regulations* (37 CFR Part II01).

ADVANTAGES OF COPYRIGHT REGISTRATION

In general, copyright registration is a legal formality intended to make a public record of the basic facts of a particular copyright. As previously noted, it is not necessary to register to establish a legal claim. Considering the simplicity and modest cost of registering, the benefits to be gained are worth the time and expense. Even though registration is not a requirement for protection, the copyright law provides several inducements or advantages to encourage copyright owners to register.

Among these are:

- Registration establishes a public record of the copyright claim.
- Before an infringement suit may be filed in federal court, registration is necessary for works of U.S. origin and for foreign works not originating in a Berne Union country.
- If made before or within five years of publication, registration will establish *prima facie* evidence in court of the validity of the copyright and of the facts stated in the certificate.

- If registration is made within three months after publication of the work or prior to an infringement of the work, statutory damages and attorneys' fees will be available to the copyright owner in court actions. Otherwise, only an award of actual damages and profits is available to the copyright owner.
- Registration allows the owner of the copyright to record the registration with the U.S. Customs Service for protection against the importation of infringing copies.

REGISTERING A COPYRIGHT

Registration may be made at any time within the life of the copyright. Unlike the law before 1978, when a work has been registered in unpublished form, it is not necessary to make another registration when the work becomes published, although the copyright owner may register the published edition, if desired.

WHO MAY FILE AN APPLICATION FOR REGISTRATION?

The following persons are legally entitled to submit an application form:

- The author
  Ownership of the copyright initially vests in the author(s). This may be the person(s) who actually created the work, the employer of an employee who created it, or other person for whom a specific type of work was prepared under a work for hire agreement or commission. Under the Act, an "author" can be individuals or business entities.
- The copyright claimant
  The copyright claimant is defined in the Office regulations as either the author of the work, or a person or organization that has obtained ownership of all the rights under the copyright initially belonging to the author. This category includes a person or organization who has obtained by contract the right to claim legal title to the copyright in an application for registration.
- The owner of exclusive right(s)
  Under the law, any of the exclusive rights that go to make up a copyright and any subdivision of them can be transferred and owned separately, even though the transfer may be limited in time, place, or effect. The term "copyright owner" with respect to any one of the exclusive rights contained in a copyright refers to the owner of that particular right. Any owner of an exclusive right may apply for registration of a claim in the work.

- The duly authorized agent
  The agent of the author, other claimant, or owner of exclusive right(s) may apply for registration on the author's behalf.
- Joint owners
  A copyright can be jointly owned. The work must be created in cooperation with another party with the intent that the individual contributions of each will be combined in the final product. Each party co-owns the copyright and (in the absence of a formal, written agreement) any one of the co-owners may license or sell the copyright with the consent of the others. However if there is a transfer of the copyright or the license to it, each of the co-owners must be compensated. In these instances a properly drafted instrument or agreement should be prepared by an attorney for all the parties.

ANONYMOUS AND PSEUDOANONYMOUS WORKS

Anonymous

An anonymous work is one for which no natural person(s) is identified as the author; an author's name does not appear on the copies or phonorecords. There is no legal requirement that the author be identified by his or her own real name on the application form. The name that appears in the copyright application and the copyright notice of an anonymous or pseudoanonymous work must be that of the copyright owner. Even though the author is anonymous or writing under a pseudonym, the owner or copyright claimant cannot be anonymous or pseudonymous. A copyright claimant must be listed. The real name of the author can be shown as claimant, or his or her pseudonym may be given and qualified as such by inclusion of his real name.

Copyright registrations are public records and available to anyone. If an author does not wish to reveal his or her identity in any way, he or she may arrange for an agent or other legal representative to file as claimant. An attorney should be consulted before this is done. If an author of a book wishes to remain anonymous, the publisher's name, by formal agreement, can appear in the copyright notice. [A historical note: During the 19th century and into the beginning of the 20th, women authors used only initials for their first and middle names or wrote anonymously for fear of discriminatory rejection of their works.]

Pseudoanonymous

A pseudonym or pen name may be used by an author of a copyrighted work. A work is pseudonymous if the author is identified on copies or phonorecords of that work by a fictitious name (nicknames or other diminutive forms of one's legal name are not considered fictitious). As is the case with other names, the pseudonym itself is not protected by copyright. (See Appendix 37, *FL 101*.)

If the author is not identified in the records of the Copyright Office, the term of copyright is 75 years from publication of the work, or 100 years from its creation, whichever term expires first. If the author's identity is later revealed in the records of the Copyright Office, the copyright term then becomes the author's life plus 50 years.

There are several other technicalities involved in this area. It would be best to contact the Office for further instructions and information. Before you decide to publish anonymously or under a pseudonym, you should be aware of the implications and legal issues that can arise from the use of either. It is advisable that you seek the advice of an attorney so that the relationship between you, as the author, and the copyright claimant can be properly documented in the Copyright Office records. For further reference see *Copyright Office Form Letter 101* (*FL 101*) in Appendix 37.

REGISTRATION PROCEDURES

The registration procedures are outlined in detail in Appendix 32, *Copyright Basics*, and will not be discussed here. However, it is important for an applicant to know the importance of sending the three specified elements of the application together as explained in *Circular 1*.

Copyright registration is effective on the day the Copyright Office receives the appropriate (1) application form, (2) deposit, and (3) filing fee. Applications and fees received without appropriate copies, phonorecords, or identifying material will not be processed and ordinarily will be returned. Unpublished deposits without applications or fees ordinarily will be returned also. In most cases, published deposits received without applications and fees can be immediately transferred to the collections of the Library of Congress. This practice is in accordance with Sections 407 and 408 of the Act that provide that the published deposit required for the collections of the Library of Congress may be used for registration only if the deposit is "accompanied by the prescribed application and fee."

After the deposit is received and transferred to another service unit of the Library for its collection or other disposition, it is no longer available to the Copyright Office. If you wish to pursue registry of the work, you must deposit additional copies or phonorecords with your application and fee. The deposit requirements vary in particular situations.

APPLICATION FORMS

Forms may be downloaded from the Copyright Office Home Page link. All forms may be downloaded and or photocopied if they meet the following criteria:

- They must be printed back to back and head to head on a single sheet of paper.
- The size of the paper must be 8½" × 11".
- The copy must look exactly as the original.

The particular application form which the Copyright Office may require will be determined by several factors. *Circular 1, Copyright Basics*, Appendix 32, discusses application forms, deposit requirements, and fees in detail.

SEARCH OF COPYRIGHT RECORDS

The records of the Copyright Office are open for inspection and searching by the public. Moreover, on request, the Office will search its records for you at the statutory rate of $20 for each hour or fraction of an hour. Office records in machine-readable form cataloged from January 1, 1978, to the present, including registration information and recorded documents, are available for searching on the Office's website. *Copyright Information Circulars 22: How to Investigate the Copyright Status of a Work* and 23: *Copyright Card Catalog and the Online Files* are available from the Office.

CONTACTING THE COPYRIGHT OFFICE

As noted throughout this chapter the Office has a variety of information circulars on particular subject matter available online. Check the Copyright Office website for the most current list. Note *Copyright Information Circular 1b Limitations/Information Furnished by Copyright Office*. Application forms as well as any circulars cited can be ordered 24 hours a day from the Copyright Office hotline. There is no charge for any of these materials.

Part IV

Appendixes

The Commissioner of Patents and Trademarks

Has received an application for a patent for a new and useful invention. The title and description of the invention are enclosed. The requirements of law have been complied with, and it has been determined that a patent on the invention shall be granted under the law.

Therefore, this

United States Patent

Grants to the person(s) having title to this patent the right to exclude others from making, using, offering for sale, or selling the invention throughout the United States of America or importing the invention into the United States of America for the term set forth below, subject to the payment of maintenance fees as provided by law.

If this application was filed prior to June 8, 1995, the term of this patent is the longer of seventeen years from the date of grant of this patent or twenty years from the earliest effective U.S. filing date of the application, subject to any statutory extension.

If this application was filed on or after June 8, 1995, the term of this patent is twenty years from the U.S. filing date, subject to any statutory extension. If the application contains a specific reference to an earlier filed application or applications under 35 U.S.C. 120, 121 or 365(c), the term of the patent is twenty years from the date on which the earliest application was filed, subject to any statutory extension.

Commissioner of Patents and Trademarks

Attest

The
United
States
of
America

US005788198A

United States Patent [19]

Sharpe

[11] **Patent Number:**   **5,788,198**

[45] **Date of Patent:**   **Aug. 4, 1998**

[54] **BRACKET FOR MOUNTING LADDER SHELF**

[76] Inventor: **Charles C. Sharpe.** 3519 Mercer Ct.. Slatington, Pa. 18080-3026

[21] Appl. No.: **606,444**

[22] Filed: **Feb. 23, 1996**

[51] Int. Cl.⁶ E06C 7/14
[52] U.S. Cl. 248/210
[58] Field of Search 248/210, 238, 248/231.41, 231.61, 222.41

[56]   **References Cited**

U.S. PATENT DOCUMENTS

2,895,700	7/1959	Johnson	248/210
3,182,749	5/1965	Girardello	248/238 X
3,309,053	3/1967	Baker	248/210
3,310,271	3/1967	King	248/222.41 X
3,710,096	1/1973	McFarlin	248/222.41 X
3,853,202	12/1974	Jarboe	248/210 X
5,060,755	10/1991	Bourdages et al.	248/238 X

FOREIGN PATENT DOCUMENTS

797732	of 1958	United Kingdom	248/222.41

Primary Examiner—Daniel P. Stodola
Assistant Examiner—Gregory J. Strimbu
Attorney, Agent, or Firm—Eckert Seamans Cherin & Mellott

[57]   **ABSTRACT**

A bracket is attachable to a ladder to form a convenience support or other attachment that attaches to the rails or rungs of a ladder, and is readily reconfigured, moved or adjusted as to angular orientation, without substantial assembly steps or tools. The bracket has at least two and preferably three mounting members, each folded at a right angle to define two flat plates, e.g., with one of the plates longer than the other. Each plate has a least one array of spaced openings for fasteners. The fasteners and some of the openings are dimensioned so that the fastener heads or nuts fit through such openings of the plates and the shanks of the fasteners engage in a slot, which can require turning non-round fastener heads for alignment with the slot before insertion, and turning the non-round heads of the fastener back after insertion, or alternatively passing the head through a larger hole joined to the slot. The mounting members are attached in a chosen configuration by affixing the fastener in the first mounting member and attaching the second mounting member to the first mounting member by passing the hole of the second mounting member over the end part of the fastener and sliding the mounting members to arrange the shank in the slot of the second mounting member such that the plates interlock and engage around rails or rungs of the ladder. additional array openings are then chosen to receive fasteners for locking the orientation of the bracket.

6 Claims, 7 Drawing Sheets

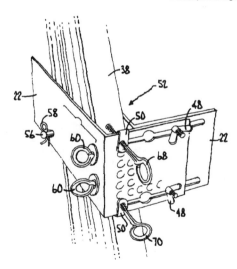

5.788.198

1

BRACKET FOR MOUNTING LADDER SHELF

BACKGROUND OF THE INVENTION

1. Field of the Invention

The invention relates to the field of ladder brackets, and concerns a structure attachable to any type and size of conventional ladder for supporting a shelf or other article for the convenience of a person using the ladder, or to enable the attachment of various items such as scaffolding connections or workpieces that need to be held level and steady regardless of the angle at which the ladder rests.

2. Prior Art

An auxiliary support, platform or the like on a ladder is useful to provide ready access to equipment, materials, tools, etc. Safety, convenience and working speed are improved if users need not climb up and down repeatedly and instead have at hand what they need to do a job. Such a support is also useful as an available workspace for operations. For example, stepladders having pivoted front and rear legs usually are equipped with a shelf pivoted at the level of the next highest rung from the top or seat. The shelf can be folded closed to reside between and in the plane of the rear legs, or folded open to horizontal (provided the stepladder is opened out) for supporting a paint can or roller tray, tools, etc., at a level below the top rung or seat. The supporting part of the shelf extends rearward from its pivot axis on the rear legs (i.e., away from the user). Two extensions extend forward from the pivot axis and bear upwardly under the rung of the front legs when the ladder is pivoted open and the shelf is folded down to a position. Due to its mounting and placement, the conventional stepladder shelf is restricted as its size, and is fixed as to the position and angle at which it deploys. Although the shelf is apt for some jobs such as indoor painting, it would be advantageous if a more versatile arrangement could be provided that can be adapted to other needs and situations than the usual stepladder shelf.

Typically, a collapsible connecting member is foldably connected between the front and rear legs of a stepladder, and fixes the separation angle of the ladder legs. The front and rear legs or rails open to a predetermined angle and the extensions of the opened shelf reach under a front rung at substantially the same elevation as the pivot axis. Thus the shelf is necessarily horizontal when deployed. Such a shelf is useful when the ladder legs are opened so the ladder is free standing, and the legs are fixed at their characteristic angle. When the stepladder is not folded open, for example being tilted against a structure while the legs are closed, the angle of the ladder is uncertain and is variable as a function of the distance between the structure and the foot of the ladder. In addition, the supporting structures for the pivoting shelf (i.e., the pivot and the rung) are not placed to interact as they do when the ladder is opened.

Extension ladders and simple ladders consisting of spaced side rails connected by rungs, are used at various, changeable angles of tilt, determined by the distance between the foot of the ladder and the structure against which the ladder leans, and the distance between the foot of the ladder and the point of contact with the structure. In different situations the ladder is set at different tilt angles. Unlike a stepladder, which is typically used in a situation where the shelf is in convenient arm's reach, an extension ladder or the like is often used in situations where the user needs to work all along the length of the ladder and not only at one height.

It would be advantageous to provide a convenient support device for any type of conventional ladder that is superior to

2

a stepladder shelf in that it is not limited to a fixed size and/or position and that accommodates a variable ladder tilt angle. The support should be movably affixed to the ladder at any desired height, and either should remain horizontal, or better yet, should be positionable at any desired angle. However, it is disadvantageous to provide a large number of nuts, bolts and adjustments, especially requiring tools. Such adjustments are not convenient for a worker because they must be loosened, moved, tightened or otherwise attended to every time the support is moved up or down, and also whenever the tilt angle of the ladder is changed.

Examples of supports attachable to ladders are disclosed in the following patents:

Des.284,513	Dyer	4,318,523	Weatherly
2,541,434	Nelson et al.	4,523,733	Lunden, Jr.
3,111,297	Conner	4,660,794	Given
3,229,943	Olsen	4,662,594	Dubis
3,822,846	Jesionowski	5,191,954	Ledford
3,829,051	Emmons	5,236,161	Haven
4,222,541	Cillis	5,342,008	Kay

As shown in these patents, an auxiliary support structure can be affixed to ladder rungs or to ladder side rails. For example, hook structures can extend over a rung and/or a clamp structure can grasp the rail or a rung. Insofar as the patents provide means for adjusting the angle of the auxiliary support structure, the adjustment typically involves releasing the platform to allow it to be moved to a new angle, where the platform is again locked. This may involve fasteners such as nuts and bolts, butterfly nuts, pins, clamps, levers, etc. The user of the ladder is required to hold the support in place while it is attached and configured. Thus the user may need to empty the support of tools, paint receptacles and similar work items so as not to spill them when releasing the support, and to make several trips up and down the ladder to remove such items, to disassemble, move, reassemble, position and lock the support, and to replace the work items needed to do the job.

It is counterproductive in a convenience support for a ladder to require tools or numerous assembly steps. It may be impractical for the user to effect all the necessary steps every time the ladder is moved. For example, a support for clamping to a rail may require the user to align two opposed clamping members, to insert a screw or bolt and attach a nut, then align the support to horizontal and tighten the nut and bolt to clamp the support in place, e.g., using wrenches. Where a support hooks over a rung, at least the angle must be adjustable if the support is to be set horizontal. If the user must empty the support of materials, obtain and use tools to build it again at another spot, and replace the tools and materials before getting back to work, the support is more trouble than it is worth.

Attempts to reduce reliance on parts that must be assembled and disassembled have had their own drawbacks. In the Lunden, Jr. patent, a support depends from a bar via a freely rotatable coupling. The attachment to the ladder is made by inserting the bar endwise into a hollow rung, with the support swinging below the bar. This is simple, but is correspondingly insecure, for example with nothing preventing the support from rocking. Dubis prevents rotation of a fitting inserted into a rung by using a lever controlled expandable fitting plug. Use of a clamping control lever is also found in Haven; however in Haven, as in others of these patents, no capability is provided to adjust the angle of attachment, e.g., as in Haven where a bowl shaped receptacle can confine articles even if tilted.

5.788.198

3

The user may desire to move the support without moving the ladder (e.g.. the working elevation may be changed without changing the ladder tilt). It would be desirable in that case to have a support that can be easily and quickly detached and removed from the ladder. or relocated and reattached as a unit at a new position where it retains its previous angular orientation. Such a support could be moved up or down on the ladder without necessarily removing work items on the support. It would also be appropriate to enable quick and easy adjustment of the orientation. for use when changing the tilt angle of the ladder or reconfiguring the support.

What is needed is an optimal compromise between complexity and adjustability in a support. The support should not rely on structural connections and fasteners that are difficult to achieve or to adjust when on a ladder. should require no tools. and should be versatile as to the nature and location of its attachment to the ladder. as well as the particular angle assumed by the support.

SUMMARY OF THE INVENTION

It is an object of the invention to provide readily attachable and detachable flanged clamping elements that are capable of alternative attachments to a ladder such as a straight ladder, extension ladder or stepladder, and are highly versatile as to the position and placement on the rungs and/or rails and as to the relative angles between the clamping elements. rungs and rails.

It is another object to arrange a plurality of right angle folded plates with hole and slot arrays making the plates attachable simply and quickly to one another anywhere over a range of angles and spacings by which the plates are attachable to a ladder in various useful configurations.

It is a further object to provide a stable and secure interlocking arrangement for the plates. such that the plates are rigidly attachable to one another and to the ladder, thereby forming a stable and secure support that can nevertheless be readily detached. moved and reattached as needed. with or without changing the configuration of the attached plates.

It is also an object to provide a support that can be quickly configured, assembled or disassembled. for optimal convenience and security in placing the support on a given ladder or ladder configuration. for moving the support on the same ladder or for moving the support to another ladder or ladder configuration.

It is another object to provide hole and slot arrays for attaching clamping plates by passing them over the heads of fasteners through a hole that opens into a slot. and engaging a shank of the fastener in the slot to thereby affix the plates without the need to assemble separate fastener elements such as nuts and bolts.

It is still another object to provide an auxiliary support or attachment to a ladder that can be configured to encompass a wide or narrow clamping span. can attach to rails or rungs. and is useful for a wide variety of clamping and support functions.

These and other objects are accomplished by a bracket attachable to a ladder for providing a convenience support or point of attachment. The bracket can be affixed to the rails or rungs of a ladder. and is readily reconfigured or adjusted as to angular orientation. preferably using two leveling bolts and two clamping bolts that are easily installed or moved without the need for tools. For a ladder that remains at a given tilt angle. the bracket can be detached from the ladder and moved without substantial disassembly (e.g.. to change

4

elevation on a fixed-angle stepladder or an extension ladder that has not been moved). When changing the tilt angle of a ladder. minimal steps are necessary to adjust the bracket for the new angle. When adapting the bracket for a new type of supporting job. the bracket can be easily reconfigured by rearranging and interlocking its parts. The bracket comprises at least two and preferably three flanged or L-shaped mounting members. each folded at a right angle to define two flat plates. Preferably one of the plates is longer. e.g.. twice as long as the other. Each of the plates has a least one array of spaced openings for fasteners. The fasteners are dimensioned to fit through the openings of the plates. and have a relatively narrower shank part and a relatively wider end part at least at one end of each fastener. The openings on the plates include a hole dimensioned to pass over the end part of the fastener. The hole being joined to a slot in the plate at least as wide as the shank part and narrower than the end part. such that the mounting members can be attached to one another in a chosen configuration by affixing a fastener in a first of the plates and attaching a second of the plates to the first plate by passing one of the holes of the second plate over the end part of the fastener and sliding the plates to arrange the shank in the slot of the second plate such that the plates interlock. Of two mounting members that clamp to a ladder. the two L-shapes are abutted directly at one of their respective plates and are spaced at the other pair of plates. which straddle around the side rail or rung of the ladder. and can be fixed by a pin. A plurality of spaced pins can abut the ladder. or more preferably. a single retaining pin is used for this purpose and only this pin needs to be removed temporarily to permit the bracket to be detached from the ladder and moved. for example to a new location or to assume a new tilt angle. The arrayed holes in the plates are such that certain of the holes will align to one another at various spacings and angles of the respective plates. Thus two spaced fasteners or pins can be placed at a required point in the array to achieve leveling. and/or a further L-shaped mounting member can be attached. for example to provide a horizontal or vertical surface as needed. In the event of a change in elevation or angle. or to attach to a different ladder. etc.. the support simply can be easily and quickly detached. relocated (or removed entirely) and moved as a unit to the new position. angle or the like. with minimal disruption of work flow. This aspect is particularly useful when moving the support to a different elevation or to a similarly inclined ladder. in that the relative angles of the plates are kept intact.

BRIEF DESCRIPTION OF THE DRAWINGS

There are shown in the drawings certain exemplary embodiments of the invention as presently preferred. It should be understood that the invention is not limited to the embodiments disclosed as examples. and is capable of variation within the scope of the appended claims. In the drawings,

FIG. 1 is a perspective illustration of a basic L-shaped folded mounting member according to the invention. two or more of which are attachable to one another and to a ladder or the like according to the invention.

FIG. 2a is a partial perspective view illustrating several alternative types of fasteners. engageable according to the invention with a combined hole-and-slot opening in one or more of the mounting members.

FIG. 2b is a partial perspective view showing attachment of two fasteners as in FIG. 2a.

FIG. 2c is a partial perspective view showing an alternative embodiment in which the fasteners are threadable into U-nuts placed over edges of a mounting member.

5,788,198

9

In various of the configurations shown in the drawings, a weight placed on the support surface of the bracket would tend to rotate it unless clamped tightly. According to the invention as shown, for example, in FIGS. 8 and 9, a bolt or pin 56 can extend through the bracket, at a position to block rotation without tight clamping. The right angle corner of one of the plates can contact a ladder side rail, or an outer edge of a plate can contact a rung. Pin 56 prevents rotation of the bracket by fixing a point spaced from the point of such contact relative to the ladder rail. The points of contact keep the bracket and its shelf horizontal although the ladder rail is tilted. No tight clamping is needed, and the bracket can be easily detached and repositioned.

The invention is widely applicable to various sizes of ladder rail and various configurations of attachment, because the array of holes 34 and hole/slot openings 30/32 provide the user with numerous potential bolt or pin entries. The user chooses available holes in the array that most closely align with the upper front and lower rear points of contact with the side rail, and places the bolts where needed. This maintains the position of the auxiliary shelf.

The L-shaped mounting members can vary with respect to the specific placement of the smaller holes 34 and the large holes 32 along slots 30. For example, slots 30 are parallel and located along the extreme edges of the plates in the embodiments shown, but could be spaced inwardly or otherwise oriented relative to one another. In any event, the heads of the fastening bolts or their nuts can be passed through the hole/slot opening without removing the nut and bolt from one another. Thus, eye bolts, thumbscrew bolts, butterfly nuts and the like are particularly useful.

FIGS. 10–15 show various uses of the invention. In FIG. 10, a flat pegboard plate 66 is carried by hooks 77 in a vertical orientation to hold tools or tool receptacles 78. In FIG. 11, a plate in a horizontal orientation the plate is useful to support tools or to provide a surface to receive a workpiece 82. Additional L-shaped bracket parts 22 can provide a restraint 80 for the workpiece. Plate 66 can have a similar arrangement of hole arrays and hole/slot combinations dimensioned the same as L-shaped mounting members 22, likewise providing a variety of options for precisely how and where the plate is mounted. Alternatively, a more generic shelf plate can be used, preferably having at least some holes spaced to complement those of the L-shaped plates for receiving fasteners whereby the plate is readily and quickly mounted or removed.

FIGS. 12–15 show some further uses. In FIG. 12, brackets on spaced ladders each connect to a horizontal beam member 84 that forms part of a scaffold-like arrangement wherein member 84 bridges between the brackets. Additional fasteners and/or fixtures 61 can be used to obtain a secure connection between the various parts. In FIG. 13, two bracket arrangements on the end of a ladder attach to pipes 92 using U-bolts 94. The pipes are arranged at an angle relative to the ladder rails for hooking over the peak of a gable roof.

In FIG. 14, a vertical post 86 is provided and clamped to the bracket of the invention, which is in turn attached to the ladder. In FIG. 15, an arrangement 88 of pipes 92 is coupled to the ladder using U-bolts 94 as in FIG. 13, coupled to a plate 66. In this case the pipes 92 extend laterally and forward such that the ladder can be tilted toward a window, and the pipes straddle the window. A third horizontal plate 66 between rungs is used to carry a PVC stabilizing pipe structure 88 having a central tee 90 and lateral arms 92, the arrangement being affixed to plate 66 with U-bolts 94. The

10

lateral arms 92 can bear against a structure, such as the walls on either side of a window. This arrangement is useful in that the ladder need not be retracted to rest against the window sill or extended well above the window to rest against the wall. Additional variations will also now be apparent.

The L-shaped members can comprise stamped steel plate and can be painted, coated with rubber or plastic, or otherwise treated or made of a material free of rust and corrosion. The thickness or gauge of the plate material is a function of the intended use. For light duty use (e.g., household), 3/32" (2.4 mm) thickness is adequate for support of paint cans, incidental tools and the like. For medium or heavy duty use, a 1/8 to 1/4" (3.2 to 6.3 mm) thickness plate is preferred. To enable a lighter and less expensive material, the edges of sheet material plates can be rolled to stiffen them. Another light duty material is injection molded plastic; but for plastic the thickness must be increased and/or flanged edges may be appropriate.

According to the embodiments shown as examples, typically a single horizontal or vertical portion of an L-shaped plate is the ultimate "working member" that is fixed relative to the ladder. The invention is also applicable to arrangements in which a plurality of such working members are affixed to the ladder. For example, two or more horizontal members can be mounted at a space to define vertically spaced shelves, shelves that protrude oppositely, etc. Combinations of horizontal and vertical plates, attachments to other structures and the like are all made possible because any two of the L-shaped plates of the invention are readily and conveniently attached anywhere over a range of relative positions and angles. Thus the structure can be readily set up, moved or removed, reconfigured and otherwise adapted to the job at hand, using minimal assembly steps, fasteners and inconveniences.

The invention having been disclosed in connection with the foregoing variations and examples, additional variations will now be apparent to persons skilled in the art. The invention is not intended to be limited to the variations specifically mentioned, and accordingly reference should be made to the appended claims rather than the foregoing discussion of preferred examples, to assess the scope of the invention in which exclusive rights are claimed.

I claim:

1. A clamping bracket for attaching an auxiliary structure to a ladder, comprising:

a first mounting member and a second mounting member, each of the mounting members having a first plate and a second plate joined at a common edge and defining an angle between the first and second plates, the common edge of the second mounting member being nested within the angle defined by the first mounting member;

means for adjustable attaching the auxiliary structure, said means secured to at least one of the mounting members, wherein one of the plates of the first mounting member is removably secured to one of the plates of the second mounting member; and,

a third mounting member removably secured to one of the first and second mounting members in a substantially horizontal orientation irrespective of an orientation of the first and second mounting members.

2. A clamping bracket for a ladder for use in front of a window, the bracket comprising:

a first mounting member and a second mounting member, each of the mounting members having a first plate and a second plate joined at a common edge and defining an angle between the first and second plates, the common

 Patent and Trademark Depository Library Program

Complete PTDL List

This PTDL list is current as of April 6, 1999 .

*** Indicates USPTO Partnership Site
** Indicates on-line APS Text Searching capability

Alabama

Auburn University: Ralph Brown Draughon Library, Auburn University **	334 844-1747
Birmingham: Birmingham Public Library	205 226-3620

Alaska

Anchorage: Z. J. Loussac Public Library, Anchorage Municipal Libraries	907 562-7323

Arizona

Tempe: Daniel E. Noble Science and Engineering Library/Science/Reference, Arizona State University **	602 965-7010

Arkansas

Little Rock: Little Rock: Arkansas State Library**	501 682-2053

California

Los Angeles: Los Angeles Public Library **	213 228-7220
Sacramento: California State Library, Library-Courts Building	916 654-0069
San Diego: San Diego Public Library	619 236-5813
San Francisco: San Francisco Public Library **	415 557-4500
Sunnyvale: Sunnyvale Center for Innovation, Invention & Ideas ***	408 730-7290

Colorado

Denver: Denver Public Library	303 640-6220

Connecticut

Hartford: Hartford Public Library	860 543-8628
New Haven: New Haven Free Public Library	203 946-8130

Delaware

Newark: University of Delaware Library	302 831-2965

District of Columbia

Washington: <u>Founders Library, Howard University</u>   202 806-7252

Florida

Fort Lauderdale: <u>Broward County Main Library</u> **   954 357-7444
Miami: <u>Miami-Dade Public Library</u> **   305 375-2665
Orlando: <u>University of Central Florida Libraries</u>   407 823-2562
Tampa: <u>Tampa Campus Library, University of South Florida</u>   813 974-2726

Georgia

Atlanta: <u>Library and Information Center, Georgia Institute of Technology</u> 404 894-4508

Hawaii

Honolulu: <u>Hawaii State Library</u> **   808 586-3477

Idaho

Moscow: <u>University of Idaho Library</u>   208 885-6235

Illinois

Chicago: <u>Chicago Public Library</u>   312 747-4450
Springfield: <u>Illinois State Library</u>   217 782-5659

Indiana

Indianapolis: <u>Indianapolis-Marion County Public Library</u>   317 269-1741
West Lafayette: <u>Siegesmund Engineering Library, Purdue University</u>   765 494-2872

Iowa

Des Moines: <u>State Library of Iowa</u>   515 281-4118

Kansas

Wichita: <u>Ablah Library, Wichita State University</u> **   316 978-3155

Kentucky

Louisville: <u>Louisville Free Public Library</u> **   502 574-1611

Louisiana

Baton Rouge: <u>Troy H. Middleton Library, Louisiana State University</u>   225 388-8875

Maine

Orono: <u>Raymond H. Fogler Library, University of Maine</u>   207 581-1678

Maryland

College Park: <u>Engineering and Physical Sciences Library, University of Maryland</u> 301 405-9157

http://www.uspto.gov/web/offices/ac/ido/ptdl/
ptdlib.htm

Massachusetts

Amherst: Physical Sciences and Engineering Library, University of Massachusetts	413 545-1370
Boston: Boston Public Library **	617 536-5400, Ext. 265

Michigan

Ann Arbor: Media Union Library, The University of Michigan	734 647-5735
Big Rapids: Abigail S. Timme Library, Ferris State University	616 592-3602
Detroit: Great Lakes Patent and Trademark Center, Detroit Public Library ***	313 833-3379

Minnesota

Minneapolis: Minneapolis Public Library & Information Center **	612 630-6120

Mississippi

Jackson: Mississippi Library Commission	601 961-4111

Missouri

Kansas City: Linda Hall Library **	816 363-4600
St. Louis: St. Louis Public Library**	314 241-2288, Ext. 390

Montana

Butte: Montana Tech of the University of Montana Library	406 496-4281

Nebraska

Lincoln: Engineering Library, Nebraska Hall, 2nd Floor West **	402 472-3411

Nevada

Reno: University Library, University of Nevada-Reno	775 784-6500, Ext. 257

New Hampshire

Concord: New Hampshire State Library	603 271-2239

New Jersey

Newark: Newark Public Library	973 733-7779
Piscataway: Library of Science and Medicine, Rutgers University	732 445-2895

New Mexico

Albuquerque: Centennial Science and Engineering Library, The University of New Mexico	505 277-4412

New York

Albany: New York State Library, Science, Industry and Business Library	518 474-5355
Buffalo: Buffalo and Erie County Public Library **	716 858-7101
New York: Science, Industry and Business Library	212 592-7000

Stony Brook: Engineering Library, State University of New York   516 632-7148

North Carolina

Raleigh: D. H. Hill Library, North Carolina State University **   919 515-2935

North Dakota

Grand Forks: Chester Fritz Library, University of North Dakota   701 777-4888

Ohio

Akron: Akron-Summit County Public Library   330 643-9075
Cincinnati: The Public Library of Cincinnati and Hamilton County   513 369-6971
Cleveland: Cleveland Public Library **   216 623-2870
Columbus: Ohio State University Libraries   614 292-6175
Toledo: Toledo/Lucas County Public Library **   419 259-5212

Oklahoma

Stillwater: Oklahoma State University **   405 744-7086

Oregon

Portland: Paul L. Boley Law Library, Lewis & Clark College   503 768-6786

Pennsylvania

Philadelphia: The Free Library of Philadelphia **   215 686-5331
Pittsburgh: The Carnegie Library of Pittsburgh   412 622-3138
University Park: Pattee Library - C207, Pennsylvania State University   814 865-4861

Puerto Rico

Mayagüez: General Library, University of Puerto Rico   787 832-4040, ext. 2022

Rhode Island

Providence: Providence Public Library   401 455-8027

South Carolina

Clemson: R. M. Cooper Library, Clemson University   864 656-3024

South Dakota

Rapid City: Devereaux Library, South Dakota School of Mines and Technology   605 394-1275

Tennessee

Memphis: Memphis & Shelby County Public Library, and Information Center   901 725-8877
Nashville: Stevenson Science and Engineering Library, Vanderbilt University   615 322-2717

Texas

Austin: McKinney Engineering Library, The University of Texas at Austin   512 495-4500

College Station: Sterling C. Evans Library, Texas A&M University ** — 409 845-5745
Dallas: Dallas Public Library ** — 214 670-1468
Houston: Fondren Library, Rice University ** — 713 527-8101, Ext. 2587
South Central Intellectual Property Partnership at Rice University (SCIPPR)*** — 713 285-5196
Lubbock: Texas Tech University — 806 742-2282

Utah

Salt Lake City: Marriott Library, University of Utah** — 801 581-8394

Vermont

Burlington: Bailey/Howe Library, University of Vermont — 802-656-2542

Virginia

Richmond: James Branch Cabell Library, Virginia Commonwealth University** — 804 828-1104

Washington

Seattle: Engineering Library, University of Washington ** — 206 543-0740

West Virginia

Morgantown: Evansdale Library, West Virginia University** — 304 293-4695, Ext. 5113

Wisconsin

Madison: Kurt F. Wendt Library, University of Wisconsin-Madison — 608 262-6845
Milwaukee: Milwaukee Public Library — 414 286-3051

Wyoming

Casper: Natrona County Public Library — 307 237-4935

| MORE INFORMATION | | USPTO HOME PAGE | | PTDL HOME PAGE |

Last Modified: Apr 12 19:35:11 1999

 **Patent and Trademark Depository Library Program**

Conducting a Patent Search at a Patent and Trademark Depository Library (PTDL)

The 7-Step Strategy

1. *Index to the U.S. Patent Classification* (paper or CD-ROM)

   Begin with this alphabetical subject index to the *Manual of Classification*. Look for common terms describing the invention and its function, effect, end-product, structure, and use. Note class and subclass numbers.

2. *Manual of Classification* (paper or CD-ROM)

   Locate class and subclass numbers in the Manual. Note where the terms fall within the U.S. Patent Classification System. Scan the entire class schedule, paying attention to the dot indent. Revise search strategy as needed.

3. *Classification Definitions* (microfiche or CD-ROM)

   Read the definitions to establish the scope of class(es) and subclass(es) relevant to the search. The definitions include important search notes and suggestions for further search.

4. **Patents BIB (CD-ROM or Automated Patent System (APS) Text)**

   Check if you are on the right path; search Patents BIB (1969-present) for a particular class/subclass; retrieve results and examine titles. Try other relevant classes/subclasses. Revise your search by using applicable keywords; note the classes and subclasses and go back to 2.

5. **Patents CLASS (CD-ROM or APS TEXT)**

   Once relevant class(es)/subclass(es) are identified, obtain a list of all patent numbers (1790-present) granted every class and subclass to be searched.

6. *Official Gazette - Patent Section* (paper or microform)

   Go to the *Gazette* and look for exemplary claim(s) and a representative drawing for all patents on the list(s) eliminate patents unrelated to the invention.

7. *Complete Patent Document* (microfilm, paper, CD-ROM, or APS IMAGE)

   Search the complete text and drawing(s) of closely related patents to determine how different they are from the invention.

| MORE INFORMATION | | USPTO HOME PAGE | | PTDL HOME PAGE |
Last Modified: Oct 15 16:52:43 1998

US PATENT AND TRADEMARK OFFICE

General Info

Patents

Trademarks

Site Index

Organization

Databases

Download Forms

Order Copies

PTO Fees

Libraries-PTDLs

FTP Data

Public Affairs

Statistics

Acquisitions

Jobs at PTO

Related Web Sites

FOIA

Document Formats

Y2k Program

Privacy Statement

Copyright (LOC)

New on the PTO Site:

- PatentIn 2.1 Training Sessions Offered (11Aug99)

- PTO Wins Procurement Lawsuit over New Facility (10Aug99)

- Public Hearings on Official Insignia of Native American Tribes (4Aug99)

- Interim Supplemental Examination Guidelines for Determining the Applicability of 35 U.S.C. section 112, paragraph 6 (4Aug99)

- President Clinton Nominates Anne Chasser to Be Assistant Commissioner for Trademarks (28Jul99)

- PTO in Forefront of Distance Learning Movement (23Jul99)

- Public Advisory Committee on Trademark Affairs Transcript, Nov 1998 (20Jul99)

- Patents Personnel Roster (20Jul99)

- Patent Statistics By Metropolitan Area/Organization & Technology Class (13Jul99)

- List of Withdrawn Patent Numbers (9Jul99)

- President Clinton Nominates Todd Dickinson to Top Post at USPTO (6Jul99)

- OG Notice: Results of April 1999 Examination for Registration to Practice (6Jul99)

- PTO Open House Program, Aug. 24/25 - Biotech, Design and Operational Issues (4Jul99)

- Fourth Annual Independent Inventors Conference, September 24/25 (3Aug99)

[Older *"New on the PTO Site"* Items]

The PTO is not yet equipped to handle general email correspondence. General inquiries should be directed by telephone to 800.786.9199 (800.PTO.9199) or 703.308.4357 (703.308.HELP), or in writing to one of the addresses specified in the **PTO Directory** *.*

Web Site Email Only!

Search US Patent Databases

Patent Applications	*Issued Patents*
PrintEFS: Enter and Print Patent Application Data	Issue Years and Patent Numbers Since 1836
Patent Application Bibliographic Data Entry Format	Withdrawn Patent Numbers
General Information Concerning Patents	Expired Patent Number Search
Frequently Asked Questions (FAQ) about Patents	Expired Patents [ftp zip file]
Guide to Filing a Utility Patent Application	Calendar Year Patent Statistics
FAQ about Design Patents	Fiscal Year Patent Statistics
Guide to Filing a Design Patent Application	Official Gazette -- Patents OG Notices
General Information About Plant Patents	Patent Maintenance Fees
Provisional Application for Patent Brochure	List of Patent Terms Extended
Disclosure Document Program	Notices to Patentees Under 37 CFR 1.607(d)
PatentIn Version 2.0 Software	Weekly Patent Data
Checker Software (pre-7/98 rules)	Patent Data and Product Sales

Manual of Classification
Patent Class Definitions
Notices and Announcements
Independent Inventors Program
Patents Personnel Roster
Search Facilities at PTO
Patent and Trademark Depository Libraries
Roster of Patent Agents and Attorneys
Examiner Handbook to the US Patent Classification System
Examination Guidelines for Computer-Related Inventions & Training Materials
Board of Patent Appeals and Interferences
Assistant Commissioner for Patents Web Pages

Mainly for Practitioners	*International*
Manual of Patent Examining Procedure	*On WIPO Site:* Search PCT Patent Gazette
Registration of Patent Agents and Attorneys	Patent Cooperation Treaty
Patent Laws on *GSA FedLaw* site	
Patent Rules, Title 37 CFR [1MB] or zip file [227kB]	
Final Rule: *Changes to Patent Practice and Procedure*	
Petitions Practice within the PTO on Patent Matters	

http://www.uspto.gov/web/menu/pats.html

US Patent and Trademark Office

HOME   SITE INDEX   SEARCH   INFO BY ORG   FEEDB

Welcome to the USPTO Web Patent Databases

Before you call or email us about either database, please **make**
sure *you have checked that database's Status and Help pages, as
well as read the important notices below.*

Database Load Status

Full-Text Database
How to access full-page images!

- Boolean Search
- Manual Search
- Patent Number Search
  List of withdrawn patent numbers

- Database Contents
- Help
- Status

Bibliographic Database
Front-page information for rapid searching.

- Boolean Search
- Advanced Search
- Patent Number Search
  List of withdrawn patent numbers

- Database Contents
- Help
- Status

Notices:

- The US Patent and Trademark Office (PTO) now offers World-Wide Web (Web) access to bibliographic and full-text patent databases. Understanding the limitations of these Web databases can help you avoid significant problems. Prior to using the PTO's patent databases on the Web, it is critical that you review the following information.

- These databases cover the period from 1 January 1976 to the most recent weekly issue date (usually each Tuesday).

- US Patent Classification data in the Full-Text Database (*Issued US Classification*) corresponds to classification data which appears on the printed patent, and may not match current classification data.

- US Patent Classification data in the Bibliographic Database (*Current US Classification*) has been updated to reflect the most current Master Classification File (1 July 1999), and may not match the classification data which appears on the printed patent.

- Changes to patent documents contained in Certificates of Correction and Re-examinations

http://www.uspto.gov/patft/index.html

Certificates are not included in the text of the patent databases, but are included as full-page images at the end of each patent's linked image pages.

- Assignment changes recorded at the PTO are not reflected in the text or image portions of either of the patent databases.

- If you have any questions about the patent application process, the PTO strongly recommends that you consult with a registered patent attorney or agent. The PTO cannot recommend attorneys or agents. For information on registered patent attorneys and agents, see Patent Attorneys and Agents Registered to Practice before the PTO.

- Additional information about the patenting process is available from PTO's Web site and at Patent and Trademark Depository Libraries located throughout the country.

- The fact that an invention cannot be found by searching in the PTO's patent databases does not mean that the invention is patentable. Both of the PTO's patent databases begin with patents granted since 1976. A complete patentability search must consider all prior art, including earlier patents, foreign patents and non-patent literature.

- The previously-offered AIDS Database has been discontinued, since it has been rendered obsolete and redundant by the availability of searchable patent full-text supplemented by full-page images. AIDS researchers can now design their own customized searches tailored to their specific needs and apply them to the full-text database.

- Please note that PTO does not record or log the parameters of search requests submitted to these databases. Such uncollected information has thus never been disclosed through sale or FOIA request, intentionally or otherwise, to any third party. PTO does not plan to change this operational policy.

- *All data provided herein is in the public domain, and may be freely used for any purpose. However, users creating their own hyperlinks to pages on this site are requested and cautioned to do so in a manner which maintains a clear distinction between the user's content and official content published by USPTO.*

USPTO HOME PAGE

Last Modified: 22 July 1999

Welcome

The Intellectual Property Network (IPN) lets you search and view patent documents from the U.S., Europe and Japan as well as patent applications published by the World Intellectual Property Organization (WIPO). For further information about our IP Network solutions, please click here or view a video presentation.

Products:

Link your patents

IPN *for Business* site
  -Description
  -Sign up

For more information about the site go to the What's New?, FAQ or background pages. For related intellectual property services please visit the Resource Page. If you have more questions, please contact us.

eviewed by

Search

Enter search words -- e.g., elevator; robot; twin-engine; Smith John; bee culture.

Select a collection from this list:

U.S. Front Pages

SEARCH   Clear

Alternate Searches   Patent Number   Boolean Text   Advanced Text

New: Browse the U.S. Classes by title or by class number

Attract att**ention invention**

Our Partners:

SMART PATENTS
by Aurigin Systems, Inc.

PatentMiner
SEARCH PATENT FULL TEXT
WITH NATURAL LANGUAGE

Gallery of Obscure Patents

Updated! Human ingenuity is unbounded. In the search for a better mousetrap, lawn mower, or golf cart, inventors come up with some pretty bizarre solutions. For a taste of the strange and wonderful, try the Gallery of Obscure Patents.

Legal　　|　　IBM

Patent Full-Page Images

The <u>Patent Full-Text Database</u> now contains hyperlinks from the full-text document display to the full-page images of each page of each patent in the database. Our goal is to make new full-page images available each issue day (Tuesday).

These full-page images are not directly viewable using most Web browsers. They are in 300 d.p.i. Tagged Image File Format (TIFF). However, there are many variants -- or "flavors" -- of TIFF, including different ways of compressing the image data within the TIFF file. The TIFF flavor used by PTO and other countries' intellectual property offices is international standard CCITT Group 4 (G4) compression. Displaying them requires either a TIFF G4 plug-in for your browser, or a properly installed and configured application to which your browser sends G4 TIFF images for display. *Note that relatively few image viewers and plug-ins handle G4 compression.*

The only free, unlimited time TIFF plug-in for **x86 PCs** of which we are presently aware is <u>Medical Informatics Engineering's *AlternaTIFF*</u> , which functions with current Netscape, Microsoft, and Opera browsers.

The only **Apple Macintosh®** plug-in we are aware of which works with our images is <u>Acordex Imaging Systems *Accel ViewTIFF*</u> , which offers a free 14-day demonstration. It is known to work in both IE 4+ and Netscape 4+ with Apple Quicktime 4.0.

If you know of other free, unlimited time TIFF Group 4 plug-ins or viewers for any computer platform, please tell us about them.

PTO cannot and will not provide direct user support for TIFF image display or printing beyond the provision of hyperlinks to known free TIFF browser plug-ins from our <u>"Document Formats" Web page</u>.

Full-page images can be accessed from each patent's full-text display by clicking on the **Images** button at the top of the patent full-text display page. If you have a properly installed G4 TIFF image viewer or plug-in, this will bring up the full-page image of the first page of the patent along with navigation buttons for retrieving the other pages of the document. These buttons include buttons for the identifiable sections of each patent: Front Page, Drawings, Specifications, Claims, Certificates of Correction (if any), and Reexaminations (if any).

- Patent images must be retrieved one page at a time.

- Patent images are only accessible from the full-text display of each patent.

- The **Images** button links are valid only for a fixed period from the time each search is conducted and the hit list generated. This period is currently set at two hours. If this time period expires, the user must execute another search to generate a hit list which will lead to valid image links.

- Successful printing of patent images is entirely dependent on the user's browser and image viewer software. PTO does not provide support for printing problems. We will suggest, however, based on our experience, that with most image viewers (including AlternaTIFF), images may best be printed using the plug-in's print button rather than the browser's print function.

Last modified: 27 May 1999

The AlternaTIFF Home Page

AlternaTIFF is a free Netscape-style browser plug-in that displays most of the common types of TIFF image files. It is compatible with Netscape Communicator 3.0 and higher, Internet Explorer 3.0 and higher, and Opera 3.51 and higher. It is a 32-bit Windows program, and requires Windows 95, Windows 98, or Windows NT 4.0, and a 32-bit browser. (It may also work other browsers, or earlier browser versions, or earlier versions of NT.)

AlternaTIFF is a product of Medical Informatics Engineering

Click one of the links below to download the latest version of AlternaTIFF (v1.2.0, 23-Apr-1999):
AlternaTIFF v1.2.0 (download site 1) - faster
AlternaTIFF v1.2.0 (download site 2)

This is a self-extracting archive file (size: 180 KB). After saving it to your computer, open it and follow the instructions. It is safest to shut down your browser first, but is not always necessary. If you would prefer to install it manually, the file can be opened with WinZip or a similar utility.

AlternaTIFF ActiveX v1.1.8 - This is an experimental ActiveX version of AlternaTIFF. However, since it is not as stable as the plug-in, and offers little if any advantage, we recommend that you use the plug-in even if you are using Microsoft Internet Explorer.

- Documentation -- Instructions for using the plug-in, and a list of features.

- FAQ - Answers to frequently asked questions.

- Refresh plug-ins -- Click here to activate your new plug-in after installing it. (If it doesn't work, try restarting your browser. If it still doesn't work, see the Troubleshooting section in the documentation.)

- Screenshots -- See what AlternaTIFF looks like running in a browser.

- Test page -- Some test images

- Release Notes -- What's new, etc.

- Receive notification when a new version is available

- IE troubleshooting -- A couple of more things to try if you absolutely must use Internet Explorer. Experts only.

- Older versions -- In case we broke something

Comments, suggestions, bug reports, requests for help, and other feedback may be sent by email to alternatiff@mieweb.com. Requests for help sent to other addresses, or via any method of communication other than email, will usually be ignored. Please read this Technical Support page before trying to contact MIE.

Other resources

- Other TIFF Plug-ins
- TIFF specification from Adobe
- Plugsy -- a utility for resolving plug-in conflicts
- Netscape's Plug-in page
- Browserwatch Plug-in Plaza
- Unisys's LZW statement
- List your currently installed plug-ins (won't work with Internet Explorer)

This page is located at http://www.mieweb.com/alternatiff/

How to Use the
Patent Classification System

- How the System is Organized
- Bases of Classification
- Classification Schedules
- How to Read Subclass Titles and Definitions
- How Subclasses are Arranged
- How Classifications are Assigned to Patents
- Alpha Subclasses, Digests, and Cross-Reference Art Collections
- Search Tools [Index to the USPCS , Manual of Classification , Class. Definitions , Class. Orders]
- Suggestions for Search

RETURN TO THE USPTO HOME PAGE

For comments on this page, e-mail *Barbara.Brown@uspto.gov*

How the System Is Organized

The U.S. Patent Classification System (USPCS) provides for the storage and retrieval of patent documents which a Patent Examiner needs to review when examining patent applications. A fundamental principle of the USPCS is that each class, or part thereof, is created by first analyzing the claimed disclosures of the U.S. patents and then creating various divisions and subdivisions on the basis of that analysis. All similar subject matter is gathered together in large groupings to create classes. These classes are then subdivided into smaller searchable units called subclasses. The sequence or pattern arrangement of the subclasses within each class is called the class schedule.

Bases of Classification

A variety of rationales have been developed over the years to subdivide the Patent and Trademark Office's (PTO) classified files into searchable units. Collections of art based on each of the following rationales can be found in the system as it exists today.

- **Industry or Use**

    This approach divides art on the basis of the industry employing the art or the use to which a device is put.

- **Proximate Function**

    To avoid the tendency to fragment art based on its industry or use, the USPTO uses the fundamental, direct, or necessary function as one of the primary bases of classification. Also, for brevity, the term "proximate" is substituted for the words fundamental, direct, or necessary. Therefore, proximate function means that similar processes or structures that achieve similar results by applying similar natural laws to similar substances are considered to have the same fundamental utility and are grouped together.

- **Effect or Product**

  This rationale collects art into industrial or trade groupings based on the result produced by the art. This result may be tangible (e.g., the product of a manufacturing process) or intangible (e.g., the communication of sound at a distance).

- **Structure**

  Simple subject matter which may have no apparent functional characteristics is classified together based upon the structural configuration or physical makeup of the object.

Classification Schedules

The order in which a subclass appears in the schedule establishes the order of superiority between the concepts provided for in the schedule. The number assigned to a subclass title merely provides an address for the storage area in which the art physically resides. The location of the subclass within a schedule hierarchy is paramount. Subject matter will be found in the first appearing coordinate subclass (or its indents) that will accept that subject matter.

Subclass titles that do not have a dot between the title and numeric designator for the subclass are referred to as "Main Line" subclasses. Indented subclasses are referred to by the number of indent levels (with each dot representing an indent level); e.g., a subclass indented one level below a Main Line subclass is referred to as a "one dot" subclass. Subclasses positioned at the same level of indentation also are referred to as "coordinate" subclasses, provided that a subclass with a lesser indent level is not located between the subclasses being compared.

A second important characteristic exhibited by the classification schedules is the inclusive nature of subclasses. This means that a subclass is proper for any claimed disclosure that at least recites the subject matter provided for in the subclass.

Query Manual of Classification [**Note:** The information in this electronic document may not be the most current available.]

How to Read Subclass Titles and Definitions

To understand the content of the material classified in a particular subclass in any given class schedule, the class title and the title(s) of any or all relevant subclass(es) under which the particular subclass is indented must be read. The following schedule is a hypothetical system to sort and classify scrap in a junk yard.

1	COMBINED BAR, LINK AND BALL
2	COMBINED BAR AND LINK
3	COMBINED BAR AND BALL
4	COMBINED LINK AND BALL
5	CHAIN
21	. With end fastener
22	. With flaccid cover
23	. . Removable
6	BAR
7	LINK
8	BALL
9	. Hollow
10	. . Perforated
11	. . Grooved
12	. Perforated
13	. Grooved
14	. Mineral
15	. . Metallic

```
16  ... Aluminum
17  ... Zinc
18  RUBBER
19  . Ivory
20  MISCELLANEOUS
```

The above schedule is similar to an outline used to write a term paper or the like. Each indented subclass further qualifies the subclass under which it is indented and, consequently, must be read as including all of the limitations of the parent subclass. For example, subclass 11 is read as a grooved hollow ball and will accept only items having at least these attributes. However, due to the superiority requirements of the system, a hollow ball that is both perforated and grooved would be located in subclass 10. The definition of any subclass includes the definition of the class and any subclasses under which it may be indented.

Arrangement of Subclasses

In most modern class schedules, subclasses are generally arranged with the most complex inventions positioned higher in the class schedule. Combined machines or processes (e.g., those which perform diverse operations such as cutting and gluing or pressing and heating) will be found higher in the class schedule than single operation machines or processes, which in turn are located higher than the individual parts of the machines (or steps in the processes). Minor details or accessories are normally found near the bottom of the class schedule, and "miscellaneous" is at the very bottom. An important exception to the ordering of subclasses by complexity is that "special" subclasses for inventions having a common unique feature may be positioned higher in the schedule, above subclasses for more complex inventions.

Assigning Classifications to Patents

Because claims define the novel disclosure(s) in a patent, each claim is assigned a classification. These are considered mandatory classifications. Once this has occurred, one of these classifications is selected as the "original" (OR) classification. If all the claims are classified in the same class, then the OR classification is the first appearing classification within the hierarchy of that class. If the claims are classified in different classes, then selection of the OR classification is achieved by considering in turn the following factors:

- selection of the most comprehensive claim
- selection among statutory categories of subject matter when claims are of equal comprehensiveness
- selection among superiority of types of subject matter
- selection among classes in "related subject" listing

The remaining mandatory classifications are designated as cross-reference(s) (XR). Additional XR classification(s) may be designated for any unclaimed subject matter which is novel and is of sufficient detail and clarity to be useful as a reference. It is important to note that OR and XR designations are merely an administrative tool and are of little consequence to the average searcher in locating subject matter.

Alpha Subclasses, Digests, Cross-Reference Art Collections, and Foreign Art Collections

As necessary, Patent Examiners create "alpha" subclasses and digests to simplify searches within their assigned arts. These are explained below.

Alpha Subclasses

A collection of patents created from those patents contained in an official, numbered subclass. This collection is then made an indented subclass under the original official subclass and given a subclass designator which is composed of the parent subclass number followed by an alpha designation (e.g., A, B, T, DD). The original subclass containing those patents not classified in the new alpha subclass(es) is given the alpha designation "R" (indicating Residual). The numeric subclass now equates to the "R" subclass plus any alpha subclasses indented thereunder. A subclass array in Class 26, TEXTILE, CLOTH FINISHING, illustrates this concept.

15R	.Shearing
16	..Ornamental
17	..With seam detector
18	..Automatic extension rests
15L	..With lubrication
15FB	..With flexible bed
18.5	SHRINKING

Alpha subclasses are not defined beyond their titles and the definition of the official numbered subclass from which they were formed. The Public Search File does not contain alpha subclasses; only those patents listed according to the official numeric classification are found in this file.

Digest or Cross-Reference Art Collection

A collection of patent copies based on a concept which relates to the concepts of a class but not to any particular subclass of that class. Digests and cross-reference art collections are listed in numeric sequence at the end of each class schedule. Although definitions exist for cross-reference art collections, in most instances digests are not defined and are not available in the Public Search Room. Neither a digest nor a cross-reference art collection can be designated as the OR classification of a patent.

Supplemental cross-reference art collections or digests have been established that are based upon the European Patent Office (EPO) Classification system, ECLA (as completely new US classes or as additions to exisitng US classes). These art collections contain only US patents that have been classified into ECLA by EPO examiners and provide optional electronic searches for the user. They are searchable on the APS Messenger System and in Groups that have image search capability. Some of the classes that have been established are Classes 930, 968, 976, 984, and 987. Examples of classes to which ECLA art collections or digests have been added are Classes 604 and 422. These ECLA classes and cross-reference art collections have no definitions associated with them, but have informational boxes at the beginning of, and sometimes embedded within, the class or art collection. Also to assist the searcher, notes are occasionally included in the titles and the ECLA subclass notations from which the subclass titles are derived are indicated in brackets at the ends of the titles.

Foreign Art Collections

The long-standing USPTO practice of classifying all foreign documents and nonpatent literature (NPL) into the US Patent Classification (USPC) system was terminated on October 1, 1995. Foreign documents in the examiners' paper search files are current through March 25, 1995. Most foreign documents after that time are searchable through on-line data bases. Foreign documents that are not reclassified are currently bieng transferred directly from the old US subclasses to foreign art collections placed at the end of the new class. These art collections are numbered with a six-character designation consisting of the letters FOR in capital letters, followed by three digits, with a space in between FOR and the three digits; e.g., FOR 701. There will be informative notes appropriately placed to assist users of the foreign art collections.

Search Tools

To locate patents pertaining to a specific field of technology or science within the U.S. Patent Classification System requires a good measure of judgment as well as the continuous and coordinated use of the following publications:

- Index to the U.S. Patent Classification System
- Manual of Classification
- Patent Classification Definitions
- Classification Orders

The **Index to the U.S. Patent Classification System** is an alphabetical listing of technical and common terms representative of arts, processes, machines, manufactures, compositions of matter, etc., along with a reference to the classification where pertinent patents or literature (prior art) can be found. As a search tool, the Index is useful as an introduction to the classification system for those who lack experience in using the classification system or for those who are unfamiliar with the particular technology that they are investigating.

To purchase the Index

The **Manual of Classification** contains a collection of the class schedules, a list of the class titles in numerical order by class number and in alphabetical order, a list of the classes by Examining Groups, and a theoretical organization of classes into major groups. Although class and subclass titles found in the Manual are as suggestive as possible about the subject matter covered, they should not be used alone to delineate subject matter. Rather, the Manual should be used only in conjunction with the class or subclass definition(s) and associated search notes.

- Query Manual of Classification [Note: The information in this on-line document may not be the most current available.]
- To purchase the Manual of Classification

The **Patent Classification Definitions** comprise statements of the scope embraced by each of the official classes, subclasses, and cross-reference art collections (exclusive of the Plant and Design Classes). Also included are search notes directing the searcher to related subject matter in other classes and subclasses. Search notes help to qualify and explain the limits of a class or subclass.

- To Browse the Classification Definitions [Note: The information in this on-line document may not be the most current available.]
- To purchase Classification Definitions

Classification Orders are issued throughout the year and contain information relating to U.S. patent classifications that are established or abolished as a result of reclassification projects. These orders are used to bridge the gap between the time a project issues (when the change is officially made) and the time that regular search tools are updated to include the new information.

For sale of these and other Classification publications, click here.

Suggestions for Search

If the Index to the U.S. Patent Classification System fails to reveal an appropriate field of search, the following suggestions should help delineate a field of search.

1. Determine what is the essential function or effect of the art or instrument being searched .
2. Scan the titles in the sections entitled "Classes Within the U.S. Classification System Arranged by Related Subjects" as well as "Classes Arranged in Alphabetical Order" in the front of the Manual of Classification .
3. Note particularly those titles that seem to include the invention being searched.
4. Inspect carefully the class definition and related notes.
5. Scan the subclass schedule of the class, if the class definition indicates that the selected class is the proper class. Review the mainline subclass titles.
6. Select the first appearing mainline (capitalized) subclass that includes a characteristic of the invention and study the definition for that subclass.
7. Scan the coordinate (i.e., same level) indented subclasses under the mainline subclass and select the first appearing title to include additional characteristic(s) of the invention.
8. Repeat this process until the most specific indented subclass is reached whose title and definition encompass the invention in question, and then review the associated documents in the search file.

If this subclass contains nothing pertinent, search the more generic subclasses under which it is indented, the miscellaneous subclasses, and those above it, the titles of which indicate the possibility that they may include the concept being searched.

Search other possible classes noted in step 2, if the pertinent art still is not found. Failure to find any pertinent art usually indicates that you have not located the proper place in the classification system. Classifiers engaged in creating new and maintaining the existing classifications are always available for consultation to outline a field of search.

U.S. PATENT AND TRADEMARK OFFICE
Office for Patent and Trademark Information

Manual of U.S. Patent Classification
April 1999

To view a listing of the classifications in a U.S. patent class, click on the class below.

List of U.S. Patent Classes

002 004 005 007 008 012 014 015 016 019 023 024 026 027 028 029 030 033 034 036 037 038 040 042
043 044 047 048 049 051 052 053 054 055 056 057 059 060 062 063 065 066 068 069 070 071 072 073
074 075 076 079 081 082 083 084 086 087 089 091 092 095 096 099 100 101 102 104 105 106 108 109
110 111 112 114 116 117 118 119 122 123 124 125 126 127 128 131 132 134 135 136 137 138 139 140
141 142 144 147 148 149 150 152 156 157 159 160 162 163 164 165 166 168 169 171 172 173 174 175
177 178 180 181 182 184 185 186 187 188 190 191 192 193 194 196 198 199 200 201 202 203 204 205
206 208 209 210 211 212 213 215 216 217 218 219 220 221 222 223 224 225 226 227 228 229 231 232
234 235 236 237 238 239 241 242 244 245 246 248 249 250 251 252 254 256 257 258 260 261 264 266
267 269 270 271 273 276 277 278 279 280 281 283 285 289 290 291 292 293 294 295 296 297 298 299
300 301 303 305 307 310 312 313 314 315 318 320 322 323 324 326 327 329 330 331 332 333 334 335
336 337 338 340 341 342 343 345 346 347 348 349 351 352 353 355 356 358 359 360 361 362 363 364
365 366 367 368 369 370 372 373 374 375 376 377 378 379 380 381 382 383 384 385 386 388 392 395
396 399 400 401 402 403 404 405 406 407 408 409 410 411 412 413 414 415 416 417 418 419 420 422
423 424 425 426 427 428 429 430 431 432 433 434 435 436 438 439 440 441 442 445 446 449 450 451
452 453 454 455 460 462 463 464 470 472 473 474 475 476 477 482 483 492 493 494 501 502 503 504
505 507 508 510 512 514 516 518 520 521 522 523 524 525 526 527 528 530 532 534 536 540 544 546
548 549 552 554 556 558 560 562 564 568 570 585 588 600 601 602 604 606 607 623 701 702 704 705
706 707 708 709 710 711 712 713 714 800 901 902 930 968 976 984 987 D01 D02 D03 D04 D05 D06
D07 D08 D09 D10 D11 D12 D13 D14 D15 D16 D17 D18 D19 D20 D21 D22 D23 D24 D25 D26 D27
D28 D29 D30 D32 D34 D99 PLT

Class	Title
002	APPAREL
004	BATHS, CLOSETS, SINKS, AND SPITTOONS
005	BEDS
007	COMPOUND TOOLS
008	BLEACHING AND DYEING; FLUID TREATMENT AND CHEMICAL MODIFICATION OF TEXTILES AND FIBERS
012	BOOT AND SHOE MAKING
014	BRIDGES
015	BRUSHING, SCRUBBING, AND GENERAL CLEANING
016	MISCELLANEOUS HARDWARE

| U.S. PATENT AND TRADEMARK OFFICE |
| Office for Patent and Trademark Information |

Manual of U.S. Patent Classification
April 1999

Class
248
SUPPORTS

class definitions may be accessed by clicking on the class title, above.
(definitions for some classes may not be available)

Subclass **Title**

ClassTitle ===> SUPPORTS

542   WITH INDICATOR OR INSPECTION MEANS

543   . Pre-set characteristic

544   WITH MEANS TO FACILITATE INSTALLATION, REPAIR, OR TRANSPORTATION, OR BROKEN PARTS RETAINER

545   . For ground insertion

546   . For support cutting or piercing

547   . . Nail guide or holder

682   ARTICLE CARRIED

683   . Mounted by vacuum, adhesive or magnet

684   . Including cutting or piercing of the article

685   . Retractable within article

686   . Embedded within article

687   . Anti-mar or nonslip e.g., cushioned

688   . Stand, foot or prop

689   . Mounted by clamping means

690   . Mounted by hook or loop

691   . . Hook pivoted to article

692   . . Open hook

693   . Including flexible suspension means

548   WITH COMPONENT FRANGIBLE OR DEFORMABLE ON IMPACT OR OVERLOAD

549   . Support for mirror- or picture-type article

550   WITH CONDITION RESPONSIVE CONTROL MEANS

551   WITH ANTI-THEFT OR ANTI-TAMPER MEANS

552   . Padlock

553   . Key operated

200 BRACKETS

200.1 . On extensible column mounted between opposed surfaces

201 . Plural, for single article

202.1 .. For swinging receptacle

205.1 . Specially mounted or attached

205.2 .. By mechanically interlocking fabric (e.g., velcro)

205.3 .. By adhesive

205.4 ... Bridged by diverse anchoring means

205.5 .. By vacuum

205.6 ... Bridged by diverse anchoring means

205.7 ... Including resilient means acting against atmospheric force

205.8 ... Including vacuum maker or breaker

205.9 .... Including valve or port

206.1 ... Including diverse abutment; e.g., brace, fulcrum

206.2 ... Including annular vacuum cup

206.3 ... Including plural vacuum cups

206.4 .... Vertically spaced

206.5 .. By magnet

207 .. Vertically or horizontally

237 .. Roof

208 .. Window

209 ... Radiator bracket

236 ... Shelf or scaffold type

210 .. Ladder

211 ... Hook type

238 ... Shelf or scaffold type

CLASS 248, SUPPORTS

CLASS DEFINITION

This class provides for devices which carry the weight of an article or articles or otherwise hold or steady it or them against the pull of gravity, and devices for holding an article to its support, which are not otherwise provided for.

(1)Note.   Devices having structural features limiting them to use in a particular art remain with the art.

(2)Note.   The line between this class and Classes 362, Illumination, 313, Electric Lamp and Discharge Devices, subclass 39, and 431, Combustion is as follows:

Class 223, Apparel Apparatus, subclass 120 for supports, bases and stands claimed in connection with means for making, repairing or maintaining in condition articles of apparel.

Class 362 takes any combination of a support with significant structure of the light distributing means or the combination of the light distributing and generating means.

Class 313, subclasses 49+ is the generic class for the combination of a support with significant structure of an electric space discharge device. See section VII of the class definition for the other classes which provide for the combination of a support and a discharge device.

The mere supporting structure goes to Class 248 and such supporting structure may include conduits for fuel or energy and mere cut-offs therefor. Supporting structures limited to use with lighting devices are in Class 362. Supports for a light generating device are in Class 248 unless a significant structure of the light generator is claimed, in which case it goes to Class 431 or 362.

The mere naming of a light or discharge device as the thing supported will not operate to take the case out of class 248. If the support is in itself an essential part of the lamp or discharge device such as are many lamp bases, it remains in the art clas See sections XI, 3 and XII, 1 of the class definition of Class 313 for the classification of an envelope with a base attached thereto.

(3)Note.   For supports for shocks of grain or hay in the field, see Class 56, Harvesters, subclass 431 and Class 211, Supports: Racks, subclass 29.

SEARCH CLASS:

4,Baths, Closets, Sinks, and Spittoons, subclasses 571.1+, 589+, 592+, 621+, and 643+ for supports limited by structure to use with basins or with bath tubs.

5,Beds, appropriate subclasses for beds and subclasses 127+ for supports limited by structure to use for supporting a hammock.

24,Buckles, Buttons, Clasps, etc., appropriate subclasses for fasteners. Fasteners such as pins, clasps, buckles, etc., are provided for in Class 24, whether simple or combined, as clasp-pin, clasp-clasp, etc. Combinations of a fastener, simple or combined with a bracket or stand, are in Class 248, and cross-referenced to Class 24 when desirable. A mere fastening means as a plate, integral with or attached to the base of a clamp, is not considered as a bracket and such combination goes to Class 24. Bracket hooks wherein the article carrying portion thereof is in the form of a hook are in Class 248.

27,Undertaking, subclass 25.1 for corpse chin supports.

30,Cutlery, subclass 231 for shears combined with a support therefor.

US PATENT & TRADEMARK OFFICE
PATENT FULL TEXT AND IMAGE DATABASE

Help	Home	Boolean	Manual	Number	Order Copy	PTDLs

Data current through 08/24/1999

Query [Help]

Term 1: [   ] in **Field 1:** [All Fields ▼]

[AND ▼]

Term 2: [   ] in **Field 2:** [All Fields ▼]

Select years [Help] [1998-1999 ▼]   [Search]   [Reset]

US PATENT & TRADEMARK OFFICE
PATENT FULL TEXT AND IMAGE DATABASE

Help	Home	Boolean	Manual	Number	Order Copy	PTDLs

Bottom

Searching 1998-1999...

Results of Search in 1998-1999 db for:
248/210: 21 patents.
Hits 1 through 21 out of 21

Jump To

Refine Search	248/210

PAT. NO.   Title

1   5,934,632   Utility can holder for use with hollow rung ladder
2   5,931,259   Safety ladder attachment
3   5,913,380   Ladder accessory
4   5,901,998   Multi-functional tool and parts carrier
5   5,873,433   Step ladder tray
6   5,865,409   Bracket support for utility basket
7   5,855,346   Self-clamping ladder caddy
8   5,853,156   Rail clamp
9   5,842,253   Ladder supported holding tray for a paint roller
10   5,836,557   Detachable utility tray for step ladder
11   5,826,844   Bucket brackets
12   5,816,549   Bracket assembly for affixing a paint roller tray to a paint bucket
13   5,816,363   Ladder bracket
14   5,813,530   Ladder mounted tool belt carrier
15   5,806,817   Attachment device for a ladder
16   5,797,571   Combined ladder hook and bracket assembly
17   5,792,312   Hook assembly for use on masking device
18   5,788,198   Bracket for mounting ladder shelf
19   5,782,314   Step ladder organizer
20   5,740,883   Tool accessory for ladder
21   5,727,649   Ladder supportable tool storage container

Top

US PATENT & TRADEMARK OFFICE
PATENT FULL TEXT AND IMAGE DATABASE

Help	Home	Boolean	Manual	Number	Order Copy	PTDLs

Data current through 08/24/1999

Enter the patent number(s) you're searching for in the box below.

Query [Help]

Examples:

Utility	: 5,146,634	Search	Reset
Design	: D339,456		
Plant	: PP8,901		
Reissue	: RE35,312		
Def. Pub.	: T109,201		
SIR	: H1,523		

US PATENT & TRADEMARK OFFICE
PATENT FULL TEXT AND IMAGE DATABASE

| Help | Home | Boolean | Manual | Number | Order Copy | PTDLs |

| Bottom |

Searching 1998-1999...

Results of Search in 1998-1999 db for:
5788198: 1 patents.
Hits   1   through   1   out of   1

| Jump To | [   ]

| Refine Search | [5788198]

PAT. NO. Title

1 5,788,198 Bracket for mounting ladder shelf

| Top |

| Help | Home | Boolean | Manual | Number | Order Copy | PTDLs |

US Patent & Trademark Office
Patent Full Text and Image Database

(136 of 224)

United States Patent	**5,788,198**
Sharpe	**August 4, 1998**

Bracket for mounting *ladder* shelf

Abstract

A *bracket* is attachable to a *ladder* to form a convenience support or other attachment that attaches to the rails or rungs of a *ladder*, and is readily reconfigured, moved or adjusted as to angular orientation, without substantial assembly steps or tools. The *bracket* has at least two and preferably three mounting members, each folded at a right angle to define two flat plates, e.g., with one of the plates longer than the other. Each plate has a least one array of spaced openings for fasteners. The fasteners and some of the openings are dimensioned so that the fastener heads or nuts fit through such openings of the plates and the shanks of the fasteners engage in a slot, which can require turning non-round fastener heads for alignment with the slot before insertion, and turning the non-round heads of the fastener back after insertion, or alternatively passing the head through a larger hole joined to the slot. The mounting members are attached in a chosen configuration by affixing the fastener in the first mounting member and attaching the second mounting member to the first mounting member by passing the hole of the second mounting member over the end part of the fastener and sliding the mounting members to arrange the shank in the slot of the second mounting member such that the plates interlock and engage around rails or rungs of the *ladder*, additional array openings are then chosen to receive fasteners for locking the orientation of the *bracket* .

Inventors:	**Sharpe; Charles C.** (3519 Mercer Ct., Slatington, PA 18080-3026)
Appl. No.:	**606444**
Filed:	**February 23, 1996**

U.S. Class:	**248/210**
Intern'l Class:	E06C 007/14
Field of Search:	248/210,238,231.41,231.61,222.41

References Cited [Referenced By]

U.S. Patent Documents

254   OFFICIAL GAZETTE   August 4, 1998

5,788,198

BRACKET FOR MOUNTING LADDER SHELF

Charles C. Sharpe, 3519 Mercer Ct., Slatington, Pa. 18080-3026

Filed Feb. 23, 1996, Ser. No. 606,444

Int. Cl.⁶ E06C 7/14

U.S. Cl. 248—210   6 Claims

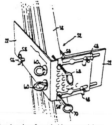

3. A clamping bracket for a ladder comprising:

a first mounting member and a second mounting member, each of the mounting members having a first plate and a second plate joined at a common edge and defining an angle between the first and second plates, the common edge of the second mounting member being nested within the angle defined by the first mounting member;

one of the plates of the first mounting member being removably secured to one of the plates of the second mounting member;

a plurality of fasteners for securing the mounting members relative to each other, the fasteners having beads and shanks extending from the heads, each of the mounting members having an array of apertures therein, said apertures having diameters at least as large as a diameter of the shanks and smaller than a diameter of the beads of the fasteners, at least two of said fasteners adapted to be placed through said apertures of both said mounting members to fix the position of the bracket relative to the ladder;

an auxiliary structure adjustable attached to at least one of said mounting members;

wherein the auxiliary structure has a portion defining a work area;

wherein the clamping bracket further comprises a means for securing the work area in a substantially horizontal position irrespective of the orientation of the mounting members,

whereby the first plates are adjustably spaced from each other so as to straddle a portion of the ladder and the second plates are positioned in contact with each other;

whereby the auxiliary structure is adapted to be positioned near the ladder when the clamping bracket is secured to the ladder.

5,788,199

EYEGLASS HOLDER MOUNTED ON A REARVIEW MIRROR

B. James Arsenault, RR 2 Ponty Pool, Ontario, Canada, L0A 1K0

Filed Jan. 16, 1997, Ser. No. 783,336

Int. Cl.⁶ A47B 96/06

U.S. Cl. 248—231.81   4 Claims

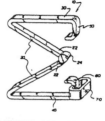

1. An eyeglass holder mounted on a rearview mirror comprising:

a resilient syncline member having a pointed end for removably engaging a rear surface of said rearview mirror when said syncline member is mounted to said rearview mirror;

an upper arm secured to an end of said syncline member opposite of said pointed end;

a lower arm secured to an end of said syncline member opposite of said upper arm forming an M-shaped structure, where said lower arm is substantially parallel to said upper arm;

an upper clasp secured to said upper arm opposite of said syncline member for removably engaging a rim of various sizes of said rearview mirror, where said upper clasp projects substantially towards said pointed end;

a lower clasp secured to said lower arm opposite of said syncline member for removably engaging said rim of various sizes of said rearview mirror, where said lower clasp projects substantially towards said pointed end; and

a loop secured to said lower clasp for receiving a temple arm from a pair of eyeglasses, wherein an axis of said loop is substantially orthogonal to a longitudinal axis of said lower arm and said loop projects away from said lower arm.

5,788,200

HIDDEN SHELF SUPPORT BRACKET

C. Reid Jones, P.O. Box 455, Taylorsville, Ky. 40071

Filed Jul. 25, 1996, Ser. No. 687,208

Int. Cl.⁶ A47F 5/08

U.S. Cl. 248—235   1 Claim

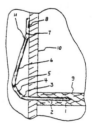

Text only | About this site | Privacy | Help | Commen

Official Federal Government Information at Your Fingertips

Site Contents

Online Bookstore

Finding Aids

Library Services

What's New Archive

Sign-up for our
OPEN FORUM

What's Available . . .

Legislative
Executive
Judicial
Regulatory
Administrative Decisions
Core Documents of U.S. Democracy

Quick Links . . .

Code of Federal Regulations
Federal Register
CBDNet
Congressional Record
U.S. Code
Other Databases

What's New on GPO Access . . .

August 3, 1999 -- Employer's Desk Guide to Child Support [$ Secure Order]

July 29, 1999 -- Shield and Sword - The United States Navy in the Persian Gulf War. Paper: [$ Secure Order]   Cloth: [$ Secure Order]

A service of the Superintendent of Documents, U.S. Government Printing Office.
Questions or comments: gpoaccess@gpo.gov.

Last updated: August 12, 1999
Page Name: http://www.access.gpo.gov/su_docs/index.html

Finding Aids

Search

- Databases Online via GPO Access
- Catalog of U.S. Government Publications (MOCAT)
- Sales Product Catalog (SPC)
- Government Information Locator Service (GILS)
- Government Information on Selected Internet Sites
- Depository Library in Your Area

Browse

- Government Information Products for Sale by Topic
- U.S. Government Subscriptions Catalog
- Electronic Government Information Products by Title
- Government Internet Sites by Topic
- Federal Agency Internet Sites
- Federal Web Sites Hosted by GPO Access
- Federal Bulletin Board Files

A service of the Superintendent of Documents, U.S. Government Printing Office.
Questions or comments: gpoaccess@gpo.gov.

Last updated: July 12, 1999
Page Name: http://www.access.gpo.gov/su_docs/tools.html

Catalog of U.S. Government Publications

A GPO Access Finding Aid

- Catalog
- About the Catalog
- Helpful Hints
- Depository Libraries

The Catalog   is a search and retrieval service that provides bibliographic records of U.S. Government information resources. Use it to link to Federal agency online resources or identify materials distributed to Federal Depository Libraries. Coverage begins with January 1994 and new records are added daily. Start searching below or learn more about the Catalog   and how to search it effectively.

Keyword | Title | SuDoc # | Item # | Stock # | Date | Search more than one field

Keyword search:

e.g., "endangered species" *or*   telev* AND children NOT advertising

Return 40 **Records**   SUBMIT   CLEAR   [More Help]
(200 Maximum)

Title search:

e.g., "Madison's Vision" *or*   budget AND United ADJ States

Return 40 **Records**   SUBMIT   CLEAR   [More Help]
(200 Maximum)

SuDoc class number search:

e.g., GP 3.2:M 26
Enter Y 3.El 2/3:2 C 76/3/(Date) as Y 3.El 2/3:2 C 76/3/996

Return 40 **Records**   [More Help]
(200 Maximum)

Depository item number search:

e.g., enter 1008-D (MF) as 1008-D MF

Return 40 **Records**   [More Help]
(200 Maximum)

GPO stock number search:

e.g., 030-001-00168-7

Return [40] **Records**   [SUBMIT] [CLEAR]   [More Help]

(200 Maximum)

Publication date search:
[1900] **TO** [2100]
e.g., 1994 to 1994
Do not leave either date field blank

Return [40] **Records**   [SUBMIT] [CLEAR]   [More Help]

(200 Maximum)

Multiple field search:
*Select the desired search fields and use the **SUBMIT** button to retrieve the search form.*

☐ Title
☐ Publication Year
☐ Superintendent of Documents Class Number
☐ Depository Item Number
☐ GPO Sales Stock Number

[SUBMIT] [CLEAR]   [More Help]

A service of the Superintendent of Documents, U.S. Government Printing Office.
Questions or comments: gpoaccess@gpo.gov.

For questions or comments about the content of this page e-mail asklps@gpo.gov.

Last updated: July 7, 1999
Page Name: http://www.gpo.gov/catalog

http://www.access.gpo.gov/su_docs/dpos/
adpos400.html

Catalog of U.S. Government Publications Search Results

The search was:

(OFFICIAL GAZETTE OF THE UNITED STATES PATENT AND TRADEMARK OFFICE)
Records returned: 40

To locate Federal depository libraries that are likely to have a publication, select [Locate Libraries]

For the cataloging information for a publication, select either TEXT (for full cataloging record) or HTML (for full cataloging record with hyperlink to an electronic document)

To go directly to an electronic document, click on the URL (if present) ex: http://

Publications with a GPO Stock Number may be available for purchase. Contact the nearest GPO Bookstore to determine if a publication is currently for sale from GPO. (Note the Title and Stock Number)

---

[1]
Budget **of the United States** Government. [Dept. ed.] 1971-. Annual. **United States**. PREX 2.8:997. GPO stock no.: 041-001-00464-5. [[0853]].
　　Rank: 1000 Locate Libraries , [Short Record] , [Full Record]

---

[2]
Budget **of the United States** Government. [Dept. ed.] 1971-. Annual. **United States**. PREX 2.8:2000. GPO stock no.: 041-001-00511-1. [[0853, 0853 (online)]].
http://purl.access.gpo.gov/GPO/LPS2343
　　Rank: 952 Locate Libraries , [Short Record] , [Full Record]

---

[3]
Budget **of the United States** Government. [Dept. ed.] 1971-. Annual. **United States**. PREX 2.8:999. GPO stock no.: 041-001-00495-5. [[0853]].
http://www.access.gpo.gov/omb/
　　Rank: 952 Locate Libraries , [Short Record] , [Full Record]

---

[4]
Budget **of the United States** Government. [Dept. ed.]. 1971-. Annual. **United States**. PREX 2.8:998. GPO stock no.: 041-001-00478-5. [[0853]].
　　Rank: 946 Locate Libraries , [Short Record] , [Full Record]

---

[5]
The budget **of the United States** Government. [computer file] /. 1995-. Annual. **United States**. PREX 2.8/1:997. GPO stock no.: 041-001-00471-8. [[0853-C]].
http://www.doc.gov/BudgetFY97/index.html.
　　Rank: 908 Locate Libraries , [Short Record] , [Full Record]

---

[6]
Budget **of the United States** Government. Dept. ed.! 1971-. Annual. **United States**. PREX 2.8:996. GPO stock no.: 041-001-00446-7. [[0853]].
　　Rank: 873 Locate Libraries , [Short Record] , [Full Record]

---

[7]
Budget **of the United States** Government. Dept. ed.! 1971-. Annual. **United States**. PREX 2.8:995. GPO stock no.: 041-001-00417-3. [[0853]].
　　Rank: 854 Locate Libraries , [Short Record] , [Full Record]

---

[8]
Budget **of the United States** Government. [Doc. ed.]. Annual. **United States**. Y 1.1/7:104-162/V.1. [[0996-A]].

http://www.access.gpo.gov/su%5Fdocs/budget/index.html
   Rank: 846 Locate Libraries , [Short Record] , [Full Record]

---

[9]
Budget **of** the **United States** Government. [Doc. ed.]. Annual. **United States.** Y 1.1/7:105-003/V.3. [[0996-A]].
http://www.access.gpo.gov/su%5Fdocs/budget/index.html
   Rank: 846 Locate Libraries , [Short Record] , [Full Record]

---

[10]
Budget **of** the **United States** Government. [Doc. ed.]. Annual. **United States.** Y 1.1/7:105-177/V.1. [[0996-A]].
http://www.access.gpo.gov/omb/
   Rank: 846 Locate Libraries , [Short Record] , [Full Record]

---

[11]
Budget **of** the **United States** Government. [Doc. ed.]. Annual. **United States.** Y 1.1/7:006-003/V.1. [[0996-A]].
http://purl.access.gpo.gov/GPO/LPS2343
   Rank: 841 Locate Libraries , [Short Record] , [Full Record]

---

[12]
The budget **of** the **United States** Government. [computer file] /. 1995-. Annual. **United States.** PREX 2.8/1:998. GPO
stock no.: 041-001-00484-0. [[0853-C]].
http://www.access.gpo.gov/omb/
   Rank: 833 Locate Libraries , [Short Record] , [Full Record]

---

[13]
Reports **of** the proceedings **of** the Judicial Conference **of** the **United States.** Microfiche. 1964-1993. Annual. Judicial
Conference **of** the **United States.** JU 10.1/2:992. [[0728 (MF)]].
   Rank: 820 Locate Libraries , [Short Record] , [Full Record]

---

[14]
Reports **of** the proceedings **of** the Judicial Conference **of** the **United States.** Microfiche. 1964-. Annual. Judicial
Conference **of** the **United States.** JU 10.1/2:991. [[0728 (MF)]].
   Rank: 801 Locate Libraries , [Short Record] , [Full Record]

---

[15]
Budget **of** the **United States** Government. Analytical perspectives. [Doc. ed.]. 1996-. Annual. **United States.** Y
1.1/7:105-003/V.2. [[0996-A]].
http://www.access.gpo.gov/su%5Fdocs/budget/index.html
   Rank: 792 Locate Libraries , [Short Record] , [Full Record]

---

[16]
The budget **of** the **United States** Government. [computer file] /. 1995-. Annual. **United States.** PREX 2.8/1:2000.
GPO stock no.: 041-001-00517-0. [[0853-C]].
   Rank: 788 Locate Libraries , [Short Record] , [Full Record]

---

[17]
Budget **of** the **United States** Government. Analytical perspectives. [Doc. ed.]. 1996-. Annual. **United States.** Y
1.1/7:106-003/V.3. [[0996-A]].
http://purl.access.gpo.gov/GPO/LPS2343
   Rank: 781 Locate Libraries , [Short Record] , [Full Record]

---

[18]
Budget **of** the **United States** Government. Appendix. Doc. ed. Annual. **United States.** Y 1.1/7:104-162/V.2.
[[0996-A]].
http://www.access.gpo.gov/su%5Fdocs/budget/index.html
   Rank: 781 Locate Libraries , [Short Record] , [Full Record]

---

[19]
Budget **of** the **United States** Government. Appendix. Doc. ed. Annual. **United States.** Y 1.1/7:105-003/V.1.
[[0996-A]].
http://www.access.gpo.gov/su%5Fdocs/budget/index.html
   Rank: 781 Locate Libraries , [Short Record] , [Full Record]

[20]
Budget of the United States Government. Appendix. Doc. ed. Annual. United States. Y 1.1/7:105-177/V.2.
[[0996-A]].
http://www.access.gpo.gov/omb/
      Rank: 781 Locate Libraries , [Short Record] , [Full Record]

[21]
Budget of the United States Government. Appendix. Doc. ed. Annual. United States. Y 1.1/7:106-003/V.2.
[[0996-A]].
http://purl.access.gpo.gov/GPO/LPS862
      Rank: 775 Locate Libraries , [Short Record] , [Full Record]

[22]
Historical tables, budget of the United States government. [Doc. ed.]. Annual. United States. Y 1.1/7:104-162/V.4.
[[0996-A]].
http://www.access.gpo.gov/su%5Fdocs/budget/index.html
      Rank: 762 Locate Libraries , [Short Record] , [Full Record]

[23]
Historical tables, budget of the United States government. [Doc. ed.]. Annual. United States. Y 1.1/7:105-003/V.4.
[[0996-A]].
http://www.access.gpo.gov/su%5Fdocs/budget/index.html
      Rank: 762 Locate Libraries , [Short Record] , [Full Record]

[24]
Historical tables, budget of the United States government. [Doc. ed.]. Annual. United States. Y 1.1/7:105-177/V.4.
[[0996-A]].
http://www.access.gpo.gov/omb/
      Rank: 762 Locate Libraries , [Short Record] , [Full Record]

[25]
Budget of the United States Government. Analytical perspectives. [Doc. ed.]. 1996-. Annual. United States. Y
1.1/7:104-162/V.3. [[0996-A]].
http://www.access.gpo.gov/su%5Fdocs/budget/index.html
      Rank: 743 Locate Libraries , [Short Record] , [Full Record]

[26]
Decisions of the Comptroller General of the United States /. 1922-. Annual. United States. GA 1.5:71. GPO stock
no.: 020-000-00264-6. [[0544]].
      Rank: 739 Locate Libraries , [Short Record] , [Full Record]

[27]
Budget of the United States Government. Analytical perspectives. [Doc. ed.]. 1996-. Annual. United States. Y
1.1/7:105-177/V.3. [[0996-A]].
http://www.access.gpo.gov/omb/
      Rank: 737 Locate Libraries , [Short Record] , [Full Record]

[28]
Decisions of the Comptroller General of the United States /. 1922-. Annual. United States. GA 1.5:66. GPO stock
no.: 020-000-00244-1. [[0544 (MF)]].
      Rank: 734 Locate Libraries , [Short Record] , [Full Record]

[29]
Decisions of the Comptroller General of the United States /. 1922-. Annual. United States. GA 1.5:72. GPO stock
no.: 020-000-00266-2. [[0544]].
      Rank: 734 Locate Libraries , [Short Record] , [Full Record]

[30]
Decisions of the Comptroller General of the United States /. 1922-. Annual. United States. GA 1.5:73. GPO stock
no.: 020-000-00270-1.
      Rank: 734 Locate Libraries , [Short Record] , [Full Record]

[31]
The budget of the **United States** Government. [computer file] /. 1995-. Annual. **United States**. PREX 2.8/1:999. GPO stock no.: 041-001-00501-3. [[0853-C, 0853-C (online)]].
http://www.access.gpo.gov/omb/
    Rank: 726 Locate Libraries , [Short Record] , [Full Record]

[32]
Budget of the **United States** Government. [computer file]. Annual. **United States**. PREX 2.8:998. GPO stock no.: 041-001-00478-5. [[0853 (online)]].
http://www.access.gpo.gov/omb/
    Rank: 719 Locate Libraries , [Short Record] , [Full Record]

[33]
Nominations of Laura S. Unger, Paul R. Carey, Dennis Dollar, Edward M. Gramlich, Roger W. Ferguson, Jr., and Ellen Seidman : hearing before the Committee on Banking, Housing, and Urban Affairs, **United States** Senate, One Hundred Fifth Congress, first session, on nominations of Laura S. Unger of New York, to be a Commissioner of the Securities and Exchange Commission; Paul R. Carey, of New York, to be a Commissioner of the Securities and Exchange Commission; Dennis Dollar, of Mississippi, to be a member of the National Credit Union Administration Board; Edward M. Gramlich, of Virginia, to be a member of the Board of Governors of the Federal Reserve System; Roger W. Ferguson, Jr., of Massachusetts, to be a member of the Board of Governors of the Federal Reserve System; Ellen Seidman, of the District of Columbia, to be the Director of the **Office of** Thrift Supervision, September 30, 1997. 1997 [i.e. 1998] **United States**. Y 4.B 22/3:S.HRG.105-544. [[1035-C]].
    Rank: 715 Locate Libraries , [Short Record] , [Full Record]

[34]
The budget of the **United States** Government. [computer file] /. 1995-. Annual. **United States**. PREX 2.8/1:996/FINAL 2. GPO stock no.: 041-001-00453-0. [[0853-A-07]].
    Rank: 702 Locate Libraries , [Short Record] , [Full Record]

[35]
The budget of the **United States** Government. [computer file] /. 1995-. Annual. **United States**. PREX 2.8/1:996. GPO stock no.: 041-001-00452-1.
    Rank: 696 Locate Libraries , [Short Record] , [Full Record]

[36]
Historical tables, budget of the **United States** government. [computer file]. Annual. **United States**. PREX 2.8/8:998. GPO stock no.: 041-001-00481-5. [[0853 (online)]].
http://www.access.gpo.gov/omb/
    Rank: 694 Locate Libraries , [Short Record] , [Full Record]

[37]
Trademark CD-ROM user's guide : **Trademark** registrations, Trademarks pending, **Trademark** assignments, **Trademark** manual of examining procedure, Goods and services manual : for use with CD answer 2.03. [1994] **United States**. C 21.31/7:R 26/GUIDE. [[0154-B-09]].
    Rank: 689 Locate Libraries , [Short Record] , [Full Record]

[38]
Budget of the **United States** Government. Analytical perspectives. [computer file]. Annual. **United States**. PREX 2.8/5:998. GPO stock no.: 041-001-00480-7. [[0855-B (online)]].
http://www.access.gpo.gov/omb/
    Rank: 688 Locate Libraries , [Short Record] , [Full Record]

[39]
The budget of the **United States** Government. Appendix. [Dept. ed.]. 1971-. Annual. **United States**. PREX 2.8:999/APP. GPO stock no.: 041-001-00496-3. [[0853]].
http://www.access.gpo.gov/su%5Fdocs/budget/index.html
    Rank: 687 Locate Libraries , [Short Record] , [Full Record]

[40]
The budget of the **United States** Government. Appendix. [Dept. ed.]. 1971-. Annual. **United States**. PREX 2.8:2000/APP. GPO stock no.: 041-001-00512-9. [[0853]].

http://purl.access.gpo.gov/GPO/LPS2343
   Rank: 681 Locate Libraries , [Short Record] , [Full Record]

Questions or comments regarding this service? Contact the *GPO Access* **User Support Team** by Internet e-mail at *gpoaccess@gpo.gov* ; by telephone at 202-512-1530; or by fax at 202-512-1262.

Page #adpos430_results May 31, 1995

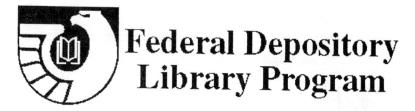

Federal Depository Library Program

Locate Federal Depository Libraries by State or Area Code

There are approximately 1,400 Federal depository libraries throughout the United States and its territories, at least one in almost every Congressional District. All provide free public access to a wide variety of Federal government information in both print and electronic formats, and have expert staff available to assist users.

NOTE: Some libraries are indicated in the search results screens as a **Regional** Library. There are currently **fifty three** (53) Regional Libraries. All states have, or are covered by, a Regional library. **REGIONAL** libraries receive all materials distributed through the Federal Depository Library Program. Other libraries select materials according to the needs of their communities.

Locate the Federal depository libraries in any state or territory by entering **ONE OR MORE** 2-letter state abbreviation(s) (within a single box) for up to 5 states.

FOR EXAMPLE: | MD | | VA | | | | |

	Locate All
	Depository
	Libraries
	Alphabetically by
Enter State Abbreviation(s)	**State and City**

For a more specific listing, enter **ONE OR MORE** 3-digit telephone area code(s) (within a single box) for up to 3 area codes.

FOR EXAMPLE: | 301 | | 703 | | |

Enter Area Code(s)

Federal Depository Libraries in Selected States

PENNSYLVANIA

0520 Muhlenberg College
Trexler Library
2400 Chew Street
Allentown, PA 18104-5586

Phone: (610) 821-3600
Fax: (610) 821-3511
http://www.muhlenberg.edu/library/govtdoc.html

0523 Altoona Area Public Library
1600 5th Avenue
Altoona, PA 16602-3693

Phone: (814) 946-0417
Fax: (814) 946-3230

0512 Bethel Park Public Library
5100 West Library Avenue
Bethel Park, PA 15102-2790

Phone: (412) 835-2207, ext. 273
Fax: (412) 835-9360

0532 Lehigh University
Fairchild-Martindale Library
8A East Packer Avenue
Bethlehem, PA 18015-3170

Phone: (610) 758-5337
Fax: (610) 758-6524
http://www.lib.lehigh.edu/depts/govdocs.dept.html

0514A Bloomsburg University of Pennsylvania
Harvey A. Andruss Library
400 East 2nd Street
Bloomsburg, PA 17815-1301

Phone: (570) 389-4204
Fax: (570) 389-3895
http://www.bloomu.edu/library/

Search US Trademark Database

Trademark Applications

Apply for a Trademark Online (TEAS)

Basic Facts about Trademarks

Frequently-Asked Questions

Registration of Internet Domain Names

Pending and Registered Trademarks

Check Trademark Status (TARR)

Official Gazette Notices

Data and Product Sales

Notices and Announcements

Acceptable Identification of Goods and Services Manual

Design Search Code Manual

Trademark Examination Guides, Notes and Announcements

Search Facilities at PTO

Patent and Trademark Depository Libraries

Assistant Commissioner for Trademarks

Trademark Trial and Appeal Board

Trademark Trial and Appeal Board Manual of Procedure

Mainly for Practitioners

Trademark Manual of Examining Procedure

US Trademark Law: Rules of Practice & Federal Statutes

Trademark Law on *GSA FedLaw* site

Trademark Law Treaty Implementation Act

Related Programs

Fastener Quality Act

RETURN TO THE USPTO HOME PAGE

Last Modified: 20 July 1999

Basic Facts About Trademarks

This pamphlet is customarily furnished in response to general information requests about trademarks received at the Patent and Trademark Office. A printed copy of this publication is provided by the PTO at no charge. You may also download this document in word processor formats or find it on our anonymous FTP server at *ftp.uspto.gov* in directory */pub/trademarks* .

Contents

As you browse this document, you will find references to the following forms, which are available for you to download, fill out, and turn in. Instructions are provided:

- Trademark/Service Mark Application (PTO Form 1478)
- Amendment to Allege Use Under 37 CFR 2.76, with Declaration (PTO Form 1579),
- Statement of Use Under 37 CFR 2.88, with Declaration (PTO Form 1580),

USPTO HOME PAGE

Last Modified: 14 May 1999

US Patent and Trademark Office

HOME   SITE INDEX   SEARCH   INFO BY ORG   FEEDBACK

Frequently Asked Questions About Trademarks

CONTENTS

Definitions

- What is a trademark?
- What is a service mark?
- What is a certification mark?
- What is a collective mark?

Basic Questions

- Do I need to register my trademark?
- What are the benefits of federal trademark registration?
- Do I have to be a U.S. citizen to obtain a federal registration?
- Where can I find trademark forms?
- Where can I get basic trademark information?
- Where can I ask a question about trademarks?
- Are there federal regulations governing the use of the designations "TM" or "SM" with trademarks?
- When can I use the federal registration symbol ® with the mark?
- Do I need an attorney to file a trademark application?
- What constitutes "interstate commerce"?
- How do I find out whether a mark is already registered?
- Is a federal registration valid outside the United States?

Searching

- Is it advisable to conduct a search of the Office records before filing an application?
- Can the Office conduct a search for an applicant?
- Can trademarks be searched on-line?
- In searching the trademark data base on the Web there are records that appear to be a registrations but the registration numbers are shown as 0000000. Is this an error?
- Where can I conduct a trademark search?
- What are "common law" rights?
- What is a "common law" search? How can I do one? Is doing a common law search necessary?

Trademarks, Patents and Copyrights

- How do I find out if I need patent, trademark and/or copyright protection?
- How do I register a copyright?

Application Process

- How do I obtain a federal trademark registration?
- Who may file an application?
- Do I have to use the application form provided by the Office?
- Can a fax copy or photocopy of an application be filed?
- Can I fax in my application?
- What is a specimen?
- What is a drawing?
- If I submit specimens, is a drawing still required?

http://www.uspto.gov/web/offices/tac/tmfaq.htm

☐ Do I need an attorney to file my application?
☐ On what bases can a foreign applicant file an application for registration?
☐ Can the Office refuse to register a mark?
☐ Can I get a refund of monies paid to the Office?
☐ How can I check on the status of a pending U.S. Trademark application?
☐ How long does it take for a mark to be registered?
☐ How long does a trademark registration last?
☐ When did the renewal period change from twenty to ten years?
☐ How long does an Intent-to-Use applicant have to allege actual use of the mark in commerce?
☐ What are the different classes of goods and services?

Other

☐ What is the Trademark Electronic Application System (TEAS)?
☐ How do I contest someone else using a trademark similar to mine?
☐ What official publications and electronic information products are available concerning trademarks?
☐ What is a PTDL (Patent and Trademark Depository Library)?
☐ How do I register to practice before the Patent and Trademark Office?
☐ Is the name of a band a trademark?
☐ Can a minor file a trademark application?
☐ Can the ownership of a trademark be assigned or transferred from one person to another?
☐ My spouse owned a trademark registration and has since died. Do I own it now?
☐ What are some suggestions to facilitate filing a trademark application and/or contacting the Office?

Definitions

What is a trademark?

A trademark includes any word, name, symbol, or device, or any combination, used, or intended to be used, in commerce to identify and distinguish the goods of one manufacturer or seller from goods manufactured or sold by others, and to indicate the source of the goods. In short, a trademark is a brand name.

Back to the Contents

What is a service mark?

A service mark is any word, name, symbol, device, or any combination, used, or intended to be used, in commerce, to identify and distinguish the services of one provider from services provided by others, and to indicate the source of the services.

Back to the Contents

What is a certification mark?

A certification mark is any word, name, symbol, device, or any combination, used, or intended to be used, in commerce with the owner's permission by someone other than its owner, to certify regional or other geographic origin, material, mode of manufacture, quality, accuracy, or other characteristics of someone's goods or services, or that the work or labor on the goods or services was performed by members of a union or other organization.

Back to the Contents

What is a collective mark?

A collective mark is a trademark or service mark used, or intended to be used, in commerce, by the members of a cooperative, an association, or other collective group or organization, including a mark which indicates membership in a union, an association, or other organization.

Back to the Contents

http://www.uspto.gov/web/offices/tac/tmfaq.htm

US Patent and Trademark Office

| HOME | SITE INDEX | SEARCH | INFO BY ORG | FEEDBACK |

Welcome to the USPTO Web Trademark Database

This page is the starting point for the USPTO's free trademark database, which includes the full bibliographic text of pending and registered trademarks. It was last updated to include data from the PTO's internal trademark database as of **July 1, 1999**. This means that marks registered and published in the *Official Gazette -- Trademarks* through that date should be included. Pending trademark applications are usually entered in the PTO database one to two months after filing; thus, pending trademark data for the preceding two months are incomplete. The next data extraction is expected during the first week of September 1999; that data should appear in this database some time later that month.

Important Notice: Limitations Regarding the Database, Database Contents, Database Currency, and Sources of More Current Data *[Click here!]*

Understanding the limitations of this Web database can help you avoid significant problems. It is critical that you review this notice before interpreting the results of searches of PTO's Web Trademark Database.

Access the Trademark Database

- **Combined Marks Search** *(Word Mark, Pseudo-Mark, and Translation)*
- **Number Search** *(Registration or Serial Number)*
- **Boolean Search** *(Graphical interface; two search terms; "AND", "OR")*
- **Manual Search** *(Type a command line search expression)*

- **Know the trademark number and can't find it in the database? Check the Trademark Status Server!**

- **Help**

- **What's New / Database Status**

Please note that PTO does not record or log the parameters of search requests submitted to these databases. Such uncollected information has thus never been disclosed through sale or FOIA request, intentionally or otherwise, to any third party. PTO does not plan to change this operational policy.

All data provided herein is in the public domain, and may be freely used for any purpose. However, users creating their own hyperlinks to pages on this site are requested and cautioned to do so in a manner which maintains a clear distinction between the user's content and official content published by USPTO.

RETURN TO THE USPTO HOME PAGE

Important Notice: Limitations Regarding The PTO's Web Trademark Database

Introduction

The U.S. Patent and Trademark Office (PTO) now offers World-Wide Web (Web) access to selected trademark information obtained from its internal trademark database. Understanding the limitations of this Web database can help you avoid significant problems. Prior to using the PTO's trademark database on the Web, it is critical that you review the following information.

This initial offering of trademark information on the PTO Web site provides access to the trademark text data currently available on two of PTO's Cassis CD-ROM products: *Trademarks Registered* and *Trademarks Pending* . Like the CD-ROM products, this text will be updated on a two-month cycle. Images will be added as they become available.

> If you have any questions regarding adoption or use of a trademark, the PTO strongly recommends that you consult with an attorney. The PTO cannot recommend attorneys.

Web Database Contents

- The fact that a mark is not present in the Web database does not necessarily mean that the mark is not currently being used as a trademark.
- The Web database contains only those trademarks that are Federally registered or that are pending (applications undergoing examination at the PTO).
- The Web database does not contain any information on state, foreign, or common law trademarks.
- The Web database does not include information on inactive applications and registrations (i.e., abandoned applications or canceled or expired registrations). Since it is possible for inactive applications or registrations to be "revived" or "reinstated," active marks that may present possible conflicts with your mark will not be retrieved if they have temporarily fallen into an "inactive" status.

Currency of the Web Database

- The PTO's trademark data on the Web is updated on a two-month cycle. Coupled with the time required for data production, this means that particular trademarks could be as much as four months out of sequence with the PTO's internal trademark database.
- The Web database does not include new applications that were filed and entered into the PTO's internal trademark database during the last two to four months.
- The Web database does not reflect changes made to the PTO's internal trademark database during the last two to four months.
- The Web database will show applications that registered after its last update as pending applications rather than registrations.
- The Web database will not include edits made to individual records after its last update.
- Images, which should exist for registered and pending trademarks with Mark Drawing Codes of "(2)" or "(3)", generally become available some months after the corresponding text is available. The availability of images in the Web database may affect your ability to evaluate trademarks that include design features.

http://www.uspto.gov/tmdb/disclaim.html

More Current Data

X-Search, the PTO's internal trademark database, may be searched for a fee at the PTO's Trademark Search Library in Arlington, VA , or at Partnership Patent and Trademark Depository Libraries located in Sunnyvale CA, Detroit MI, and Houston TX . You may also update your search by consulting the *Official Gazette: Trademarks* , which can be found at over 80 Patent and Trademark Depository Libraries and at selected Federal depository libraries throughout the country. The Official Gazette does not list all marks that are in pending applications. It contains only registered marks and marks published for opposition.

Any perceived error or inconsistency in these records must be resolved by examining the official record, which is the physical application/registration file.

RETURN TO THE USPTO HOME PAGE

Last Modified: 1 December 1998

US PATENT & TRADEMARK OFFICE
TRADEMARK TEXT AND IMAGE DATABASE

| Help | Home | Marks | Boolean | Manual | Number | Order Copy | PTDLs |

Check Status

Word Mark	*LADDERMASTER*
Pseudo Mark	LADDER-MASTER
Owner Name	(REGISTRANT) Viking Manufacturing Inc.
Owner Address	5717 Albatros Boise IDAHO 83705 CORPORATION IDAHO
Serial Number	75-038179
Registration Number	2033683
Filing Date	12/28/1995
Registration Date	01/28/1997
Mark Drawing Code	(1) TYPED DRAWING
Register	PRINCIPAL
Published for Opposition	11/05/1996
Type of Mark	TRADEMARK

International Class	006
Goods and Services	ladder accessories, namely automatic metal ladder leveler; DATE OF FIRST USE: 1995.05.15; DATE OF FIRST USE IN COMMERCE: 1995.06.05

US PATENT & TRADEMARK OFFICE
TRADEMARK TEXT AND IMAGE DATABASE

| Help | Home | Marks | Boolean | Manual | Number | Order Copy | PTDLs |

(1 of 1)

Check Status

Ladder Witch

Word Mark	*LADDER WITCH*
Owner Name	(REGISTRANT) Pate, Ivan G.
Owner Address	160 West Moody Knoxville TENNESSEE 37920 INDIVIDUAL UNITED STATES
Attorney of Record	Robert O. Fox
Serial Number	74-498424
Registration Number	1986061
Filing Date	03/08/1994
Registration Date	07/09/1996
Design Search Code	04.01.25; 14.09.02; 26.03.02
Section 1(B) indicator	SECTION 1 (B)
Mark Drawing Code	(3) DESIGN PLUS WORDS, LETTERS, AND/OR NUMBERS
Disclaimer	NO CLAIM IS MADE TO THE EXCLUSIVE RIGHT TO USE "LADDER" APART FROM THE MARK AS SHOWN
Register	PRINCIPAL
Published for Opposition	06/20/1995

http://trademarks.uspto.gov/cgi-bin/ifetch4?ENG+
REG+3+944327+0+0+267830+F+1+1+1+

Type of Mark   TRADEMARK
_____

International Class   007

Goods and Services   hoist systems for use with extension ladders comprised of a winch and pulley block, all
                         sold as a unit; DATE OF FIRST USE: 1995.08.30; DATE OF FIRST USE IN
                         COMMERCE: 1995.09.30
_____

1 of 1)

International Schedule of Classes of Goods and Services

Goods

1. Chemicals used in industry, science and photography, as well as in agriculture, horticulture and forestry; unprocessed artificial resins, unprocessed plastics; manures; fire extinguishing compositions; tempering and soldering preparations; chemical substances for preserving foodstuffs; tanning substances; adhesives used in industry.

2. Paints, varnishes, lacquers; preservatives against rust and against deterioration of wood; colorants; mordants; raw natural resins; metals in foil and powder form for painters, decorators, printers, and artists.

3. Bleaching preparations and other substances for laundry use; cleaning, polishing, scouring and abrasive preparations; soaps, perfumery, essential oils, cosmetics, hair lotions; dentifrices.

4. Industrial oils and greases; lubricants; dust absorbing, wetting and binding compositions; fuels (including motor spirit) and illuminants; candles, wicks.

5. Pharmaceutical, veterinary and sanitary preparations; dietetic substances adapted for medical use, food for babies; plasters, materials for dressings; material for stopping teeth, dental wax, disinfectants; preparations for destroying vermin; fungicides, herbicides.

6. Common metals and their alloys; metal building materials; transportable buildings of metal; materials of metal for railway tracks; non-electric cables and wires of common metal; ironmongery, small items of metal hardware; pipes and tubes of metal; safes; goods of common metal not included in other classes; ores.

7. Machines and machine tools; motors and engines (except for land vehicles); machine coupling and transmission components (except for land vehicles); agricultural implements; incubators for eggs.

8. Hand tools and implements (hand operated); cutlery; side arms; razors.

9. Scientific, nautical, surveying, electric, photographic, cinematographic, optical, weighing, measuring, signalling, checking (supervision), life-saving and teaching apparatus and instruments; apparatus for recording, transmission or reproduction of sound or images; magnetic data carriers, recording discs; automatic vending machines and mechanisms for coin operated apparatus; cash registers, calculating machines, data processing equipment and computers; fire-extinguishing apparatus.

10. Surgical, medical, dental and veterinary apparatus and instruments, artificials limbs, eyes and teeth; orthopedic articles; suture materials.

11. Apparatus for lighting, heating, steam generating, cooking, refrigerating, drying, ventilating, water supply and sanitary purposes.

12. Vehicles; apparatus for locomotion by land, air, or water.

13. Firearms; ammunition and projectiles; explosives; fireworks.

14. Precious metals and their alloys and goods in precious metals or coated therewith, not included in other classes; jewellery, precious stones; horological and chronometric instruments.

15. Musical instruments.

16. Paper, cardboard and goods made from these materials, not included in other classes; printed matter; bookbinding material; photographs; stationery; adhesives for stationery or household purposes; artists' materials; paint brushes; typewriters and office requisites (except furniture); instructional and teaching material (except apparatus); playing cards; printers' type; printing blocks.

17. Rubber, gutta-percha, gum asbestos, mica and goods made from these materials and not included in other classes; plastics in extruded form for use in manufacture; packing, stopping and insulating materials; flexible pipes, not of metal.

18. Leather and imitations of leather, and goods made of these materials and not included in other classes; animal skins, hides; trunks and travelling bags; umbrellas, parasols and walking sticks; whips, harness and saddlery.

19. Building materials (non-metallic); rigid pipes for building; asphalt, pitch and bitumen; non-metallic transportable buildings; monuments, not of metal.

20. Furniture, mirrors, picture frames; goods (not included in other classes) of wood, cork, reed, cane, wicker, horn, bone, ivory, whalebone, shell, amber, mother-of-pearl, meeschaum and substitutes for all these materials, or of plastics.

21. Household or kitchen utensils and containers (not of precious metal or coated therewith); combs and sponges; brushes (except paint brushes); brush-making materials; articles for cleaning purposes; steelwool; unworked or semiworked glass (except glass used in building); glassware, porcelain and earthenware not included in other classes.

22. Ropes, string, nets, tents, awnings, tarpaulins, sails, sacks and bags (not included in other classes); padding and stuffing materials (except of rubber or plastics); raw fibrous textile materials.

23. Yarns and threads, for textile use.

24. Textiles and textile goods, not included in other classes; bed and table covers.

25. Clothing, footwear, headgear.

26. Lace and embroidery, ribbons and braid; buttons, hooks and eyes, pins and needles; artificial flowers.

27. Carpets, rugs, mats and matting, linoleum and other materials for covering existing floors; wall hangings (non-textile).

28. Games and playthings; gymnastic and sporting articles not included in other classes; decorations for Christmas trees.

29. Meat, fish, poultry and game; meat extracts; preserved, dried and cooked fruits and vegetables; jellies, jams, fruit sauces; eggs, milk and milk products; edible oils and fats.

30. Coffee, tea, cocoa, sugar, rice, tapioca, sago, artificial coffee; flour and preparations made from cereals, bread, pastry and confectionery, honey, treacle; yeast, baking-powder; salt, mustard; vinegar, sauces (condiments); spices; ice.

31. Agricultural, horticultural and forestry products and grains not included in other classes; live animals; fresh fruits and vegetables; seeds, natural plants and flowers; foodstuffs for animals, malt.

32. Beers; mineral and aerated waters and other non-alcoholic drinks; fruit drinks and fruit juices; syrups and other preparations for making beverages.

33. Alcoholic beverages (except beers).

34. Tobacco; smokers articles; matches.

Services

35. Advertising; business management; business administration; office functions.

36. Insurance; financial affairs; monetary affairs; real estate affairs.

37. Building construction; repair, installation services.

38. Telecommunications.

39. Transport; packaging and storage of goods; travel arrangement.

40. Treatment of materials.

41. Education; providing of training; entertainment; sporting and cultural activities.

42. Providing of food and drink; temporary accommodation; medical, hygienic and beauty care; veterinary and agricultural services; legal services; scientific and industrial research; computer programming; services that cannot be placed in other classes.

TRADEMARK/SERVICE MARK APPLICATION, PRINCIPAL REGISTER, WITH DECLARATION	MARK (Word(s) and/or Design)	CLASS NO. (If known)

TO THE ASSISTANT COMMISSIONER FOR TRADEMARKS:

APPLICANT'S NAME:

APPLICANT'S MAILING ADDRESS:

(Display address exactly as it should appear on registration)

APPLICANT'S ENTITY TYPE: (Check one and supply requested information)

	Individual - Citizen of (Country):
	Partnership - State where organized (Country, if appropriate): _____ Names and Citizenship (Country) of General Partners: _____
	Corporation - State (Country, if appropriate) of Incorporation:
	Other (Specify Nature of Entity and Domicile):

GOODS AND/OR SERVICES:

Applicant requests registration of the trademark/service mark shown in the accompanying drawing in the United States Patent and Trademark Office on the Principal Register established by the Act of July 5, 1946 (15 U.S.C. 1051 et. seq., as amended) for the following goods/services **(SPECIFIC GOODS AND/OR SERVICES MUST BE INSERTED HERE)**

BASIS FOR APPLICATION (Check boxes which apply, but never both the first AND second boxes, and supply requested information related to each box checked.)

[ ]	Applicant is using the mark in commerce on or in connection with the above identified goods/services. (15 U.S.C. 1051(a), as amended.) Three specimens showing the mark as used in commerce are submitted with this application. • Date of first use of the mark in commerce which the U.S. Congress may regulate (for example, interstate or between the U.S. and a foreign country): _____ • Specify the type of commerce: _____ (for example, interstate or between the U.S. and a specified foreign country) • Date of first use anywhere (the same as or before use in commerce date): _____ • Specify manner or mode of use of mark on or in connection with the goods/services: _____ (for example, trademark is applied to labels, service mark is used in advertisements)
[ ]	Applicant has a bona fide intention to use the mark in commerce on or in connection with the above identified goods/services. (15 U.S.C. 1051(b), as amended.) • Specify intended manner or mode of use of mark on or in connection with the goods/services: _____ (for example, trademark will be applied to labels, service mark will be used in advertisements)
[ ]	Applicant has a bona fide intention to use the mark in commerce on or in connection with the above identified goods/services, and asserts a claim of priority based upon a foreign application in accordance with 15 U.S.C. 1126(d), as amended. • Country of foreign filing: _____ •Date of foreign filing: _____
[ ]	Applicant has a bona fide intention to use the mark in commerce on or in connection with the above identified goods/services and, accompanying this application, submits a certification or certified copy of a foreign registration in accordance with 15 U.S.C 1126(e), as amended. • Country of registration: _____ • Registration number: _____

NOTE: Declaration, on Reverse Side, MUST be Signed

PTO Form 1478 (REV 6/96)   U.S. DEPARTMENT OF COMMERCE/Patent and Trademark Office
OMB No. 0651-0009 (Exp. 06/30/98) There is no requirement to respond to this collection of information unless a currently valid OMB Number is displayed.

DECLARATION

The undersigned being hereby warned that willful false statements and the like so made are punishable by fine or imprisonment, or both, under 18 U.S.C. 1001, and that such willful false statements may jeopardize the validity of the application or any resulting registration, declares that he/she is properly authorized to execute this application on behalf of the applicant; he/she believes the applicant to be the owner of the trademark/service mark sought to be registered, or if the application is being filed under 15 U.S.C. 1051(b), he/she believes the applicant to be entitled to use such mark in commerce; to the best of his/her knowledge and belief no other person, firm, corporation, or association has the right to use the above identified mark in commerce, either in the identical form thereof or in such near resemblance thereto as to be likely, when used on or in connection with the goods/services of such other person, to cause confusion, or to cause mistake, or to deceive; and that all statements made of his/her own knowledge are true and that all statements made on information and belief are believed to be true.

DATE

SIGNATURE

TELEPHONE NUMBER

PRINT OR TYPE NAME AND POSITION

INSTRUCTIONS AND INFORMATION FOR APPLICANT

TO RECEIVE A FILING DATE, THE APPLICATION MUST BE COMPLETED AND SIGNED BY THE APPLICANT AND SUBMITTED ALONG WITH:

1. The prescribed **FEE ($245.00)** for each class of goods/services listed in the application;
2. A **DRAWING PAGE** displaying the mark in conformance with 37 CFR 2.52;
3. If the application is based on use of the mark in commerce, **THREE (3) SPECIMENS** (evidence) of the mark as used in commerce for each class of goods/services listed in the application. All three specimens may be the same. Examples of good specimens include: (a) labels showing the mark which are placed on the goods; (b) photographs of the mark as it appears on the goods, (c) brochures or advertisements showing the mark as used in connection with the services.
4. An **APPLICATION WITH DECLARATION** (this form) - The application must be signed in order for the application to receive a filing date. Only the following persons may sign the declaration, depending on the applicant's legal entity: (a) the individual applicant; (b) an officer of the corporate applicant; (c) one general partner of a partnership applicant; (d) all joint applicants.

SEND APPLICATION FORM, DRAWING PAGE, FEE, AND SPECIMENS (IF APPROPRIATE) TO:

Assistant Commissioner for Trademarks
Box New App/Fee
2900 Crystal Drive
Arlington, VA 22202-3513

Additional information concerning the requirements for filing an application is available in a booklet entitled **Basic Facts About Registering a Trademark,** which may be obtained by writing to the above address or by calling: (703) 308-HELP.

Help   Home   Marks   Number   Boolean   Manual   Order Copy   PTDLs

Tips on Fielded Searching

This page contains definitions of search fields and tips on the use of fields in your searches.

The PTO's Web Trademark database contains many searchable fields. By narrowing your search to terms in a field that you specify, you can greatly decrease the likelihood of retrieving extraneous documents.

This page shows a list of all the available fields, defines each field, shows the abbreviated field name or code, and provides examples of how do field searching.

- Affidavits
- Amended Supplemental Registration
- Attorney of Record
- Change in Registration
- Description of Mark
- Design Search Code
- Disclaimer
- Filing Date
- Goods and Services
- International Class
- Mark Drawing Code
- Mark Search
- Other Data
- Other Registration Information
- Owner Address
- Owner Name
- Priority Date
- Pseudo Mark
- Published for Opposition
- Register
- Registration Date
- Registration Number
- Renewals
- Section 1(b) Indicator
- Section 2(f) Limitation
- Section 44 Indicator
- Serial Number
- Translation
- Type of Mark
- Word Mark

Affidavits (AF)

This field contains notations on the types of affidavits filed on registrations. It refers to either or both Sec. 8 and Sec. 15 of the trademark law (Lanham Act, as amended), or to Section 12(c) for pre-1946 registrations.

Section 8: These affidavits are required for both the Supplemental and Principal Registers to show continuous use of the mark since registration. A Section 8 Affidavit must be filed between the fifth and sixth year anniversary of the registration date in order to maintain the registration.

Section 15: These affidavits apply only to the Principal Register. They must be filed within one year of any five-year period of continuous use to confer a status of incontestability in the registration.

Section 12(c): This affidavit may be filed for a registration that registered under trademark legislation that was in effect prior to the Lanham Act which was enacted in 1946. By filing this affidavit the registration takes on the benefits as well as the responsibilities (such as the requirement to file a Section 8 affidavit) of the 1946 Lanham Act.

TIP: Enter one of the following terms (using quotation marks) in the text entry box: **Sect 8** , **Sect 15** or **Sect 12c**.

(This field applies only to Registered marks.)

US Patent and Trademark Office

| HOME | SITE INDEX | SEARCH | INFO BY ORG | FEEDBACK |

Trademark Acceptable Identification of Goods and Services Manual

The information available consists of five data fields:

- a single-character, either "G" for Goods or "S" for Services;
- a 1-3 character alphanumeric trademark classification;
- a single-character status: "A" for added, "D" for deleted, or "M" for modified;
- the effective date of that status;
- a description of the Goods or Services.

The trademark classification number should and the description of goods or services must be included in a trademark application. The other three data elements do not need to be referred to in the application.

| Search | Browse - 642 KB |

Nice Agreement, Seventh Edition: Trademark Class Changes

USPTO HOME PAGE

Last Modified: 19 May 1999

http://www.uspto.gov/go/tac/doc/gsmanual/

Trademark Acceptable Identification
of Goods and Services Manual

Table of Contents

Goods

The **S** field indicates the status of the record: **A=added, M=modified, D=deleted**. The **Date** field indicates the date of that status. Minor corrections to an entry, e.g., typos, are not considered changes in status.

```
T       IC      S       Date    Goods
-----------------------------------------------------------------------------

G       009     A       2/20/96 Abacuses
G       010     A       4/2/91  Abdominal belts
G       010     A       4/2/91  Abdominal corsets
G       010     A       4/2/91  Abdominal pads
G       001     A       4/2/91  Abrasive [indicate specific use or industry] (Auxiliary fluids for
G       001     A       4/2/91  Abrasive compositions used in the manufacture of metal polish
G       021     A       1/1/95  Abrasive liner for cat litter boxes
G       007     A       4/2/91  Abrasive wheels (Power operated)
G       005     A       4/2/91  Abrasives (Dental)
G       001     A       4/2/91  Absorbing carbons [indicate specific use or industry]
G       005     A       4/2/91  Acaricides for [indicate specific area of use, e.g., agricultural,
G       015     A       4/2/91  Accordions
G       016     A       4/2/91  Account books
G       016     A       4/2/91  Accounting forms
G       005     A       1/1/95  Acetaminophen [for relief of pain]
G       017     A       4/2/91  Acetate, for use in [indicate specific field of use] (Semi-processe
G       011     A       4/2/91  Acetylene burners
G       011     A       4/2/91  Acetylene flares
G       009     A       4/2/91  Acid hydrometers
G       029     A       4/2/91  Acidophilus milk
G       005     A       4/2/91  Acne medications
G       005     A       4/2/91  Acne treatment preparations
G       015     A       4/2/91  Acoustic guitars
G       017     A       4/2/91  Acoustical insulation barrier panels
G       017     A       4/2/91  Acoustical insulation for buildings
G       017     A       4/2/91  Acoustical panels for buildings
G       022     A       4/2/91  Acrylic fibers
G       017     A       4/2/91  Acrylic molded plastic substances, for use in [indicate specific fi
G       017     A       4/2/91  Acrylic resin sheeting for use in the manufacture of laminated glas
G       001     A       4/2/91  Acrylic resins [indicate specific use or industry](Unprocessed)
G       017     A       4/2/91  Acrylic sheeting for use in the manufacture of [indicate specific i
G       009     A       4/2/91  Actinometers
G       028     A       4/2/91  Action balls (Rubber)
G       028     A       4/2/91  Action figures and accessories therefor
G       028     A       4/2/91  Action figures
G       028     A       4/2/91  Action skill games
```

US PATENT & TRADEMARK OFFICE
TRADEMARK TEXT AND IMAGE DATABASE

| Help | Home | Marks | Boolean | Manual | Number | Order Copy | PTDLs |

Searching REG...

[Search Summary]
Results of Search in REG for:
MS/"ladder lackey": 0 trademarks.

No trademarks have matched your query

| Refine Search | MS/"ladder lackey" |

Search Summary

MS/"ladder lackey": 0 occurrences in 0 trademarks.

Search Time: 0.07 seconds.

US PATENT & TRADEMARK OFFICE
TRADEMARK TEXT AND IMAGE DATABASE

Help	Home	Marks	Boolean	Manual	Number	Order Copy	PTDLs

Searching REG...

[Search Summary]
Results of Search in REG for:
MS/"ladder lackey": 0 trademarks.

No trademarks have matched your query

Refine Search	MS/"ladder lackey"

Search Summary

MS/"ladder lackey": 0 occurrences in 0 trademarks.

Search Time: 0.1 seconds.
▲

US PATENT & TRADEMARK OFFICE
TRADEMARK TEXT AND IMAGE DATABASE

| Help | Home | Marks | Boolean | Manual | Number | Order Copy | PTDLs |

This page provides an interface for advanced searching of the U.S. Trademark Database.

Select Database:
○ Pending ● Registered ○ Both

Query:

[   ]

[Search]   [Reset]

US Trademark Field Codes

Field Code	Field Name	Field Code	Field Name
MS	Combined Marks	MD	Mark Drawing Code
WM	Word Mark	DS	Disclaimer
PM	Pseudo Mark	RG	Register
TL	Translation	S4	Sec. 44 Indicator
DC	Design Search Code	PD	Priority Date
ON	Owner Name	OR	Other Reg. Info
OA	Owner Address	2F	Sec. 2(f) Limitation
SN	Serial Number	PU	Published for Oppos.
RN	Registration Number	AF	Affidavits
FD	Filing Date	CR	Change in Reg.
RD	Registration Date	TM	Type of Mark
IC	International Class	RE	Renewals
GS	Goods & Services	EF	Amended Sup. Reg.
DE	Description of Mark	AT	Attorney of Record
IU	Sec. 1(b) Indicator	OD	Other Data

US PATENT & TRADEMARK OFFICE
TRADEMARK TEXT AND IMAGE DATABASE

Help	Home	Marks	Boolean	Manual	Number	Order Copy	PTDLs

Searching ALL...

[Search Summary]
Results of Search in ALL for:
(ladder AND lackey): 0 trademarks.

No trademarks have matched your query

[Refine Search]   `ladder and lackey`

Search Summary

ladder: 473 occurrences in 317 trademarks.
lackey: 438 occurrences in 436 trademarks.
(ladder AND lackey): 0 trademarks.

Search Time: 0.14 seconds.
▲

US PATENT & TRADEMARK OFFICE
TRADEMARK TEXT AND IMAGE DATABASE

Help	Home	Marks	Boolean	Manual	Number	Order Copy	PTDLs

This page provides a simplified interface for performing basic searches in the Word Mark, Pseudo Mark, and Translation fields of the U.S. Trademark database.

Select Database:
◯ Pending ⬤ Registered ◯ Both

Words in the Marks: [   ]

Results must contain: [All of these words ▼]   [Search] [Reset]

US PATENT & TRADEMARK OFFICE
TRADEMARK TEXT AND IMAGE DATABASE

Help	Home	Marks	Boolean	Manual	Number	Order Copy	PTDLs

Searching ALL...

[Search Summary]
Results of Search in ALL for:
MS/ladder: 87 trademarks.
Hits 1 through 50 of 87

Final 37 Hits   **Start At** [＿＿＿＿＿＿]

Refine Search | MS/ladder

No.	Trademark
1.	2243393 -- IT'S HARD TO CLIMB THE CORPORATE *LADDER* WHEN YOU HAVE CHEST PAIN
2.	2232000 -- LADDERMATE
3.	2179553 -- PENGUIN PLATFORM *LADDER*
4.	2165639 -- *LADDER* OF OPPORTUNITY
5.	2116442 -- EMOTIONAL *LADDER*
6.	2077176 -- CERTIFIED WERNER *LADDER* SALES EXPERT
7.	2077174 -- *LADDER* POWER
8.	2077173 -- *LADDER* POWER
9.	2049854 -- *LADDER* CLAW
10.	2041427 -- *LADDER* LASH
11.	2036151 -- FOX PRODUCTS, INC. THE FOX PLATFORM *LADDER*
12.	2033683 -- LADDERMASTER
13.	2004336 -- *LADDER* RAX
14.	1986061 -- *LADDER* WITCH
15.	1981343 -- LADDERTRACK
16.	1969782 -- POWR *LADDER*
17.	1961061 -- *LADDER* -LOC
18.	1949148 -- COOK & *LADDER*
19.	1939688 -- *LADDER* MULTIMEDIA
20.	1924491 -- STABILADDER
21.	1924423 -- TUFLADDER
22.	1882107 -- *LADDER* -MATE
23.	1878176 -- THE QUALITY *LADDER*
24.	1873329 -- THE SOCIAL *LADDER* IN OLD MONEY WE TRUST SOCIETY'S GAME OF CLASS STRUGGLE
25.	1858622 -- *LADDER* -CINCH

United States • Copyright Office
The Library *of* Congress

"To promote the Progress of Science and useful Arts, by
securing for limited Times to Authors and Inventors the
exclusive Right to their respective Writings and Discoveries"
(U.S. Constitution, Article 1 Section 8)

What's New

Current Developments
Vessel Hull Design
Study on Encryption
Legislation
Copyright regulations
Fee changes
Distance education
Press releases

About the Office

Register of Copyrights
Location and hours
Contact Information
Historical overview

Library of Congress

Visit the Library of Congress to
access information and
materials from its collections.

Library of Congress

U.S. Copyright Office
Library of Congress
101 Independence Ave. S.E.
Washington, D.C. 20559-6000

Comments: copyinfo@loc.gov
07/30/99

General Information

Copyright Basics

Registration Procedures

(FAQ) Frequently Asked Questions

CORDS (Copyright Office Electronic Registration,
Recordation & Deposit System)

Copyright Arbitration Royalty Panels

CARP and Licensing

Freedom of Information Act Requests

Fax on Demand

Mandatory Deposit

Copyright Records

Search Registrations/Documents

Service Provider Agents
NIE Lists

Announcements

Federal Register Notices

Press Releases

NewsNet List

Copyright Links

Related Resources
GPO Access (Federal Documents)

Publications

Application Forms

Information Circulars

Form Letters/Factsheets

Federal Regulations

Compendium II Copyright O

Office Reports

Legislation

Copyright Law

New/Pending Legislation

Register's Testimony

Digital Millennium Copyright
(version: pdf)

International

International Copyright

WIPO (World Intellectual Prope
Diplomatic Conference--
Preparatory Documents
New Treaties

URAA amends U.S. law

http://lcweb.loc.gov/copyright/

United States Copyright Office

Copyright

Basics

WHAT IS COPYRIGHT?

Copyright is a form of protection provided by the laws of the United States (title 17, U.S. Code) to the authors of "original works of authorship," including literary, dramatic, musical, artistic, and certain other intellectual works. This protection is available to both published and unpublished works. Section 106 of the 1976 Copyright Act generally gives the owner of copyright the exclusive right to do and to authorize others to do the following:

- *To reproduce* the work in copies or phonorecords;
- To prepare *derivative works* based upon the work;
- *To distribute copies or phonorecords* of the work to the public by sale or other transfer of ownership, or by rental, lease, or lending;
- *To perform the work publicly*, in the case of literary, musical, dramatic, and choreographic works, pantomimes, and motion pictures and other audiovisual works;
- *To display the work publicly,* in the case of literary, musical, dramatic, and choreographic works, pantomimes, and pictorial, graphic, or sculptural works, including the individual images of a motion picture or other audiovisual work; and
- In the case of **sound recordings, to perform the work publicly** by means of a **digital audio transmission.**

In addition, certain authors of works of visual art have the rights of attribution and integrity as described in section 106A of the 1976 Copyright Act. For further information, request Circular 40, "Copyright Registration for Works of the Visual Arts."

It is illegal for anyone to violate any of the rights provided by the copyright law to the owner of copyright. These rights, however, are not unlimited in scope. Sections 107 through 121 of the 1976 Copyright Act establish limitations on these rights. In some cases, these limitations are specified exemptions from copyright liability. One major limitation is the doctrine of "fair use," which is given a statutory basis in section 107 of the 1976 Copyright Act. In other instances, the limitation takes the form of a "compulsory license" under which certain limited uses of copyrighted works are permitted upon payment of specified royalties and compliance with statutory conditions. For further information about the limitations of any of these rights, consult the copyright law or write to the Copyright Office.

WHO CAN CLAIM COPYRIGHT?

Copyright protection subsists from the time the work is created in fixed form. The copyright in the work of authorship *immediately* becomes the property of the author who created the work. Only the author or those deriving their rights through the author can rightfully claim copyright.

In the case of works made for hire, the employer and not the employee is considered to be the author. Section 101 of the copyright law defines a "work made for hire" as:

(1) a work prepared by an employee within the scope of his or her employment; or

(2) a work specially ordered or commissioned for use as a contribution to a collective work, as a part of a motion picture or other audiovisual work, as a translation, as a supplementary work, as a compilation, as an instructional text, as a test, as answer material for a test, or as an atlas, if the parties expressly agree in a written instrument signed by them that the work shall be considered a work made for hire....

The authors of a joint work are co-owners of the copyright in the work, unless there is an agreement to the contrary.

Copyright in each separate contribution to a periodical or other collective work is distinct from copyright in the collective work as a whole and vests initially with the author of the contribution.

Two General Principles

• Mere ownership of a book, manuscript, painting, or any other copy or phonorecord does not give the possessor the copyright. The law provides that transfer of ownership of any material object that embodies a protected work does not of itself convey any rights in the copyright.

• Minors may claim copyright, but state laws may regulate the business dealings involving copyrights owned by minors. For information on relevant state laws, consult an attorney.

COPYRIGHT AND NATIONAL ORIGIN OF THE WORK

Copyright protection is available for all unpublished works, regardless of the nationality or domicile of the author.

Published works are eligible for copyright protection in the United States if *any* one of the following conditions is met:

• On the date of first publication, one or more of the authors is a national or domiciliary of the United States, or is a national, domiciliary, or sovereign authority of a treaty party,* or is a stateless person wherever that person may be domiciled; or

• The work is first published in the United States or in a foreign nation that, on the date of first publication, is a treaty party. For purposes of this condition, a work that is published in the United States or a treaty party within 30 days after publication in a foreign nation that is not a treaty party shall be considered to be first published in the United States or such treaty party, as the case may be; or

• The work is a sound recording that was first fixed in a treaty party; or

• The work is a pictorial, graphic, or sculptural work that is incorporated in a building or other structure, or an architectural work that is embodied in a building and the building or structure is located in the United States or a treaty party; or

• The work is first published by the United Nations or any of its specialized agencies, or by the Organization of American States; or

• The work is a foreign work that was in the public domain in the United States prior to 1996 and its copyright was restored under the Uruguay Round Agreements Act (URAA). Request Circular 38b, "Highlights of Copyright Amendments Contained in the Uruguay Round Agreements Act (URAA-GATT)," for further information.

• The work comes within the scope of a Presidential proclamation.

* A treaty party is a country or intergovernmental organization other than the United States that is a party to an international agreement.

WHAT WORKS ARE PROTECTED?

Copyright protects "original works of authorship" that are fixed in a tangible form of expression. The fixation need not be directly perceptible so long as it may be communicated 'ith the aid of a machine or device. Copyrightable works ıclude the following categories:

(1) literary works
(2) musical works, including any accompanying words
(3) dramatic works, including any accompanying music
(4) pantomimes and choreographic works
(5) pictorial, graphic, and sculptural works
(6) motion pictures and other audiovisual works
(7) sound recordings
(8) architectural works

These categories should be viewed broadly. For example, computer programs and most "compilations" may e registered as "literary works"; maps and architectural lans may be registered as "pictorial, graphic, and sculptural works."

VHAT IS NOT PROTECTED BY COPYRIGHT?

Several categories of material are generally not eligible ɔr federal copyright protection. These include among others:

Works that have **not** been fixed in a tangible form of expression, (for example, choreographic works that have not been notated or recorded, or improvisational speeches or performances that have not been written or recorded)

Titles, names, short phrases, and slogans; familiar symbols or designs; mere variations of typographic ornamentation, lettering, or coloring; mere listings of ingredients or contents

Ideas, procedures, methods, systems, processes, concepts, principles, discoveries, or devices, as distinguished from a description, explanation, or illustration

Works consisting **entirely** of information that is common property and containing no original authorship (for example: standard calendars, height and weight charts, tape measures and rulers, and lists or tables taken from public documents or other common sources)

IOW TO SECURE A COPYRIGHT

:opyright Secured Automatically Upon Creation

The way in which copyright protection is secured is frequently misunderstood. No publication or registration or ther action in the Copyright Office is required to secure opyright. (See following NOTE.) There are, however, certain definite advantages to registration. See "Copyright Registration" on page 7.

Copyright is secured **automatically** when the work is created, and a work is "created" when it is fixed in a copy or phonorecord for the first time. "Copies" are material objects from which a work can be read or visually perceived either directly or with the aid of a machine or device, such as books, manuscripts, sheet music, film, videotape, or microfilm. "Phonorecords" are material objects embodying fixations of sounds (excluding, by statutory definition, motion picture soundtracks), such as cassette tapes, CDs, or LPs. Thus, for example, a song (the "work") can be fixed in sheet music ("copies") or in phonograph disks ("phonorecords"), or both.

If a work is prepared over a period of time, the part of the work that is fixed on a particular date constitutes the created work as of that date.

PUBLICATION

Publication is no longer the key to obtaining federal copyright as it was under the Copyright Act of 1909. However, publication remains important to copyright owners.

The 1976 Copyright Act defines publication as follows:

"Publication" is the distribution of copies or phonorecords of a work to the public by sale or other transfer of ownership, or by rental, lease, or lending. The offering to distribute copies or phonorecords to a group of persons for purposes of further distribution, public performance, or public display constitutes publication. A public performance or display of a work does not of itself constitute publication.

NOTE: Before 1978, federal copyright was generally secured by the act of publication with notice of copyright, assuming compliance with all other relevant statutory conditions. U.S. works in the public domain on January 1, 1978, (for example, works published without satisfying all conditions for securing federal copyright under the Copyright Act of 1909) remain in the public domain under the 1976 Copyright Act.

Certain foreign works originally published without notice had their copyrights restored under the Uruguay Round Agreements Act (URAA). Request Circular 38b and see the "Notice of Copyright" section on page 4 of this publication for further information.

Federal copyright could also be secured before 1978 by the act of registration in the case of certain unpublished works and works eligible for ad interim copyright. The 1976 Copyright Act automatically extends to full term (section 304 sets the term) copyright for all works, including those subject to ad interim copyright if ad interim registration has been made on or before June 30, 1978.

A further discussion of the definition of "publication" can be found in the legislative history of the 1976 Copyright Act. The legislative reports define "to the public" as distribution to persons under no explicit or implicit restrictions with respect to disclosure of the contents. The reports state that the definition makes it clear that the sale of phonorecords constitutes publication of the underlying work, for example, the musical, dramatic, or literary work embodied in a phonorecord. The reports also state that it is clear that any form of dissemination in which the material object does not change hands, for example, performances or displays on television, is *not* a publication no matter how many people are exposed to the work. However, when copies or phonorecords are offered for sale or lease to a group of wholesalers, broadcasters, or motion picture theaters, publication does take place if the purpose is further distribution, public performance, or public display.

Publication is an important concept in the copyright law for several reasons:

- Works that are published in the United States are subject to mandatory deposit with the Library of Congress. See discussion on "Mandatory Deposit for Works Published in the United States" page 9.

- Publication of a work can affect the limitations on the exclusive rights of the copyright owner that are set forth in sections 107 through 121 of the law.

- The year of publication may determine the duration of copyright protection for anonymous and pseudonymous works (when the author's identity is not revealed in the records of the Copyright Office) and for works made for hire.

- Deposit requirements for registration of published works differ from those for registration of unpublished works. See discussion on "Registration Procedures" page 7.

- When a work is published, it may bear a notice of copyright to identify the year of publication and the name of the copyright owner and to inform the public that the work is protected by copyright. Copies of works published before March 1, 1989, *must* bear the notice or risk loss of copyright protection. See discussion on "Notice of Copyright" below.

NOTICE OF COPYRIGHT

The use of a copyright notice is no longer required under U.S. law, although it is often beneficial. Because prior law did contain such a requirement, however, the use of notice is still relevant to the copyright status of older works.

Notice was required under the 1976 Copyright Act. This requirement was eliminated when the United States adhered to the Berne Convention, effective March 1, 1989. Although works published without notice before that date could have entered the public domain in the United States, the Uruguay Round Agreements Act (URAA) restores copyright in certain foreign works originally published without notice. For further information about copyright amendments in the URAA, request Circular 38b.

The Copyright Office does not take a position on whether copies of works first published with notice before March 1, 1989, which are distributed on or after March 1, 1989, must bear the copyright notice.

Use of the notice may be important because it informs the public that the work is protected by copyright, identifies the copyright owner, and shows the year of first publication. Furthermore, in the event that a work is infringed, if a proper notice of copyright appears on the published copy or copies to which a defendant in a copyright infringement suit had access, then no weight shall be given to such a defendant's interposition of a defense based on innocent infringement in mitigation of actual or statutory damages, except as provided in section 504(c)(2) of the copyright law. Innocent infringement occurs when the infringer did not realize that the work was protected.

The use of the copyright notice is the responsibility of the copyright owner and does not require advance permission from, or registration with, the Copyright Office.

Form of Notice for Visually Perceptible Copies

The notice for visually perceptible copies should contain all the following three elements:

1. *The symbol* © (the letter C in a circle), or the word "Copyright," or the abbreviation "Copr."; and

2. *The year of first publication* of the work. In the case of compilations or derivative works incorporating previously published material, the year date of first publication of the compilation or derivative work is sufficient. The year date may be omitted where a pictorial, graphic, or sculptural work, with accompanying textual matter, if any, is reproduced in or on greeting cards, postcards, stationery, jewelry, dolls, toys, or any useful article; and

3. *The name of the owner of copyright* in the work, or an abbreviation by which the name can be recognized, or a generally known alternative designation of the owner.

Example: © 1999 John Doe

The "C in a circle" notice is used only on "visually perceptible copies." Certain kinds of works—for example, musical, dramatic, and literary works—may be fixed not in "copies" but by means of sound in an audio recording. Since audio recordings such as audio tapes and phonograph disks are "phonorecords" and not "copies," the "C in a circle" notice is not used to indicate protection of the underlying musical, dramatic, or literary work that is recorded.

Form of Notice for Phonorecords of Sound Recordings*

The notice for phonorecords embodying a sound recording should contain all the following three elements:

1. *The symbol* ℗ (the letter P in a circle); and

2. *The year of first publication* of the sound recording; and

3. *The name of the owner of copyright* in the sound recording, or an abbreviation by which the name can be recognized, or a generally known alternative designation of the owner. If the producer of the sound recording is named on the phonorecord label or container and if no other name appears in conjunction with the notice, the producer's name shall be considered a part of the notice.

Example: ℗ 1999 A.B.C. Records, Inc.

NOTE: Since questions may arise from the use of variant forms of the notice, you may wish to seek legal advice before using any form of the notice other than those given here.

Position of Notice

The copyright notice should be affixed to copies or phonorecords in such a way as to "give reasonable notice of the claim of copyright." The three elements of the notice should ordinarily appear together on the copies or phonorecords or on the phonorecord label or container. The Copyright Office has issued regulations concerning the form and position of the copyright notice in the *Code of Federal Regulations* (37 CFR Part 201.20). For more information, request Circular 3, "Copyright Notice."

Publications Incorporating U.S. Government Works

Works by the U.S. Government are not eligible for U.S. copyright protection. For works published on and after March 1, 1989, the previous notice requirement for works consisting primarily of one or more U.S. Government works has been eliminated. However, use of a notice on such a

work will defeat a claim of innocent infringement as previously described *provided* the notice also includes a statement that identifies either those portions of the work in which copyright is claimed or those portions that constitute U.S. Government material.

Example: © 1999 Jane Brown. Copyright claimed in Chapters 7-10, exclusive of U.S. Government maps

Copies of works published before March 1, 1989, that consist primarily of one or more works of the U.S. Government *should* have a notice and the identifying statement.

Unpublished Works

The author or copyright owner may wish to place a copyright notice on any unpublished copies or phonorecords that leave his or her control.

Example: Unpublished work © 1999 Jane Doe

Omission of Notice and Errors in Notice

The 1976 Copyright Act attempted to ameliorate the strict consequences of failure to include notice under prior law. It contained provisions that set out specific corrective steps to cure omissions or certain errors in notice. Under these provisions, an applicant had 5 years after publication to cure omission of notice or certain errors. Although these provisions are technically still in the law, their impact has been limited by the amendment making notice optional for all works published on and after March 1, 1989. For further information, request Circular 3.

HOW LONG COPYRIGHT PROTECTION ENDURES

Works Originally Created On or After January 1, 1978

A work that is created (fixed in tangible form for the first time) on or after January 1, 1978, is automatically protected from the moment of its creation and is ordinarily given a term enduring for the author's life plus an additional 70 years after the author's death. In the case of "a joint work prepared by two or more authors who did not work for hire," the term lasts for 70 years after the last surviving author's death. For works made for hire, and for anonymous and pseudonymous works (unless the author's identity is revealed in Copyright Office records), the duration of copyright will be 95 years from publication or 120 years from creation, whichever is shorter.

Works Originally Created Before January 1, 1978, But Not Published or Registered by That Date

These works have been automatically brought under the statute and are now given federal copyright protection. The duration of copyright in these works will generally be computed in the same way as for works created on or after Janu-

---

* Sound recordings are defined in the law as "works that result from the fixation of a series of musical, spoken, or other sounds, but not including the sounds accompanying a motion picture or other audiovisual work." Common examples include recordings of music, drama, or lectures. A sound recording is not the same as a phonorecord. A phonorecord is the physical object in which works of authorship are embodied. The word "phonorecord" includes cassette tapes, CDs, LPs, 45 r.p.m. disks, as well as other formats.

ary 1, 1978: the life-plus-70 or 95/120-year terms will apply to them as well. The law provides that in no case will the term of copyright for works in this category expire before December 31, 2002, and for works published on or before December 31, 2002, the term of copyright will not expire before December 31, 2047.

Works Originally Created and Published or Registered Before January 1, 1978

Under the law in effect before 1978, copyright was secured either on the date a work was published with a copyright notice or on the date of registration if the work was registered in unpublished form. In either case, the copyright endured for a first term of 28 years from the date it was secured. During the last (28th) year of the first term, the copyright was eligible for renewal. The Copyright Act of 1976 extended the renewal term from 28 to 47 years for copyrights that were subsisting on January 1, 1978, or for pre-1978 copyrights restored under the Uruguay Round Agreements Act (URAA), making these works eligible for a total term of protection of 75 years. Public Law 105-298, enacted on October 27, 1998, further extended the renewal term of copyrights still subsisting on that date by an additional 20 years, providing for a renewal term of 67 years and a total term of protection of 95 years.

Public Law 102-307, enacted on June 26, 1992, amended the 1976 Copyright Act to provide for automatic renewal of the term of copyrights secured between January 1, 1964, and December 31, 1977. Although the renewal term is automatically provided, the Copyright Office does not issue a renewal certificate for these works unless a renewal application and fee are received and registered in the Copyright Office.

Public Law 102-307 makes renewal registration optional. Thus, filing for renewal registration is no longer required in order to extend the original 28-year copyright term to the full 95 years. However, some benefits accrue from making a renewal registration during the 28th year of the original term.

For more detailed information on renewal of copyright and the copyright term, request Circular 15, "Renewal of Copyright"; Circular 15a, "Duration of Copyright"; and Circular 15t, "Extension of Copyright Terms."

TRANSFER OF COPYRIGHT

Any or all of the copyright owner's exclusive rights or any subdivision of those rights may be transferred, but the transfer of **exclusive** rights is not valid unless that transfer is in writing and signed by the owner of the rights conveyed or such owner's duly authorized agent. Transfer of a right on a nonexclusive basis does not require a written agreement.

A copyright may also be conveyed by operation of law and may be bequeathed by will or pass as personal property by the applicable laws of intestate succession.

Copyright is a personal property right, and it is subject to the various state laws and regulations that govern the ownership, inheritance, or transfer of personal property as well as terms of contracts or conduct of business. For information about relevant state laws, consult an attorney.

Transfers of copyright are normally made by contract. The Copyright Office does not have any forms for such transfers. The law does provide for the recordation in the Copyright Office of transfers of copyright ownership. Although recordation is not required to make a valid transfer between the parties, it does provide certain legal advantages and may be required to validate the transfer as against third parties. For information on recordation of transfers and other documents related to copyright, request Circular 12, "Recordation of Transfers and Other Documents."

Termination of Transfers

Under the previous law, the copyright in a work reverted to the author, if living, or if the author was not living, to other specified beneficiaries, provided a renewal claim was registered in the 28th year of the original term.* The present law drops the renewal feature except for works already in their first term of statutory protection when the present law took effect. Instead, the present law permits termination of a grant of rights after 35 years under certain conditions by serving written notice on the transferee within specified time limits.

For works already under statutory copyright protection before 1978, the present law provides a similar right of termination covering the newly added years that extended the former maximum term of the copyright from 56 to 95 years. For further information, request Circulars 15a and 15t.

INTERNATIONAL COPYRIGHT PROTECTION

There is no such thing as an "international copyright" that will automatically protect an author's writings throughout the entire world. Protection against unauthorized use in a particular country depends, basically, on the national laws of that country. However, most countries do offer protection to foreign works under certain conditions, and these conditions have been greatly simplified by international copyright treaties and conventions. For further information and

---

*The copyright in works eligible for renewal on or after June 26, 1992, will vest in the name of the renewal claimant on the effective date of any renewal registration made during the 28th year of the original term. Otherwise, the renewal copyright will vest in the party entitled to claim renewal as of December 31st of the 28th year.

a list of countries that maintain copyright relations with the United States, request Circular 38a, "International Copyright Relations of the United States."

COPYRIGHT REGISTRATION

In general, copyright registration is a legal formality intended to make a public record of the basic facts of a particular copyright. However, registration is not a condition of copyright protection. Even though registration is not a requirement for protection, the copyright law provides several inducements or advantages to encourage copyright owners to make registration. Among these advantages are the following:

- Registration establishes a public record of the copyright claim.

- Before an infringement suit may be filed in court, registration is necessary for works of U.S. origin.

- If made before or within 5 years of publication, registration will establish prima facie evidence in court of the validity of the copyright and of the facts stated in the certificate.

- If registration is made within 3 months after publication of the work or prior to an infringement of the work, statutory damages and attorney's fees will be available to the copyright owner in court actions. Otherwise, only an award of actual damages and profits is available to the copyright owner.

- Registration allows the owner of the copyright to record the registration with the U.S. Customs Service for protection against the importation of infringing copies. For additional information, request Publication No. 563 from: Commissioner of Customs, ATTN: IPR Branch, U.S. Customs Service, 1300 Pennsylvania Avenue, N.W., Washington, D.C. 20229.

Registration may be made at any time within the life of the copyright. Unlike the law before 1978, when a work has been registered in unpublished form, it is not necessary to make another registration when the work becomes published, although the copyright owner may register the published edition, if desired.

REGISTRATION PROCEDURES

Original Registration
To register a work, send the following three elements *in the same envelope or package* to:

Library of Congress
Copyright Office
Register of Copyrights
101 Independence Avenue, S.E.
Washington, D.C. 20559-6000

1. A properly completed application form.
2. A nonrefundable filing fee of $30 (effective through June 30, 2002) for each application.

NOTE: For current information on fees, please write the Copyright Office, check the Copyright Office Website at www.loc.gov/copyright, or call (202) 707-3000.

3. A nonreturnable deposit of the work being registered. The deposit requirements vary in particular situations. The *general* requirements follow. Also note the information under "Special Deposit Requirements" on page 8.

- If the work is unpublished, one complete copy or phonorecord.

- If the work was first published in the United States on or after January 1, 1978, two complete copies or phonorecords of the best edition.

- If the work was first published in the United States before January 1, 1978, two complete copies or phonorecords of the work as first published.

- If the work was first published outside the United States, one complete copy or phonorecord of the work as first published.

- If sending multiple works, all applications, deposits, and fees should be sent in the same package. If possible, applications should be attached to the appropriate deposit. Whenever possible, number each package (e.g., 1 of 3, 2 of 4) to facilitate processing.

What Happens if the Three Elements Are Not Received Together
Applications and fees received without appropriate copies, phonorecords, or identifying material will **not** be processed and ordinarily will be returned. Unpublished deposits without applications or fees ordinarily will be returned, also. In most cases, published deposits received without applications and fees can be immediately transferred to the collections of the Library of Congress. This practice is in accordance with section 408 of the law, which provides that the published deposit required for the collections of the Library of Congress may be used for registration only if the deposit is "accompanied by the prescribed application and fee...."

---

*For the fee structure for application Form SE/GROUP, Form GATT, Form GATT/GRP, and Form G/DN, see the instructions on these forms.

After the deposit is received and transferred to another service unit of the Library for its collections or other disposition, it is no longer available to the Copyright Office. If you wish to register the work, you must deposit additional copies or phonorecords with your application and fee.

Renewal Registration
To register a renewal, send:

1. A properly completed application Form RE and
2. A nonrefundable filing fee of $45 without Addendum; $60 with Addendum for each application. Filing fees are effective through June 30, 2002.

> **NOTE: Complete the application form using black ink pen or type.** You may photocopy blank application forms. **However,** photocopied forms submitted to the Copyright Office must be clear, legible, on a good grade of 8½-inch by 11-inch white paper suitable for automatic feeding through a photocopier. The forms should be printed, preferably in black ink, head-to-head so that when you turn the sheet over, the top of page 2 is directly behind the top of page 1. **Forms not meeting these requirements may be returned resulting in delayed registration.**

Special Deposit Requirements
Special deposit requirements exist for many types of works. The following are prominent examples of exceptions to the general deposit requirements:

- If the work is a motion picture, the deposit requirement is one complete copy of the unpublished or published motion picture *and* a separate written description of its contents, such as a continuity, press book, or synopsis.

- If the work is a literary, dramatic, or musical work *published only in a phonorecord,* the deposit requirement is one complete phonorecord.

- If the work is an unpublished or published computer program, the deposit requirement is one visually perceptible copy in source code of the *first 25 and last 25 pages* of the program. For a program of fewer than 50 pages, the deposit is a copy of the entire program. For more information on computer program registration, including deposits for revised programs and provisions for trade secrets, request Circular 61, "Copyright Registration for Computer Programs."

- If the work is in a CD-ROM format, the deposit requirement is one complete copy of the material, that is, the CD-ROM, the operating software, and any manual(s) accompanying it. If registration is sought for the computer program on the CD-ROM, the deposit should also include

a printout of the first 25 and last 25 pages of source cod for the program.

In the case of works reproduced in three-dimension; copies, identifying material such as photographs or drawing is ordinarily required. Other examples of special deposit re quirements (but by no means an exhaustive list) includ many works of the visual arts such as greeting cards, toys fabrics, oversized materials (request Circular 40a, "Depos Requirements for Registration of Claims to Copyright in V sual Arts Material"); video games and other machine-read able audiovisual works (request Circular 61); automate databases (request Circular 65, "Copyright Registration fc Automated Databases"); and contributions to collectiv works. For information about deposit requirements for grou registration of serials, request Circular 62, "Copyright Reg istration for Serials on Form SE."

If you are unsure of the deposit requirement for you work, write or call the Copyright Office and describe th work you wish to register.

Unpublished Collections
Under the following conditions, a work may be registere in unpublished form as a "collection," with one applicatio form and one fee:

- The elements of the collection are assembled in an or derly form;
- The combined elements bear a single title identifying th collection as a whole;
- The copyright claimant in all the elements and in the col lection as a whole is the same; and
- All the elements are by the same author, or, if they are b different authors, at least one of the authors has contrib uted copyrightable authorship to each element.

> **NOTE: A Library of Congress Catalog Card Number** is different from a copyright registration number. The Cataloging in Publication (CIP) Division of the Library of Congress is responsible for assigning LC Catalog Card Numbers and is operationally separate from the Copyright Office. A book may be registered in or deposited with the Copyright Office but not necessarily cataloged and added to the Library's collections. For information about obtaining an LC Catalog Card Number, see the following homepage: www.lcweb2.loc.gov/pcn. For information on International Standard Book Numbering (ISBN), write to: ISBN, R.R. Bowker, 121 Chanlon Road, New Providence, NJ 07974. Call (908) 665-6770. For further information and to apply online, see www.bowker.com/standards/. For information on International Standard Serial Numbering (ISSN), write to: Library of Congress, National Serials Data Program, Serial Record Division, Washington, D.C. 20540-4160. Call (202) 707-6452. Or obtain information via the World Wide Web at *www.loc.gov/issn/*.

An unpublished collection is not indexed under the individual titles of the contents but under the title of the collection.

EFFECTIVE DATE OF REGISTRATION

A copyright registration is effective on the date the Copyright Office receives all the required elements in acceptable form, regardless of how long it then takes to process the application and mail the certificate of registration. The time the Copyright Office requires to process an application varies, depending on the amount of material the Office is receiving.

If you apply for copyright registration, you will not receive an acknowledgment that your application has been received the Office receives more than 600,000 applications annually), but you can expect:

› A letter or a telephone call from a Copyright Office staff member if further information is needed or

› A certificate of registration indicating that the work has been registered, or if the application cannot be accepted, a letter explaining why it has been rejected.

Requests to have certificates available for pickup in the Public Information Office or to have certificates sent by Federal Express or another mail service cannot be honored.

If you want to know the date that the Copyright Office receives your material, send it by registered or certified mail and request a return receipt.

CORRECTIONS AND AMPLIFICATIONS OF EXISTING REGISTRATIONS

To correct an error in a copyright registration or to amplify the information given in a registration, file a supplementary registration form—Form CA—(filing fee of $65 effective through June 30, 2002) with the Copyright Office. The information in a supplementary registration augments but does not supersede that contained in the earlier registration. Note also that a supplementary registration is not a substitute for an original registration, for a renewal registration, or for recording a transfer of ownership. For further information about supplementary registration, request Circular 8, "Supplementary Copyright Registration."

MANDATORY DEPOSIT FOR WORKS PUBLISHED IN THE UNITED STATES

Although a copyright registration is not required, the Copyright Act establishes a mandatory deposit requirement for works published in the United States. See the definition of "publication" on page 3. In general, the owner of copyright or the owner of the exclusive right of publication in the work has a legal obligation to deposit in the Copyright Office, within 3 months of publication in the United States, two copies (or in the case of sound recordings, two phonorecords) for the use of the Library of Congress. Failure to make the deposit can result in fines and other penalties but does not affect copyright protection.

Certain categories of works are *exempt entirely* from the mandatory deposit requirements, and the obligation is reduced for certain other categories. For further information about mandatory deposit, request Circular 7d, "Mandatory Deposit of Copies or Phonorecords for the Library of Congress."

USE OF MANDATORY DEPOSIT TO SATISFY REGISTRATION REQUIREMENTS

For works published in the United States, the copyright law contains a provision under which a single deposit can be made to satisfy both the deposit requirements for the Library and the registration requirements. In order to have this dual effect, the copies or phonorecords must be accompanied by the prescribed application form and filing fee.

WHO MAY FILE AN APPLICATION FORM?

The following persons are legally entitled to submit an application form:

● **The author.** This is either the person who actually created the work or, if the work was made for hire, the employer or other person for whom the work was prepared.

● **The copyright claimant.** The copyright claimant is defined in Copyright Office regulations as either the author of the work or a person or organization that has obtained ownership of all the rights under the copyright initially belonging to the author. This category includes a person or organization who has obtained by contract the right to claim legal title to the copyright in an application for copyright registration.

- **The owner of exclusive right(s).** Under the law, any of the exclusive rights that make up a copyright and any subdivision of them can be transferred and owned separately, even though the transfer may be limited in time or place of effect. The term "copyright owner" with respect to any one of the exclusive rights contained in a copyright refers to the owner of that particular right. Any owner of an exclusive right may apply for registration of a claim in the work.

- **The duly authorized agent** of such author, other copyright claimant, or owner of exclusive right(s). Any person authorized to act on behalf of the author, other copyright claimant, or owner of exclusive rights may apply for registration.

There is no requirement that applications be prepared or filed by an attorney.

APPLICATION FORMS

For Original Registration

Form PA: for published and unpublished works of the performing arts (musical and dramatic works, pantomimes and choreographic works, motion pictures and other audiovisual works)

Form SE: for serials, works issued or intended to be issued in successive parts bearing numerical or chronological designations and intended to be continued indefinitely (periodicals, newspapers, magazines, newsletters, annuals, journals, etc.)

Form SR: for published and unpublished sound recordings

Form TX: for published and unpublished nondramatic literary works

Form VA: for published and unpublished works of the visual arts (pictorial, graphic, and sculptural works, including architectural works)

Form G/DN: a specialized form to register a complete month's issues of a daily newspaper when certain conditions are met

Short Form/SE and Form SE/GROUP: specialized SE forms for use when certain requirements are met

Short Forms TX, PA, and VA: short versions of applications for original registration. For further information about using the short forms, request publication SL-7.

Form GATT and Form GATT/GRP: specialized forms to register a claim in a work or group of related works in which U.S. copyright was restored under the 1994 Uruguay Round Agreements Act (URAA). For further information, request Circular 38b.

For Renewal Registration

Form RE: for claims to renew copyright in works copyrighted under the law in effect through December 31, 1977 (1909 Copyright Act)

For Corrections and Amplifications

Form CA: for supplementary registration to correct or amplify information given in the Copyright Office record of an earlier registration

For a Group of Contributions to Periodicals

Form GR/CP: an adjunct application to be used for registration of a group of contributions to periodicals in addition to an application Form TX, PA, or VA

How to Obtain Application Forms

See "For Further Information" on page 11.

You must have Adobe Acrobat Reader® installed on your computer to view and print the forms accessed on the Internet. Adobe Acrobat Reader may be downloaded free from Adobe Systems Incorporated through links from the same Internet site from which the forms are available.

Print forms head to head (top of page 2 is directly behind the top of page 1) on a single piece of good quality, 8½-inch by 11-inch white paper. To achieve the best quality copies of the application forms, use a laser printer.

FEES

All remittances should be in the form of drafts, that is, checks, money orders, or bank drafts, payable to: **Register of Copyrights.** Do not send cash. Drafts must be redeemable without service or exchange fee through a U. S. institution, must be payable in U.S. dollars, and must be imprinted with American Banking Association routing numbers. International Money Orders and Postal Money Orders that are negotiable only at a post office are not acceptable.

If a check received in payment of the filing fee is returned to the Copyright Office as uncollectible, the Copyright Office will cancel the registration and will notify the remitter.

The filing fee for processing an original, supplementary, or renewal claim is nonrefundable, whether or not copyright registration is ultimately made.

Do not send cash. The Copyright Office cannot assume any responsibility for the loss of currency sent in payment of copyright fees. For further information, request Circular 4, "Copyright Fees."

> **NOTE:** Registration filing fees and search fees are effective through June 30, 2002. For information on the fee changes, please write the Copyright Office, check the Copyright Office Website at www.loc.gov/copyright, or call (202) 707-3000.

SEARCH OF COPYRIGHT OFFICE RECORDS

The records of the Copyright Office are open for inspection and searching by the public. Moreover, on request, the Copyright Office will search its records for you at the statutory hourly rate of $65 (effective through June 30, 2002) for each hour or fraction of an hour. (See NOTE above.) For information on searching the Office records concerning the copyright status or ownership of a work, request Circular 22, "How to Investigate the Copyright Status of a Work," and Circular 23, "The Copyright Card Catalog and the Online Files of the Copyright Office."

Copyright Office records in machine-readable form cataloged from January 1, 1978, to the present, including registration and renewal information and recorded documents, are now available for searching on the Internet. These files may be examined through LOCIS (Library of Congress Information System). Access to LOCIS requires Telnet support. If your online service provider supports Telnet, you can connect to LOCIS through the World Wide Web or directly by using Telnet.

World Wide Web: www.loc.gov/copyright/rb.html

Telnet: locis.loc.gov

If your online service provider does not support Telnet, address your concerns directly to the provider.

FOR FURTHER INFORMATION

Information via the Internet: Frequently requested circulars, announcements, regulations, other related materials, and all copyright application forms are available via the Internet. You may access these via the Copyright Office homepage at www.loc.gov/copyright.

Information by fax: Circulars and other information (but not application forms) are available by Fax-on-Demand at (202)707-2600.

Information by telephone: For general information about copyright, call the Copyright Public Information Office at (202)707-3000. The TTY number is (202)707-6737. Information specialists are on duty from 8:30 a.m. to 5:00 p.m., eastern time, Monday through Friday, except federal holidays. Recorded information is available 24 hours a day. Or, if you know which application forms and circulars you want, request them from the Forms and Publications Hotline at (202)707-9100 24 hours a day. Leave a recorded message.

Information by regular mail: Write to:

> Library of Congress
> Copyright Office
> Publications Section, LM-455
> 101 Independence Avenue, S.E.
> Washington, D.C. 20559-6000

For a list of other material published by the Copyright Office, request Circular 2, "Publications on Copyright."

> The Copyright Office provides a free electronic mailing list, *NewsNet*, that issues periodic email messages on the subject of copyright. The messages alert subscribers to hearings, deadlines for comments, new and proposed regulations, new publications, and other copyright-related subjects of interest. *NewsNet* is not an interactive discussion group. To subscribe, send a message to LISTSERV@RS8.LOC.GOV. In the body of the message say: SUBSCRIBE USCOPYRIGHT. You will receive a standard welcoming message indicating that your subscription to *NewsNet* has been accepted.

The Copyright Public Information Office is open to the public 8:30 a.m. to 5:00 p.m. Monday through Friday, eastern time, except federal holidays. The office is located in the Library of Congress, James Madison Memorial Building, Room 401, at 101 Independence Avenue, S.E., Washington, D.C., near the Capitol South Metro stop. Information specialists are available to answer questions, provide circulars, and accept applications for registration. Access for disabled individuals is at the front door on Independence Avenue, S.E.

The Copyright Office is not permitted to give legal advice. If information or guidance is needed on matters such as disputes over the ownership of a copyright, suits against possible infringers, the procedure for getting a work published, or the method of obtaining royalty payments, it may be necessary to consult an attorney.

U.S. Copyright Office   **Library of Congress**

Home · Forms · Records · Registration · Law · Comments · Library of Congress

QUESTIONS FREQUENTLY ASKED
IN THE COPYRIGHT OFFICE PUBLIC INFORMATION SECTION

The answers to the following frequently asked questions should be read as introductory rather than as definitive. Please consult the references cited in the answers. References noted by colored links are available in full text online. Other cited materials are available by telephoning the U.S. Copyright Office, Public Information Office, Monday through Friday (except legal holidays) between 8:30 a.m. - 5:00 p.m. eastern time. (202) 707-3000. TTY (202) 707-6737.

1. What does copyright protect?
2. When is my work protected?
3. What is your **telephone number**?
4. What is your **mailing address**?
5. What are your **visiting address and hours** of operation?
6. Where can I get **application forms**?
7. When will **I get my certificate**?
8. Can you **provide me with copies** of my application and my work?
9. How can I obtain **copies of someone else's work** and/or registration certificate?
10. **I lost my certificate**; can I get a new one?
11. Do you have a **list of songs** or movies in the **public domain**?
12. What is **mandatory deposit**?
13. Do **I have to register** with your office to be protected?
14. Why **should I register my work** if copyright protection is automatic?
15. Are you the **only place I can go to register** a copyright?
16. **How do I register** my copyright?
17. **How long** does the registration process take?
18. What is the registration **fee**?
19. Can I make **copies of the application** form?
20. What is a **deposit**?
21. How can I **know if you received** my application for registration?
22. Can I find out **what is happening** with my registration?
23. Do I have to send in my work? Do I get it back?
24. May I register more than one work on the same application? Where do I list the titles?
25. What is the **difference between** form PA and form SR?
26. Do I have to **renew** my copyright?
27. Can I submit my manuscript on a **computer disk**?
28. Can I submit a **CD-ROM** of my work?
29. How do I protect my **recipe**?
30. Does copyright now protect **architecture**?
31. Can I register a diary I found in my grandmother's attic?
32. Do you have special **mailing** requirements?
33. Can **foreigners register** their works in the U.S.?
34. Who is an **author**?
35. What is a **work made for hire**?
36. Can a **minor** claim copyright?
37. Do I have to use my real name on the form? Can I use a **stage name** or a **pen name**?
38. What is **publication**?
39. Does my work have to be **published** to be protected?
40. How do I get my work **published**?
41. Are copyrights **transferable**?
42. Do you have any **forms for transfer** of copyrights?
43. Can I copyright the **name** of my band?
44. How do I copyright a **name, title, slogan, or logo**?
45. How do I protect my **idea**?
46. How long does **copyright last**?

http://www.loc.gov/copyright/faq.html

47. How much of someone else's work can I use **without getting permission**?
48. How much do I have to **change in my own work** to make a new claim of copyright?
49. How much do I have to **change in order to claim copyright** in someone else's work?
50. How do I get my work **into the Library of Congress**?
51. What is a **Library of Congress number**?
52. What is an **ISBN** number?
53. What is a **copyright notice**? How do I put a copyright notice on my work? ·
54. How do I collect **royalties**?
55. Somebody **infringed** my copyright: What can I do?
56. Is my copyright good in **other countries**?
57. How do I get on your mailing list or e-mail list?
58. How do I protect **my sighting of Elvis**?
59. How do I **get permission** to use somebody else's work?
60. Could I be **sued** for using somebody else's work? How about **quotes or samples**?

---

1. **What does copyright protect?**

Copyright, a form of intellectual property law, protects original works of authorship including literary, dramatic, musical, and artistic works such as poetry, novels, movies, songs, computer software and architecture. Copyright does not protect facts, ideas, systems, or methods of operation, although it may protect the way these things are expressed. See Circular 1, section *What Works Are Protected.*

2. **When is my work protected?**

Your work is under copyright protection the moment it is created and fixed in a tangible form so that it is perceptible either directly or with the aid of a machine or device.

3. **What is your telephone number?**

The Public Information Office telephone number is (202) 707-3000. To order application forms, the number is (202) 707-9100. TTY is (202) 707-6737.

4. **What is your mailing address?**

Our mailing address is Copyright Office, Library of Congress, 101 Independence Avenue, S.E.,Washington, D.C. 20559-6000.

5. **What are your visiting address and hours of operation?**

The Copyright Office is located at 101 Independence Avenue, S.E., Washington, D.C., in the James Madison Memorial Building, Room LM-401, of the Library of Congress. Hours of service are 8:30 a.m. to 5:00 p.m. eastern time, Monday through Friday, except Federal holidays. The nearest Metro stop is Capitol South.

6. **Where can I get application forms?**

You may get forms from the U.S. Copyright Office in person, by mailing in a request, or by calling our 24-hours-per-day forms hotline: (202) 707-9100. Some public libraries may carry our forms but we do not maintain a list of those libraries. Forms may also be downloaded from our website.

7. **When will I get my certificate?**

The time the Copyright Office requires to process an application varies, depending on the amount of material the Office is receiving. You may generally expect a certificate of registration within approximately 8 months of submission .

8. **Can you provide me with copies of my application and my work?**

Contact the Certifications and Documents Section of the Copyright Office (202) 707-6787 or see Circular 6 for details.

9. **How can I obtain copies of someone else's work and/or registration certificate?**

The Copyright Office will not honor a request for a copy of someone else's work without written authorization from the owner or from his or her designated agent if that work is still under copyright protection, unless the work is involved in litigation. Written permission from the copyright owner or a litigation statement is required before copies can be made available. A certificate of registration for any registered work can be obtained for a fee of $25. Circular 6 provides additional information.

10. **I lost my certificate: Can I get a new one?**

Yes, we can produce additional certificates for a fee of $25. See Circular 6 for details on how to make such a request.

11. **Do you have a list of songs or movies in the public domain?**

No, we neither compile nor maintain such a list. A search of our records, however, may reveal whether a particular work has fallen into the public domain. We will conduct a search of our records by the title of a work, an author's name, or a claimant's name. The search fee is $65 per hour. You may also search the records in person without paying a fee.

12. **What is mandatory deposit?**

Copies of all works under copyright protection that have been published in the United States are required to be deposited with the Copyright Office within three months of the date of first publication. See Circular 7d and the Deposit Regulation 96 202.19.

13. **Do I have to register with your office to be protected?**

No. In general, registration is voluntary. Copyright exists from the moment the work is created. You will have to register, however, if you wish to bring a lawsuit for infringement of a U.S. work. See Circular 1, section *Copyright Registration.*

14. **Why should I register my work if copyright protection is automatic?**

Registration is recommended for a number of reasons. Many choose to register their works because they wish to have the facts of their copyright on the public record and have a certificate of registration. Registered works may be eligible for statutory damages and attorney's fees in successful litigation. Finally, if registration occurs within five years of publication, it is considered prima facie evidence in a court of law. See Circular 1, section *Copyright Registration* and Circular 38b on non-U.S. works.

15. **Are you the only place I can go to register a copyright?**

Although copyright application forms may be available in public libraries and some reference books, the U.S. Copyright Office is the only office that can accept applications and issue registrations.

16. **How do I register my copyright?**

To register a work, you need to submit a completed application form, a non-refundable filing fee of $30, and a non-returnable copy or copies of the work to be registered. See Circular 1, section *Registration Procedures.*

17. **How long does the registration process take?**

The time the Copyright Office requires to process an application varies, depending on the amount of material the Office is receiving. You may generally expect a certificate of registration within approximately 8 months of submission .

18. **What is the registration fee?**

The current filing fee is $30 per application. Generally, each work requires a separate application. See Circular 4.

19. **Can I make copies of the application form?**

Yes, you can make copies of copyright forms if they meet the following criteria: photocopied back to back and head to head on a single sheet of 8 1/2 by 11 inch white paper. In other words, your copy must look just like the original.

20. What is a deposit?

A deposit is usually one copy (if unpublished) or two copies (if published) of the work to be registered for copyright. In certain cases such as works of the visual arts, identifying material such as a photograph may be used instead. See Circular 40a. The deposit is sent with the application and fee and becomes the property of the Library of Congress.

21. How can I know if you received my application for registration?

If you want to know when the Copyright Office receives your material, you should send it by registered or certified mail and request a return receipt from the post office. Allow at least five weeks for the return of your receipt.

22. Can I find out what is happening with my registration?

Copyright registration is effective on the day we receive the appropriate form, copy or copies of the work, and the $30 filing fee. The time the Copyright Office requires to process an application varies, depending on the amount of material the Office is receiving. You may generally expect a certificate of registration within approximately 8 months of submission . In the event we need further information, a letter or telephone call from our office, will be received during this time period. We are not able to provide status information for submissions that were received less than eight months ago. If it is imperative that you have this information sooner, you may pay the appropriate fees and request that the Certifications and Documents Section conduct an in-process search. The current in-process search fee is $65 per hour.

23. Do I have to send in my work? Do I get it back?

Yes, you must send the required copy or copies of the work to be registered. These copies will not be returned. Upon their deposit in the Copyright Office, under sections 407 and 408 of the Copyright law, all copies, phonorecords, and identifying material, including those deposited in connection with claims that have been refused registration, are the property of the United States Government.

24. May I register more than one work on the same application? Where do I list the titles?

You may register unpublished works as a collection on one application with one title for the entire collection if certain conditions are met. It is not necessary to list the individual titles in your collection, although you may do so by completing a Continuation Sheet. Published works may only be registered as a collection if they were actually first published as a collection and if other requirements have been met. See Circular 1, section *Registration Procedures.*

25. What is the difference between form PA and form SR?

These forms are for registering two different types of copyrightable subject matter that may be embodied in a recording. Form PA is used for the registration of music and/or lyrics (as well as other works of the performing arts), even if your song is on a cassette. Form SR is used for registering the performance and production of a particular recording of sounds. See Circular 50 and Circular 56a.

26. Do I have to renew my copyright?

No. Works created on or after January 1, 1978, are not subject to renewal registration (see Circular 15). As to works published or registered prior to January 1, 1978, renewal registration is optional after 28 years but does provide certain legal advantages. For information on how to file a renewal application as well as the legal benefit for doing so, see Circular 15 and Circular 15a.

27. Can I submit my manuscript on a computer disk?

No. There are many different software formats and the Copyright Office does not have the equipment to accommodate all of them. Therefore, the Copyright Office still generally requires a printed copy or audio recording of the work for deposit.

28. Can I submit a CD-ROM of my work?

Yes, you may. The deposit requirement consists of the best edition of the CD-ROM package of any work, including the accompanying operating software, instruction manual and a printed version, if included in the package. See Circular 55.

29. How do I protect my recipe?

A mere listing of ingredients is not protected under copyright law. However, where a recipe or formula is accompanied by substantial literary expression in the form of an explanation or directions, or when there is a collection of recipes as in a cookbook, there may be a basis for copyright protection. See FL 122.

30. Does copyright now protect architecture?

Yes. Architectural works became subject to copyright protection on December 1, 1990. The copyright law defines "architectural work" as "the design of a building embodied in any tangible medium of expression, including a building, architectural plans, or drawings." Copyright protection extends to any architectural work created on or after December 1, 1990, and any architectural work that on December 1, 1990, was unconstructed and embodied in unpublished plans or drawings. Architectural works embodied in buildings constructed prior to December 1, 1990, are not eligible for copyright protection. See, Circular 41.

31. Can I register a diary I found in my grandmother's attic?

You can register copyright in the diary only if you are the transferee (by will, by inheritance). Copyright is the right of the author of the work or the author's heirs or assignees, not of the one who only owns or possesses the physical work itself. See Circular 1, section Who Can Claim Copyright.

32. Do you have special mailing requirements?

Our only requirement is that all three elements, the application, the copy or copies of the work, and the $30 filing fee, be sent in the same package. Many people send their material to us by certified mail, with a return receipt request, but this is not necessary.

33. Can foreigners register their works in the U.S.?

Any work that is protected by U.S. copyright law can be registered. This includes many works of foreign origin. All works that are unpublished, regardless of the nationality of the author, are protected in the United States. Works that are first published in the United States or in a country with which we have a copyright treaty or that are created by a citizen or domiciliary of a country with which we have a copyright treaty are also protected and may therefore be registered with the U.S. Copyright Office. See Circular 38a for the status of specific countries.

34. Who is an author?

Under the copyright law, the creator of the original expression in a work is its author. The author is also the owner of copyright unless there is a written agreement by which the author assigns the copyright to another person or entity, such as a publisher. In cases of works made for hire (see Circular 9), the employer or commissioning party is considered to be the author.

35. What is a work made for hire?

Although the general rule is that the person who creates the work is its author, there is an exception to that principle; the exception is a work made for hire, which is a work prepared by an employee within the scope of his or her employment; or a work specially ordered or commissioned in certain specified circumstances. When a work qualifies as a work made for hire, the employer or commissioning party is considered to be the author. See Circular 9.

36. Can a minor claim copyright?

Minors may claim copyright, and the Copyright Office does issue registrations to minors, but state laws may regulate the business dealings involving copyrights owned by minors. For information on relevant state laws, consult an attorney.

37. **Do I have to use my real name on the form? Can I use a stage name or a pen name?**

There is no legal requirement that the author be identified by his or her real name on the application form. For further information, see FL 101. If filing under a fictitious name, check the "Pseudonymous" box at space 2.

38. **What is publication?**

Publication has a technical meaning in copyright law. According to the statute, "Publication is the distribution of copies or phonorecords of a work to the public by sale or other transfer of ownership, or by rental, lease, or lending. The offering to distribute copies or phonorecords to a group of persons for purposes of further distribution, public performance, or public display constitutes publication. A public performance or display of a work does not of itself constitute publication." Generally, publication occurs on the date on which copies of the work are first made available to the public. For further information see Circular 1, section *Publication.*

39. **Does my work have to be published to be protected?**

Publication is not necessary for copyright protection.

40. **How do I get my work published?**

Publication occurs at the discretion and initiative of the copyright owner. The Copyright Office has no role in the publication process.

41. **Are copyrights transferable?**

Yes. Like any other property, all or part of the rights in a work may be transferred by the owner to another. See Circular 1, section *Transfer of Copyright* , for a discussion of ownership.

42. **Do you have any forms for transfer of copyrights?**

There are no forms provided by the Copyright Office to effect a copyright transfer. The Office does, however, keep records of transfers if they are submitted to us. If you have executed a transfer and wish to record it, the Copyright Office can provide a Document Cover Sheet, which can help to expedite the processing of the recordation. See Circular 12.

43. **Can I copyright the name of my band?**

No. Names are not protected by copyright law. Some names may be protected under trademark law. Contact the U.S. Patent & Trademark Office, (800) 786-9199, for further information.

44. **How do I copyright a name, title, slogan or logo?**

Copyright does not protect names, titles, slogans, or short phrases. In some cases, these things may be protected as trademarks. Contact the U.S. Patent & Trademark Office at (800) 786-9199 for further information. However, copyright protection may be available for logo art work that contains sufficient authorship. In some circumstances, an artistic logo may also be protected as a trademark.

45. **How do I protect my idea?**

Copyright does not protect ideas, concepts, systems, or methods of doing something. You may express your ideas in writing or drawings and claim copyright in your description, but be aware that copyright will not protect the idea itself as revealed in your written or artistic work.

46. **How long does copyright last?**

The Sonny Bono Copyright Term Extension Act, signed into law on October 27, 1998, amends the provisions concerning duration of copyright protection. Effective immediately, the terms of copyright are generally extended for an additional 20 years. Specific provisions are as follows:

* For works created after January 1, 1978, copyright protection will endure for the life of the author plus an additional 70 years. In the case of a joint work, the term lasts for 70 years after the last surviving author's death. For anonymous and pseudonymous works and works made for hire, the term will be 95 years from the year of first publication or 120 years from the year of creation, whichever expires first;

* For works created but not published or registered before January 1, 1978, the term endures for life of the author plus 70 years, but in no case will expire earlier than December 31, 2002. If the work is published before December 31, 2002, the term will not expire before December 31, 2047;

* For pre-1978 works still in their original or renewal term of copyright, the total term is extended to 95 years from the date that copyright was originally secured. For further information see Circular 15a.

47. How much of someone else's work can I use without getting permission?

Under the fair use doctrine of the U.S. copyright statute, it is permissible to use limited portions of a work including quotes, for purposes such as commentary, criticism, news reporting, and scholarly reports. There are no legal rules permitting the use of a specific number of words, a certain number of musical notes, or percentages of a work. Whether a particular use qualifies as fair use depends on all the circumstances. See Circular 21 and FL 102.

48. How much do I have to change in my own work to make a new claim of copyright?

You may make a new claim in your work if the changes are substantial and creative -- something more than just editorial changes or minor changes. This would qualify as a new derivative work. For instance, simply making spelling corrections throughout a work does not warrant a new registration -- adding an additional chapter would. See Circular 14 for further information.

49. How much do I have to change in order to claim copyright in someone else's work?

Only the owner of copyright in a work has the right to prepare, or to authorize someone else to create a new version of that work. Accordingly, you cannot claim copyright to another's work, no matter how much you change it, unless you have the owner's consent. See Circular 14.

50. How do I get my work into the Library of Congress?

Copies of works deposited for copyright registration or in fulfillment of the mandatory deposit requirement are available to the Library of Congress for its collections. The Library reserves the right to select or reject any published work for its permanent collections based on the research needs of Congress, the nation's scholars, and of the nation's libraries. If you would like further information on the Library's selection policies, you may contact: Library of Congress, Collections Policy Office, 101 Independence Avenue, S.E., Washington, D.C. 20540.

51. What is a Library of Congress number?

The Library of Congress Card Catalog Number is assigned by the Library at its discretion to assist librarians in acquiring and cataloging works. For further information call the Cataloging in Publication Division at (202) 707-6345.

52. What is an ISBN number?

The International Standard Book Number is administered by the R. R. Bowker Company (908) 665-6770. The ISBN is a numerical identifier intended to assist the international community in identifying and ordering certain publications.

53. What is a copyright notice? How do I put a copyright notice on my work?

A copyright notice is an identifier placed on copies of the work to inform the world of copyright ownership. While use of a copyright notice was once required as a condition of copyright protection, it is now optional. Use of the notice is the responsibility of the copyright owner and does not require advance permission from, or registration with, the Copyright Office. See Circular 3, *Copyright Notice* for requirements for works published before March 1, 1989 and for more information on the form and position of the copyright notice.

54. **How do I collect royalties?**

The collection of royalties is usually a matter of private arrangements between an author and publisher or other users of the author's work. The Copyright Office plays no role in the execution of contractual terms or business practices. There are copyright licensing organizations and publications rights clearinghouses that distribute royalties for their members.

55. **Somebody infringed my copyright. What can I do?**

A party may seek to protect his or her copyrights against unauthorized use by filing a civil lawsuit in Federal district court. If you believe that your copyright has been infringed, consult an attorney. In cases of willful infringement for profit, the U.S. Attorney may initiate a criminal investigation.

56. **Is my copyright good in other countries?**

The United States has copyright relations with more than 100 countries throughout the world, and as a result of these agreements, we honor each other's citizens' copyrights. However, the United States does not have such copyright relationships with every country. For a listing of countries and the nature of their copyright relations with the United States, see Circular 38a, *International Copyright Relations of the United States*.

57. **How do I get on your mailing list?**

The Copyright Office does not maintain a mailing list. The Copyright Office sends periodic e-mail messages via NewsNet, a free electronic mailing list. Important announcements and new or changed regulations and the like are published in the Federal Register. Most will also appear on the Copyright Office website on the Internet.

58. **How do I protect my sighting of Elvis?**

Copyright law does not protect sightings. However, copyright law will protect your photo (or other depiction) of your sighting of Elvis. Just send it to us with a form VA application and the $30 filing fee. No one can lawfully use your photo of your sighting, although someone else may file his own photo of his sighting. Copyright law protects the original photograph, not the subject of the photograph.

59. **How do I get permission to use somebody else's work?**

You can ask for it. If you know who the copyright owner is, you may contact the owner directly. If you are not certain about the ownership or have other related questions, you may wish to request that the Copyright Office conduct a search of its records for a fee of $65 per hour. Additional information can be found in Circular 22.

60. **Could I be sued for using somebody else's work? How about quotes or samples?**

If you use a copyrighted work without authorization, the owner may be entitled to bring an infringement action against you. There are circumstances under the fair use doctrine where a quote or a sample may be used without permission. However, in cases of doubt, the Copyright Office recommends that permission be obtained.

U.S. Copyright Office   Library of Congress

Home · Forms · Records · Registration · Law · Comments · Library of Congress

Copyright Information Circulars
and Form Letters

The Copyright Office information circulars are available in the Adobe Acrobat PDF format. You must have the Adobe Acrobat Reader installed on your computer to view and print the circulars. The Adobe Acrobat Reader is available for free from Adobe Systems Incorporated.

Circulars
1 - Copyright Basics   Version: PDF
1b - Limitations on Information Furnished by the Copyright Office   Version: PDF
2 - Publications on Copyright   Version: PDF
3 - Copyright Notice   Version: PDF
4 - Copyright Fees   Version: PDF
5 - How to Open and Maintain a Deposit Account in the U.S. Copyright Office   Version: PDF
6 - Access to and Copies of Copyright Records and Deposit   Version: PDF
7b - "Best Edition" of Published Copyrighted Works for the Collection of the Library of Congress   Version: PDF
7c - Effects of not Replying within 120 Days to Copyright Office Correspondence   Version: PDF
7d - Mandatory Deposit of Copies of Phonorecords   Version: PDF
8 - Supplementary Copyright Registration   Version: PDF
9 - Work-Made-For-Hire Under the 1976 Copyright Act   Version: PDF
10 - Special Handling   Version: PDF
12 - Recordations of Transfers and Other Documents   Version: PDF

14 - Copyright Registration for Derivative Works
Version: PDF

15 - Renewal of Copyright
Version: PDF

15a - Duration of Copyright: Provisions of the Law Dealing with the Length of Copyright   Protection
Version: PDF

15t - Extension of Copyright Term
Version: PDF

21 - Reproductions of Copyrighted Works by Educators and Librarians
Version: PDF

22 - How to Investigate the Copyright Status of a Work
Version: PDF

23 - Copyright Card Catalog and the Online Files
Version: PDF

31 - Ideas, Methods, or Systems
Version: PDF

32 - Blanks Forms and Other Works Not Protected by Copyright
Version: PDF

33 - Computing and Measuring Devices
Version: PDF

34 - Names, Titles, Short Phrases not Copyrightable
Version: PDF

38a - International Copyright Relations of the United States
Version: PDF

38b - Highlights of Copyright Amendments Contained in the URAA
Version: PDF

40 - Copyright Registration for Works of the Visual Arts
Version: PDF

40a - Deposit Requirements in Visual Arts Material
Version: PDF

41 - Copyright Claims in Architectural Works
Version: PDF

44 - Cartoons and Comic Strips
Version: PDF

45 - Motions Pictures including Video Recordings
Version: PDF

50 - Musical Compositions
Version: PDF

55 - Copyright Registration for Multimedia Works
Version: PDF

http://www.loc.gov/copyright/circs/index.html#circ1

56 - Copyright for Sound Recordings
   Version: PDF

56a - Copyright Registration of Musical Compositions
   Version: PDF

61 - Copyright Registration for Computer Programs
   Version: PDF

62 - Copyright Registration for Serials on Form SE
   Version: PDF

62b - Group Registration for Daily Newspapers
   Version: PDF

64 - Copyright Registration for Secure Tests
   Version: PDF

65 - Copyright Registration for Automated Databases
   Version: PDF

66 - Copyright Registration for Online Works
   Version: PDF

73 - Compulsory License For Making and Distributing Phonorecords
   Version: PDF

74 - How To Make Compulsory License Royalty Payments Via Electronic Transfer of Funds
   Version: PDF

75 - The Licensing Division of the Copyright Office
   Version: PDF

100 - Federal Statutory Protection for Mask Works
   Version: PDF

Factsheets (SL's and Form Letters)
SL 4 - Fee Changes Version: PDF
SL 10 - Get It Quick Over the Net Version: PDF
SL 15 - New Terms for Copyright Protection Version: PDF
Satellite Network Television Factsheet Version: PDF
International Copyright (FL100) Version: PDF
Pseudonyms (FL101) Version: PDF
Fair Use (FL102) Version: PDF
Useful Articles (FL103) Version: PDF
Music (FL105) Version: PDF
Poetry (FL106) Version: PDF
Photographs (FL107) Version: PDF
Games (FL108) Version: PDF
Books, Manuscripts, and Speeches (FL109) Version: PDF
Visual Arts (FL115) Version: PDF
Dramatic Works: Scripts, Pantomimes & Choreography (FL119) Version: PDF
Recipes (FL122) Version: PDF

IN ANSWER TO YOUR QUERY

FL
108

LIBRARY
OF
CONGRESS

GAMES

COPYRIGHT
OFFICE

The idea for a game is not protected by copyright. The same is true of the name or title given to the game and of the method or methods for playing it.

Copyright protects only the particular manner of an author's expression in literary, artistic, or musical form. Copyright protection does not extend to any idea, system, method, device, or trademark material involved in the development, merchandising, or playing of a game. Once a game has been made public, nothing in the copyright law prevents others from developing another game based on similar principles.

Some material prepared in connection with a game may be subject to copyright if it contains a sufficient amount of literary or pictorial expression. For example, the text matter describing the rules of the game, or the pictorial matter appearing on the game-board or container, may be registrable.

101 Independence
Avenue, S.E.

In order to register the copyrightable portions of a game, you must send the Library of Congress, Copyright Office, 101 Independence Avenue S.E., Washington, D.C. 20559-6000, the following elements **in the same envelope or package:**

    1. A completed application form. If your game includes any written element, such as instructions or directions, we recommend using Form TX, which can be used to register all copyrightable parts of the game, including any pictorial elements. When the copyrightable elements of the game consist predominantly of pictorial matter, Form VA should be used.

Washington, D.C.
20559-6000

    2. A nonrefundable filing fee of $30*.

    3. A deposit of the material to be registered. The deposit requirements will vary depending on whether the work has been published at the time of registration.

If the game is *published*, the proper deposit is one complete copy of the work. If, however, the game is published in a box larger than 12 x 24 x 6 inches (or a total of 1728 cubic inches) then identifying material must be submitted in lieu of the entire game. (See "identifying material" below). If the game is published and contains fewer than three 3-dimensional elements, then identifying material for those parts must be submitted in lieu of those parts.

If the game is *unpublished*, either one copy of the game OR identifying material should be deposited.

Identifying material deposited to represent the game or its 3-dimensional parts shall usually consist of photographs, photostats, slides, drawings, or other 2-dimensional representations of the work. The identifying material shall include as many pieces as necessary to show the entire copyrightable content of the work including the copyright notice if it appears on the work. All pieces of identifying material other than transparencies must be no less than 3 x 3 inches in size, and not more than 9 x 12 inches, but preferably 8 x 10 inches. At least one piece of identifying material must, on its front, back, or mount, indicate the title of the work and an exact measurement of one or more dimensions of the work.

Sincerely yours,

Register of Copyrights

* Fees are effective through June 30, 2002. For the latest fee information, write the Copyright Office, check the Copyright Office Website at www.loc.gov/copyright, or call (202) 707-3000.

Enclosures

IN ANSWER TO YOUR QUERY

LIBRARY
OF
CONGRESS

FAIR USE

One of the rights accorded to the owner of copyright is the right to reproduce or to authorize others to reproduce the work in copies or phonorecords. This right is subject to certain limitations found in sections 107 through 118 of the copyright act (title 17, U.S.

COPYRIGHT
OFFICE

Code). One of the more important limitations is the doctrine of "fair use." Although fair use was not mentioned in the previous copyright law, the doctrine has developed through a substantial number of court decisions over the years. This doctrine has been codified in section 107 of the copyright law.

Section 107 contains a list of the various purposes for which the reproduction of a particular work may be considered "fair," such as criticism, comment, news reporting, teaching, scholarship, and research. Section 107 also sets out four factors to be consid-

101 Independence
Avenue, S.E.

ered in determining whether or not a particular use is fair:

(1) the purpose and character of the use, including whether such use is of commercial nature or is for nonprofit educational purposes;

(2) the nature of the copyrighted work;

(3) the amount and substantiality of the portion used in relation to the copyrighted work as a whole; and

Washington, D.C.
20559-6000

(4) the effect of the use upon the potential market for or value of the copyrighted work.

The distinction between "fair use" and infringement may be unclear and not easily defined. There is no specific number of words, lines, or notes that may safely be taken without permission. Acknowledging the source of the copyrighted material does not substitute for obtaining permission.

The 1961 *Report of the Register of Copyrights on the General Revision of the U.S. Copyright Law* cites examples of activities that courts have regarded as fair use: "quotation of excerpts in a review or criticism for purposes of illustration or comment; quotation of short passages in a scholarly or technical work, for illustration or clarification of the author's observations; use in a parody of some of the content of the work parodied; summary of an address or article, with brief quotations, in a news report; reproduction by a library of a portion of a work to replace part of a damaged copy; reproduction by a teacher or student of a small part of a work to illustrate a lesson; reproduction of a work in legislative or judicial proceedings or reports; incidental and fortuitous reproduction, in a newsreel or broadcast, of a work located in the scene of an event being reported."

Copyright protects the particular way an author has expressed himself; it does not extend to any ideas, systems, or factual information conveyed in the work.

The safest course is always to get permission from the copyright owner before using copyrighted material. The Copyright Office cannot give this permission.

When it is impracticable to obtain permission, use of copyrighted material should be avoided unless the doctrine of "fair use" would clearly apply to the situation. The Copyright Office can neither determine if a certain use may be considered "fair" nor advise on possible copyright violations. If there is any doubt, it is advisable to consult an attorney.

Sincerely yours,

Register of Copyrights

Enclosures

IN ANSWER TO YOUR QUERY

LIBRARY
OF
CONGRESS

PSEUDONYMS

COPYRIGHT
OFFICE

A pseudonym or pen name may be used by an author of a copyrighted work. A work is pseudonymous if the author is identified on copies or phonorecords of that work by a fictitious name (nicknames or other diminutive forms of one's legal name are not considered "fictitious"). As is the case with other names, the pseudonym itself is not protected by copyright.

If you are writing under a pseudonym but wish to be identified by your legal name in the records of the Copyright Office, you should give your legal name followed by your pseudonym at the "name of author" line at space 2 of the application (example: "Judith Barton whose pseudonym is Madeline Elster"). You should also check "yes" in the box at space 2 which asks "Was this author's contribution to the work pseudonymous?" If the author is identified in the records of the Copyright Office, the term of the copyright is the author's life plus 70 years.

101 Independence
Avenue, S.E.

If you are writing under a pseudonym but do not wish to have your identity revealed in the records of the Copyright Office, you should give your pseudonym and identify it as such (example: "Huntley Haverstock, pseudonym") or you may leave the "name of author" space blank. You must, however, identify the citizenship or domicile of the author.

Washington, D.C.
20559-6000

In no case should space 4 (name of copyright claimant) be left blank. You may use a pseudonym in completeing the claimant space, but you should also be aware that if a copyright is held under a fictitious name, business dealings involving that property may raise questions of ownership of the copyright property. You should consult an attorney for legal advice on these matters.

If the author is not identified in the records of the Copyright Office, the term of copyright is 95 years from publication of the work, or 120 years from its creation, whichever term expires first. If the author's identity is later revealed in the records of the Copyright Office, the copyright term then becomes the author's life plus 70 years.

Sincerely yours,

Register of Copyrights

Enclosures

Pseudonyms
June 1999—10,000

List of Websites

GENERAL

American Patent and Trademark Law Center
http://www.patentpending.com

Answers to Patent, Copyright, Trademark Questions
http://www.ucc.uconn.edu/~bxb95001/

Federal Trade Commission: "Operation Mousetrap"
http://www.ftc.gov/opa/1977/9707/mouse.htm

Frequently Asked Questions about Intellectual Property Law: Patents,Trademarks, and Copyright
http://www.patents.com/faq.sht

Frequently Asked Questions (and Answers!) about Patents and Trademarks
http://weber.u.washington.edu/~englib/ptdl/faq.html

Gallery of Obscure Patents: IBM Intellectual Property Network
http://www.patents.ibm.com/gallery.html

Inventor Net
http://www.inventornet.com

Inventors Awareness Group, Inc.
http://www.fplc.edu/iag/

Red Flags
http://www.fplc.edu/iag/iag3.htm#red

National Inventor Fraud Center
http://www.inventorfraud.com

Patent, Trademark, and Copyright Resources: University of California, Berkeley
http://www-library.lbl.gov/Library/text/sci/patents.html

Ronald J. Riley's Home Page: Inventor & Entrepreneur Links to resources for inventor
http://www.rjriley.com/site-index

Ronald J. Riley's Invention Promoter Caution List
http://www.rjriley.com/caution

Selected Patent and Trademark Information Available via the WWW
http://www.lib.washington.edu/engineering/ptdl/

Totally Absurd Patents
http://totallyabsurd.com/absurd.htm

U.S. Government Printing Office
http://www.access.gpo.gov/su_docs/

You Want to Be an Inventor
http://www.rjriley.com/new.html

PATENT

Community of Science: Patent database, patent classifications
http://www.cos.com/
(Select: "US Patents")

Frequently Asked Questions about the Patents Database
http://concord.cnidr.org/help/help-faq.html

IBM Intellectual Property Network: searchable patent database, January 5, 1971, to present
http://www.patents.ibm.com/

Patent and Trademark Information: University of Texas
http://www.lib.utexas.edu/Libs/ENG/uspat.html

Patent Classification Numbers: Identifying
http://weber.u.washington.edu/~englib/ptdl/patents/class-numb.html

Patent FAQ
http://www.sccsi.com/DaVinci/patentfaq.html

Patent Law Links: Legal Information Institute, Cornell University Law School
http://isl-garnet.uah.edu/techlaw/patent_law.html

Patent Law Materials: Cornell University Law School
http://www.law.cornell.edu/topics/patent.html

Patent Portal, Resources on the Internet: Villanova University Law School
http://www.law.vill.edu/~rgruner/patport.htm

Patent Resources on the Internet via ICE
http://www.englib.cornell.edu/ice/lists/patents.html

Patent Searching on the Internet: Rice University
http://is.rice.edu/~spare/patentlink.html

Patent Searching: University of Washington
http://weber.u.washington.edu/~englib.ptdl/patents/pt.html

Selected Patent Information via the Internet: University of Washington
http://weber.u.washington.edu/~englib/ptdl/webpat.html

Shadow Patent Office (SPO):
http://www.spo.eds.com/patent.html

STO Internet Patent Search System: University of North Carolina
http://metalab.unc.edu/patents/intropat.html

Index to *Manual of Classification*
http://metalab.unc.edu/patents/intropat.html

Manual of Classification
Class/subclass definition and search, patent number search
http://metalab.unc.edu/patents/intropat.html

Index to all U.S. patent classes
http://metalab.unc.edu/patents/classes.html

Example of "dot-indent" system
http://metalab.unc.edu/patents/class/

Want to Try a Patent Search?: Michigan Technology University.
http://www.sas.it.mtu.edu/rgs/ip_tl/search.html

Yahoo's List of Patent Sites
http://www.yahoo.com/Government/Law/Intellectual_Property/Patents/

UNITED STATES PATENT AND TRADEMARK OFFICE SITES

Boolean Search
http://164.195.100.11/netahtml/search-bool.html

Classification Definitions
http://www1.uspto.gov/web/offices/pac/clasdefs/index.html

Forms online
http://www.uspto.gov/web/forms/

General Information Concerning Patents
http://www.uspto.gov/web/offices/pac/doc/general/

General PTO Reference and Data Collections
http://www.uspto.gov/web/menu/menu4.htmll

How to order copies of US patents and trademarks
http://www.uspto.gov/web/offices/ac/ido/opr/ptcs/

Independent Inventor Resources
  http://www.uspto.gov/web/offices/com/iip/indextst.htm

Patent and Trademark Depository Libraries: List:
  Select the link on the USPTO Home Page, or:
  http://www.uspto.gov/web/offices/ac/ido/ptdlib/index.html

Patent Attorneys and Agents Registered to Practice before the USPTO
  http://www.uspto.gov/web/offices/dcom/olia/oed/roster/

Patent attorneys and agents: Listings by geographic region:
  http://www.uspto.gov/web/offices/dcom/olia/oed/roster/region/

Patent Bibilographic Search Help Information
  http://128.109.179.23/help/help.html

Patent Information
  http://www.uspto.gov/web/menu/pats.html

Patent Number Search
  http://164.195.100.11/netahtml/orchrum.htm

Publications of the Patent and Trademark Office
  http://www.uspto.gov/web/offices/pac/doc/general/public.htm

The 7-Step Strategy for Patent Searching
  http://www.uspto.gov/web/offices/ac/ido/ptdl/step7.htm

USPTO: Home Page
  http://www.uspto.gov

USPTO: Site Index:
  http://www.uspto.gov/web/navaids/siteindx.htm

USPTO Web Patent Databases: U.S. Patent Full Text Database, U.S. Patent
  Bibliographic Database
  http://www.uspto.gov/patft/index.htm

TRADEMARK

Basic Facts About Registering a Trademark
  http://www.uspto.gov/web/offices/tac/doc/basic

Frequently Asked Questions About Trademarks
  http://www.uspto.gov/web/offices/tac/tmfaq.htm

How to Order Copies of U.S. Trademarks
  http://www.uspto.gov/web/offices/ac/ido/opr/ptcs/

TEAS: Trademark Electronic ApplicationSystem
http://www.uspto.gov/teas/e-TEAS/index.html

Tips on Fielded Searching
http://www.uspto.gov/tmdb/helpflds.html

Trademark Acceptable Identification of Goods and Services Manual
http://www.uspto.gov/web/offices/tac/doc/gsmanual

Trademark Acceptable Identification of Goods and Services Manual: Table
of Contents
http://www.uspto.gov/web/offices/tac/doc/gsmanual/manual.html

Trademark Information
http://www.uspto.gov/web/menu/tm.html

USPTO Web Trademark Database
http:www.uspto.gov/tmdb/index.html

COPYRIGHT

COPYRIGHT OFFICE: LIBRARY OF CONGRESS

Copyright Basics
http://lcweb.gov/copyright/circs/circ1.html

Copyright forms
http://lcweb.loc.gov/copyright/forms.html

Copyright Law: Library of Congress
http://lcweb.loc.gov/copyright/title17/1-107.html

Copyright Office: Library of Congress
http://lcweb.loc.gov/copyright

Copyright Office Circulars: On-line
http://lcweb.gov/copyright/circs/

Frequently Asked Questions: Copyright
http://lcweb.loc.gov/copyright/faq.html

Suggested Readings

Ardis, Susan. *An Introduction to U.S. Patent Searching: The Process*. Libraries Unlimited, 1991.

Battle, Carl. *The Patent Guide: A Friendly Guide to Protecting and Profiting from Patents*. Watson-Guptill, 1997.

Besenjak, Cheryl. *Copyright Plain and Simple*. Career Press, 1997.

Carr, Fred. *Patents Handbook: A Guide for Inventors and Researchers to Searching Patent Documents and Preparing and Making an Application*. Jefferson, N.C.: McFarland, 1995.

Donaldson, Michael. *The E-Z Legal Guide to Trademarks & Copyrights*. Garrett, 1995.

Fishman, Steven. *The Copyright Handbook: How to Protect & Use Written Works*, 4th ed. Nolo Press, 1997.

Foster, Frank H., and Robert L. Shook. *Patents, Copyrights & Trademarks*. John Wiley & Sons, 1993.

Fowler, Mavis. *The Law of Copyright*. Oceana, 1996.

_____. *The Law of Patents*. Oceana, 1996.

Hitchcock, David. *Patent Searching Made Easy: How to Do Patent Searches on the Internet and in the Library*. Nolo Press, 1998.

Lehman, Bruce. *Remarks of Bruce A. Lehman, Assistant Secretary of Commerce, and Commissioner of Patents and Trademarks Before the American Bar Association*. June 25, 1998. Text online: http://www.uspto.gov.

Library of Congress. *Copyright Basics*. Online: http://lcweb.loc.gov/copyright/circs/circ1.html

McGrath, Kate, et al. *Trademark: Legal Care for Your Business & Product Name*. 3rd ed. Nolo Press, 1998.

Pressman, David. *Patent It Yourself*. 7th ed. Nolo Press, 1999.

Rosenbaum, David. *Patents, Trademarks, & Copyrights*. Chelsea House, 1997.

Smith, Martin. *How to Avoid Patent, Marketing & Invention Company Scams*. Rainbow Books, 1995.

United States Patent and Trademark Office.
> *Basic Facts about Registering a Trademark*. Text online:
> http://www.uspto.gov/web/offices/tac/doc/basic.
> *Frequently Asked Questions about Trademarks*. Text online:
> http://www.uspto.gov/web/offices/tac/tmfaq.htm.
> *General Information Concerning Patents*. Text online:
> http://www.uspto.gov/web/offices/pac/doc/general/.
> Independent Inventor Resources
> http://www.uspto.gov/web/offices/com/iip/indextst.htm

Warda, Mark. *How to Register Your Own Copyright*, 2d ed. Sourcebooks, 1997.

_____. *How to Register Your Own Trademark*. 2d ed. Sourcebooks, 1997.

Wherry, Timothy Lee. *Patent Searching for Librarians and Inventors*. American Library Association Editions, 1995.

Wilson, Lee. *The Trademark Guide*. Watson-Guptill, 1998.

_____. *The Copyright Guide: A Friendly Handbook for Protecting and Profiting from Copyrights*. Allworth Press, 1996.

Index